EU development cooperation

EU development cooperation

From model to symbol

edited by
Karin Arts and Anna K. Dickson

Manchester University Press
Manchester and New York

distributed exclusively in the USA by Palgrave

Copyright © Manchester University Press 2004, 2009

While copyright in the volume as a whole is vested in Manchester University Press, copyright in individual chapters belongs to their respective authors, and no chapter may be reproduced in whole or in part without the express permission in writing of both author and publisher.

Published by Manchester University Press
Oxford Road, Manchester M13 9NR, UK
and Room 400, 175 Fifth Avenue, New York, NY 10010, USA
www.manchesteruniversitypress.co.uk

Distributed exclusively in the USA by
Palgrave, 175 Fifth Avenue, New York NY 10010, USA

Distributed exclusively in Canada by
UBC Press, University of British Columbia, 2029 West Mall,
Vancouver, BC, Canada V6T 1Z2

British Library Cataloguing-in-Publication Data
A catalogue record for this book is available from the British Library

Library of Congress Cataloging-in-Publication Data
A catalog record for this book is available from the Library of Congress

ISBN 13: 978 0 7190 6299 5

First published in hardback 2004 by Manchester University Press
This edition first published 2009

Printed by Lightning Source

Contents

Notes on contributors—vi
Acknowledgements—viii
List of abbreviations—x

1	EU development cooperation: from model to symbol? *Karin Arts and Anna K. Dickson*	1
2	From uniqueness to uniformity? An assessment of EU development aid policies *William Brown*	17
3	The unimportance of trade preferences *Anna K. Dickson*	42
4	The ACP in the European Union's network of regional relationships: still unique or just one in the crowd? *Karen E. Smith*	60
5	Changing European concerns: security and complex political emergencies instead of development *Gorm Rye Olsen*	80
6	Changing interests in EU development cooperation: the impact of EU membership and advancing integration *Karin Arts*	101
7	'Sense and sensibility': the role of France and French interests in European development policy since 1957 *Anne-Sophie Claeys*	113
8	The Commission and development policy: bureaucratic politics in EU aid – from the Lomé leap forward to the difficulties of adapting to the twenty-first century *Adrian Hewitt and Kaye Whiteman*	133
9	Conclusions: the potential and limits of EU development cooperation policy *Karin Arts and Anna K. Dickson*	149

Index—153

Notes on contributors

Karin Arts is Associate Professor in International Law and Development at the Institute of Social Studies (ISS) in The Hague, The Netherlands. She is author of *Integrating Human Rights into Development Cooperation: The Case of the Lomé Convention* (Kluwer Law International, 2000) and served as adviser to Women in Development Europe (WIDE) and other NGOs. Her research interests include ACP–EU relations, and human rights and development cooperation.

William Brown is Lecturer in Government and Politics at the Open University in the UK. He is author of *The European Union and Africa: The Restructuring of North–South Relations* (IB Tauris, 2002). Current research interests focus on the political economy of Africa in the international system and the continent's relations with international donors.

Anne-Sophie Claeys is Assistant Lecturer at the Institute of Political Studies (IEP), Bordeaux, France, and a PhD student at the Centre d'Etudes d'Afrique Noire (CEAN), also in Bordeaux. Her current research interests include EU and French development policies, and regionalisation processes.

Anna K. Dickson is Lecturer in Politics at the University of Durham, UK. Recent publications include 'Bridging the gap: great expectations for EU development policy', *Current Politics and Economics of Europe*, 9:3 (2000) and 'The demise of the Lomé protocols: revising European development policy', *European Foreign Affairs Review*, 5:2 (2000). Her research interests focus on EU–ACP relations, trade policy and Caribbean international relations.

Adrian Hewitt has been Deputy Director of the Overseas Development Institute (ODI) for a decade and runs the ODI Fellowship Scheme, operating in partnership with nearly twenty developing country governments. His current research work covers international trade policy, aid and global public goods, as well as institutional development questions – not least European development policy reform.

Notes on contributors

Gorm Rye Olsen is Head of the European Studies Department, Institute for International Studies, Copenhagen, Denmark. Recent publications include: 'Europe and Africa in the 1990s: European policies towards a poor continent in an era of globalisation', *Global Society*, 15:4 (2001) and 'European public opinion and aid to Africa: is there a link?', *The Journal of Modern African Studies*, 39:4 (2001). His main research interests focus on European–African relations in the post-Cold War era.

Karen E. Smith is Senior Lecturer in International Relations at the London School of Economics. She is the co-editor of *Ethics and Foreign Policy* (CUP, 2001) and of *European Foreign Policy: Key Documents* (Routledge, 2000). Her research interests include European external human rights policy, the CFSP and enlargement.

Kaye Whiteman is currently the Editor in Chief of *Business Confidential*, Lagos. He has previously been the Director of Information and Public Affairs at the Commonwealth Secretariat and was for many years in charge of *West Africa* magazine. From 1973 to 1982 he worked for the European Commission in Brussels, in its Information Directorate-General (X). He currently works as a consultant.

Acknowledgements

This book is the result of hard work on the part of the contributors, the editors and of course the publishers. The book spans debates that are found in the realm of development studies, European politics, political economy and international relations. This perhaps makes it slightly more difficult to market, but reflects the reality of the processes at work over the period which do not fit neatly into a single academic discipline. The main ideas for the book came into being at a wonderful research group meeting in Uppsala, Sweden, sponsored by the European Consortium for Political Research (ECPR) and the University of Uppsala. On that occasion several of the contributors to this volume met for the first time. We exchanged ideas on European Union development cooperation policy and brainstormed a lot about the options for bringing them together in a single volume in a manner that was useful, novel and interesting. Thanks to the great hospitality and generosity of our sponsors we were able to combine these activities with enjoying some elements of academic life in Uppsala, and sampling as many of the culinary delights of Sweden as possible. Our thanks go out to the ECPR and Uppsala University for this possibility.

A year later another meeting of contributors took place at the Centre for Development Research (CDR) in Copenhagen, Denmark. We understand that the CDR is to be closed and merged into a larger foreign policy institute. We nevertheless gratefully acknowledge the contribution of the CDR to this project, and especially the enthusiastic support of Gorm Rye Olsen, who made possible the Copenhagen meeting and who was a perfect host, both academically and personally.

The idea for this book was very much a joint effort on the part of all the contributors. We have tried to create something that reflects our shared thoughts on explanations of current European development policy and on its future. As we have written, there have been many changes to EU development policy and we have tried to keep up to date. Most chapters consider developments until early 2002. Nevertheless, some things might have passed us by

Acknowledgements

and we apologise for any such errors. The editors each had significant distractions on the way to finishing this book and it is to these new-born distractions, Fabian and Ramon Biondina and Rafe Wendelken-Dickson, that we wish to dedicate this book.

Karin Arts and Anna K. Dickson

List of abbreviations

AAMS	Associated African and Malagasy States
ACP	African, Caribbean and Pacific
ALA	Asia and Latin America
ASEAN	Association of South East Asian Nations
ASEM	Asia–Europe Meeting
CAP	Common Agricultural Policy
CBEA	Caribbean Banana Exporters' Association
CDF	comprehensive development framework
CFA	Communauté Financière Africaine
CFSP	Common Foreign and Security Policy
DG	Directorate-General
EC	European Community
ECHO	European Community Humanitarian Office
ECU	European Currency Unit
EDF	European Development Fund
EEC	European Economic Community
EPC	European Political Cooperation
ESAF	enhanced structural adjustment facility
EU	European Union
GATT	General Agreement on Tariffs and Trade
GSP	Generalised System of Preferences
HIPC	highly indebted poor countries
IFI	international financial institution
IMF	International Monetary Fund
LDC	least developed country
MEDA	Euro-Mediterranean Assistance Programme
MFN	Most Favoured Nation
NAFTA	North American Free-Trade Agreement
NGO	Non-Governmental Organisation

List of abbreviations

NIC	Newly Industrialising Country
NIEO	New International Economic Order
NIP	National Indicative Programme
OAU	Organisation of African Unity
OCT	Overseas Countries and Territories
ODA	Official Development Assistance
OECD	Organisation for Economic Cooperation and Development
OPEC	Organisation of Petroleum Exporting Countries
PCA	Partnership and Cooperation Agreement
PR	Permanent Representation
PRGF	poverty reduction growth facility
PRSP	Poverty Reduction Strategy Paper
REPAs	Regional Economic Partnership Agreements
SAARC	South Asian Association for Regional Cooperation
SAF	structural adjustment facility
SAP	structural adjustment programme
SDA	Social Dimensions of Adjustment Programmes
Stabex	System for the Stabilisation of Export Earnings
Sysmin	System for the Promotion of Mineral Production and Exports
TACIS	Technical Assistance to the Commonwealth of Independent States
TEU	Treaty on European Union
WEU	Western European Union
WTO	World Trade Organisation

1

EU development cooperation: from model to symbol?

Karin Arts and Anna K. Dickson

At the beginning of the twenty-first century, the European Union (EU) stands out as an important regional organisation. It entertains formalised relations with almost all other (groups of) states. Although much of its attention is devoted to internal integration, obviously the European Union cannot and does not wish to be an isolated entity. Instead it has expressed the desire and ambition to take up a prominent place in the working of international relations. In addition to the general goal of forging good relations with (potential) political and economic partners across the globe, the Union also wishes to use its place in international relations as a vehicle for advocating some of the values it considers important. Among these values are democracy, social welfare, human rights and liberalism.

The EU perceives development cooperation policy as an important tool to serve both missions. Accordingly, an impressive and unique record of development cooperation activities and of structural and comprehensive policy has been built over time. Until the 1990s, the African, Caribbean and Pacific (ACP) states unequivocally were Europe's most preferred developing country partners, and ACP–EU relations were the most visible and important component of the EU development cooperation programme. ACP–EU relations started at the very creation of the European Economic Community in 1957 and were elaborated first in the Yaoundé and then in the Lomé Conventions and the 2000 Cotonou Agreement. In many peoples' eyes the Lomé Convention came to symbolise EU development cooperation, more so than any other agreement (Grilli, 1993). It linked the EU with a large group of developing countries, many among the poorest, in an innovative agreement which declared itself to operate on the basis of equality of partners. In the 1970s the Lomé Convention was held up as a model for the future of North–South relations in general and EU development policy in particular. The Convention embodied many novel features which seemed to suggest that the EU was prepared to buck the trend in international development and take on board some of the arguments put forward by the Third World in its quest for a New International Economic Order (NIEO). Examples include the contractual approach, the non-reciprocal trade preferences extended by the EU to the ACP countries and the creation of a semi-automatic system of financial compensation for unstable export earnings from agricultural commodities and mining products, the so-called Stabex and Sysmin mechanisms (Arts, 2000: 127–34).

The high hopes engendered by the Lomé Convention have not been realised. Lomé has not been replicated, and its mixed results have initiated a process of rethinking the concepts underlying ACP–EU relations and the instruments available to shape them. As a result, the most recent ACP–EU general cooperation treaty – the Cotonou Agreement of June 2000 – breaks rather drastically with the Lomé past, both in terms of content and approach. It introduces greater differentiation in the packages of benefits offered to ACP countries, to be decided on the basis of need and merit. Moreover, many of the unique preferential trade aspects of the past will disappear for all but the least developed. ACP–EU relations clearly are no longer the automatic centrepiece they used to be.

For a long time there were no real incentives to change EU development policy and activities. The external Cold War context did not, in its stability, predispose the EU to make radical changes to development policy. Internal influencing factors were either non-existent or too weak to exert real pressure. After the end of the Cold War the scene changed completely as external and internal influencing factors became mutually reinforcing in support of change (see below).

Firstly, since the late 1990s, under the pressure of various simultaneous developments (including the poor results of EU development cooperation efforts thus far and the changed constellation of the world after the end of the Cold War), the Union embarked on a process of evaluation, reconsideration and reform of both the content and organisation of its development cooperation agenda and activities. Secondly, despite the fact that the EU is the largest collective donor, it does not necessarily have proportionate influence in relevant international development fora. EU policies have been largely peripheral in their influence compared with US and Bretton Woods institutions. This dissonance has been significant in the determination of a number of new policies, including the increased use of political conditionality, the desire to create new regional free trade agreements and the new emphasis on conflict resolution. Thirdly, matters such as the enlargement process and the finalisation of Economic and Monetary Union create internal preoccupations that take away political priority and attention from some aspects of the Union's external relations.

As a result of the combination of developments referred to above, EU development cooperation policy has shifted away from making substantive and innovative attempts to contribute to the North–South dialogue, which was the case during the 1970s and 1980s. Instead, since the 1990s EU development cooperation policy has appeared to follow global trends much more than before and is at risk of perpetuating an ineffective agenda. This book contends that, taken as a whole, changes over the period represent a substantive change in the nature of EU development cooperation. That change is characterised as a move from a policy which was, certainly in 1975, unique and held up as a model for the future of North–South relations, to a policy which is neither unique nor successful. More specifically, the contention here is that development cooperation policy in relation to the ACP has become a symbolic gesture from the EU, primarily useful to demonstrate its breadth of commitment to, and relationship with, the South. In so doing it seeks to enhance its perceived role as an important international actor.

Considering these significant changes, it is appropriate and timely to assess the rationale for, and impact of, EU development cooperation so far. That assessment will help us to understand why the Union continues to place so much emphasis on its development cooperation profile, despite the obvious difficulties involved and the modest tangible returns. It will also provide a basis for answering the question of whether the European Union is now moving in the right direction and whether it has the means to realise its ambitions in the realm of development cooperation. These means include political will and the capacity to become what Christopher Hill (1993) termed 'the bridge between the rich and the poor'.

Why EU development policy?

EU development cooperation is an understudied area of European politics, despite its economic and political significance. Perhaps the European Union does not sufficiently publicise its achievements and failings in this field, or perhaps they appear unimportant compared with the dilemmas of the integration process. Nevertheless, over the years there have been a number of important studies in this area. Ten years ago Grilli (1993), a World Bank economist, published a much cited volume already referred to above, *The European Community and the Developing Countries*, which examined Europe's relationship with the developing world from a historical, comparative and thematic perspective. Grilli was critical of the ad hoc approach to development which led the EU to have close ties with Africa but not India or China, or even Eastern Europe. For Grilli, development policy seemed to be more the result of chance than of design: 'apart from the top preference reserved for Africa, who got what, when and why among the other developing countries never had a clear and consistent rationale' (1993: 337). It would be difficult to match the breadth of Grilli's study here and we have not tried to do so. Instead we have chosen to isolate those factors which we consider to be the most significant determining factors in the nature of EU development policy.

More recently, in 1997, Marjorie Lister, who has been writing on this topic for many years, published a volume entitled *The European Union and the South*.

In this book she argues that Europe could play an important role as champion of the South. From her perspective the long institutional relationship between Europe and most of the developing world, and Africa in particular, makes the Community an ideal partner for, and defender of, the South. Furthermore, this role would provide an appropriate complement to the integration process.

In *The European Union and the Third World* (2002), Holland seeks to answer the question of whether the EU plays a distinct role in development policy. He does this through an examination of Europe's relationship with different regions and by interrogating the explanatory potential of different integration theories. Like Lister he argues that development policy can enhance the integration process. Like the authors in this volume he recognises that EU development policy is understudied and given only sporadic attention in the European policy-making debates.

There are two recent volumes which look at Europe and the wider world and for which development policy forms one part of this relationship. Brian White's *Understanding European Foreign Policy* (2001) is specifically concerned with the utility of foreign policy analysis. Bretherton and Vogler (1999), in *The European Union as a Global Actor*, provide a more detailed and critical account of development policy although their ambit is much wider.

The Commission Green Paper of 1997 declared that the colonial and post-colonial period was behind us and that Europe would be seeking to create a new external environment for its relationship with the developing world. There are a number of articles which specifically address aspects of EU development policy (see, for example, Parfitt, 1996; Watts, 1998; Dickson, 2000; Hurt, 2003). All agree that the post-2000 arrangements represent above all the loss of many of the benefits secured initially in 1975.

The central question addressed in this book is: why, given the above mentioned circumstances, does the EU still maintain its development policy? That question is justified by an exploration of the manifest changes which have occurred in EU development cooperation policy through the years. This will be done through an analysis of the various external and internal factors that the authors believe have significantly influenced EU development policy, and have directed changes in scope and coverage of that policy. Among the external factors are, firstly, changes in the international environment e.g. the end of the Cold War, the emergence of Central and Eastern Europe, globalisation/liberalisation (in particular in relation to trade) and increasing civil conflict (ethnic rivalry, failed states). Secondly, other international actors, notably the World Bank, the International Monetary Fund (IMF) and the World Trade Organisation (WTO), and the ideas and concepts they have developed have had an impact on EU policy making in the realm of development. The internal factors considered by this book include, firstly, the changes in the relations between EU member states brought about by the various waves of enlargement. Secondly, there is the influence of the advancing process of European integration. Thirdly, the book looks into the impact of France, as the individual member state that historically has influenced European development policy most strongly of all. Fourthly, there are bureaucratic interests of the Commission in keeping up its development profile and activities.

These factors are identified as being key determining factors in the evolution of EU development policy and, it is argued, they explain many of the changes which have taken place over the period. This approach, which differs from other books on the topic, which tend to adopt a historical, regional or policy-making approach, has the advantage of allowing the authors to study in depth one particular factor and apply it more widely to the field of development cooperation. There is no single theoretical approach expounded here although of course we all have our own particular preferences.

The authors of this book contend that, unless the EU recognises and takes account of the factors which have so far determined the parameters of EU development policy, it is unlikely that future policy will have a more significant impact on development.

EU development cooperation: member states' or common policy?

In practice Europe's relations with the South comprise the bilateral policies of member states plus the collective policies of the Community, at times referred to as a 'mixed system' (Groux and Manin, 1985). The relationship between the two is one of the defining features of EU development cooperation policy in general and of the Lomé Convention/Cotonou Agreement in particular. Development cooperation is a Community policy, although certain member states (the UK and France in particular) have a greater interest in, and influence over, it. Other members of the EU would prefer a more globally oriented policy, notably Austria, the Netherlands, Greece and Germany (Council Ministers, 1997). This debate is not new. Since the 1960s there has been an ongoing discussion about whether development policy should become more globally focused or retain its geographical selectivity based on historical, national rather than Community-wide interests (Faber, 1982; Arts, 2000: 100). The terms of the Cotonou Agreement suggest that internal pressures between the globalists and the regionalists have been decided in favour of the globalists, as the new agreement effectively ends the ACP's status as the EU's most preferred partner. Instead, as is argued in chapter 4, ACP relations are on the way to becoming normalised, that is, they are being brought more in tune with the types of agreement offered to other groups of states. More importantly, the historical basis for support has been deemed less relevant. Instead the EU will offer pro-poor policies targeted at the poorest developing countries (the UN category of least developed countries, LDCs) and other policies more in line with the neoliberal slant for all other developing and transitional economies.

The mixed system can lead to a cumbersome bargaining process in which short-term national goals can prevail over Community values and goals (Edwards and Regelsberger, 1990). Alternatively, member states may sign up for Community policies which they have no intention of, or capacity to, implement. This means that what appears to be a united front initially may in practice disintegrate as member states refuse to play by the rules they created themselves (Peterson, 1998).

Different member states' interests also permeate the Commission, particularly at higher levels. Commissioners have to find a balance between Community interests and the European impartiality they are supposed to display, and national allegiances. This is particularly difficult where member states view their appointments in the Commission as representative of the national interest. This balancing game is coupled with the fact that within each Directorate-General (DG) members do not share common nationalities or party loyalties. This set-up makes the establishment of a collective European interest difficult (Middlemas, 1995; Peterson, 1998).

Like many aspects of EU policy making, decisions about development cooperation are often created by compromise – by attempting to get a majority or, if this is not possible, some kind of compromise position. The results are often either watered down solutions or solutions reached at great expense to one or other interested party. A prerequisite for the EU to exercise greater influence in international affairs is to have a common (i.e. coordinated) approach perceptible to outsiders. In his 1993 analysis of the relationship between the EU and the developing world, Grilli argued that there had never been a coherent development policy. Rather there has been a series of ad hoc responses to particular situations: 'The sequencing of . . . relations with different groups of developing countries, and of their development cooperation content, appear to have been haphazard, reactive and more dictated by events, and sometimes fashions, than by plans, principles or even a broad strategy' (Grilli, 1993: 337–8).

This is one of the key issues the Commission addressed in its 1992 report, 'Development Policy in the Run Up to 2000' (or 'Horizon 2000'). Here the Commission argued for greater complementarity between, and coordination of, objectives in the development policies of the member states and those of the Community as a means of making development assistance more effective (referred to as 'coordination shortfall'). The report noted a 'gap between the Community's importance as an export market for the developing countries and as a donor of official development assistance on the one hand and its still modest role in the management of the international economic system on the other' (CEC, 1992: 40). The Community as a whole at the time already provided more than half of world aid and, according to the Commission, was well placed to influence the shape of international development policy. However, the report continues, 'by not always acting together in these institutions [the IMF and World Bank] the member states and the Community frequently pass the initiative to the US' (CEC 1992: 41).

In 1992 the Treaty on European Union (TEU) for the first time set out the objectives of a common European development policy as part of an attempt to reduce inconsistencies between different policies (then Title XVII, Article 130u; after the entry into force of the Amsterdam Treaty, Title XX, Articles 179–81). The purpose is not to create a single development policy but rather to make the bilateral policies of the fifteen member states consistent and complementary with the common policy. Thus Article 130x reads: 'The Community and the member states shall coordinate their policies on development cooperation and shall consult each other on their aid programmes . . .'. In theory this would provide a level playing field for the many partners with which the EU and its member states have agreements. However, practice is utterly different.

Within the internal workings of the EU the Commission is the chief initiator of policy and implementor of EU development policy, which falls mainly under the economic and commercial policies of the EU and also has Common Foreign and Security Policy (CFSP) aspects. Although only the Commission has the right to initiate policy, it is often viewed as the civil service of the member states. While the Commission seeks to expand its competencies, the Council often seeks to curtail Commission aspirations (Middlemas, 1995: 210–27). The result is that the Commission has been criticised for putting forward grandiose plans without the necessary capacity to deliver (Committee of Independent Experts Report, 1999). This has been compounded by staff problems, in terms of quality and numbers, in the sections relevant to traditional development cooperation.

The Commission is aware that development policy and other facets of Community policy are not always consistent (and referred to this as 'linkage shortfall') (CEC, 1992: 42). This is another issue which needs to be addressed if the Community is to increase its effectiveness in international development. The lack of cohesion between different policies, directorates and services means that while overall the Commission may have a formal commitment to the elimination of poverty in the South, sections within the Commission may have competing priorities. Although internal mechanisms for coordination exist they are not effective. The lack of consistency promotes the appearance of a confused, unfocused actor and has prompted calls for a single external relations Commissioner within a reformed Commission.

Nevertheless, there is a noticeable trend towards enlarging the scope of activities carried out at the Community level (Edwards and Regelsberger, 1990: 4). The Community now has relations with almost all developing countries. Some are with individual states, for example Cuba. Others are with regional organisations, for example the Association of South East Asian Nations (ASEAN) and Mercado Comun del Sur (MERCOSUR; the Southern common market). Yet others apply to groups of trans-regional states such as the ACP.

The impact of the end of the Cold War

High expectations generated by the end of the Cold War led optimists to hope for a peace dividend: finance previously tied up in the arms race could now be used to help the poor, and aid would no longer be based on Cold War rivalries but on need. These hopes proved to be misplaced. While the end of the ideological and political division that dominated international relations, within and outside Europe, was a determining factor for many changes in development cooperation, it has not brought forth any significant additional aid to traditional recipients and political conditionality has only increased.

However, the end of the Cold War directly initiated a process of change in EU development cooperation. The changed geo-political situation that emerged during the 1990s had a profound impact on the European Union's external cooperation priorities. This was put straightforwardly in the April 2000 Commission document 'Communication on the European Community's Development Policy' (CEC, 2000a: 4):

> Development policy is today one of the three principal components of the EU's external action, alongside trade policy and the political dimension. In addition to the objectives specific to development policy, other factors – such as geopolitics, trade, and global environmental problems – affect the EU's external choices. ... In this context, the EU's objective interests have led it to give priority to the stability and development of neighbouring countries and to aid for countries in crisis in the regions nearest to the EU.

Within the changed post-Cold War political constellation, the European Union caught sight of an unprecedently large group of 'new' countries in its immediate vicinity in need of assistance. Politically, and perhaps economically too, it had no choice but to approach them sympathetically. The reunification of Germany, the disintegration of the Soviet Union and the outbreak of large-scale armed conflict in, and the falling apart of, the former Yugoslavia further increased the weight of intra-European problems on the EU's agenda. This took away space that previously was available for addressing development challenges in other parts of the world.

While overall apparently there is no hard evidence of shifts of development aid resources from the South to the East (Cox and Chapman, 1999: 76; Raffer, 1999), clear re-orientations have emerged in aid allocation patterns. As a direct result of the changing interests and priorities, the traditional developing country cooperation partners of the European Union, notably the ACP countries, have lost out significantly on their previously largely unchallenged share of structural European Community development aid. For example, the share of sub-Saharan Africa in total allocable EC aid has gone down from 70 per cent at the beginning of the 1970s, to 60 per cent at the beginning of the 1980s, to some 30 per cent over 1996–97. In contrast, during the period 1990–97, the Central and Eastern European countries and the new independent states of the former Soviet Union built up a share of 19 per cent of allocable Community aid. This trend had begun by the start of the Phare programme in 1990 and rapidly extended thereafter. The Middle East's and non-EU southern European's share in total allocable EC aid doubled from 6 per cent in the 1970s and 1980s to 14 per cent over 1996–97 (Cox and Chapman, 1999: 2 and 101 ff.).

Another major change that occurred in the 1990s relates to the issue of political conditionality of Community development assistance. The end of the Cold War brought about changes in the tone and orientation of global and inter-regional debates on human rights and development. A slightly more open climate emerged for addressing issues in this realm. Controversy over the interrelationship between human rights, development and democratisation gradually reduced somewhat, although it certainly did not disappear (Arts, 2000: e.g. 28–31 and 110–11). Accordingly, from the early 1990s, human rights, democracy, and later also governance considerations, became increasingly important determinants in the European Union's external relations as a whole.

The November 1991 Council of Ministers 'Resolution on human rights, democracy and development' set the main agenda to be pursued through European Community development cooperation and the basic approaches through which this was to be done (Council of Ministers, 1991). Thereafter, the Community, at a breathtaking pace, formulated a large number of specific human rights and governance-related conditions and criteria for its development assistance. Many of these were developed through jointly negotiated clauses in newly concluded cooperation treaties, including the Lomé IV and Lomé IV-bis Conventions, and the Europe Agreements. However, the Community did not hesitate to introduce and specify additional conditionalities unilaterally. At least three means were used for this purpose. Firstly, the various Community Regulations that set the legal framework for development cooperation gradually came to include specific references and procedures for taking up human rights and democracy concerns. Examples include the regulations on financial and technical assistance to developing countries in Asia and Latin America (ALA), and on the Generalised System of Preferences (GSP). Secondly, throughout the 1990s a regular stream of Council of Ministers' resolutions and Commission documents defined the Community's understanding of certain human rights-related terms and concepts, or further specified Community priorities and criteria (Arts, 2000: 118–26 and 134–6). Thirdly, more and more often during the 1990s the Community resorted to the application of sanctions against developing countries that it deemed to have disrespected human rights, democracy or governance norms.

Particularly on the latter aspect – that is, in its human rights-related sanctions practice – the European Community regularly pushed matters too far, even up to the extent of violating international law. For example, the early practice of suspending the Lomé Convention because of alleged disrespect for human rights or democracy (i.e. at least until Lomé IV of 1989, the main text of which contained an elaborate human rights provision), and the more recent such punitive practice in response to 'bad' governance, amounted to straightforward violations of relevant international law (Arts, 2000: 193–200 and 321–48). This position is based on the fact that the international law norms governing the integration of human rights and democracy considerations into development cooperation are relatively clear and enjoy solid legal definition and status. Good governance, on the other hand, lacks international legal definition and is perhaps not an international legal principle at all (Arts, 2000: 40–1 and 50). Rather than drawing conclusions from this situation and changing its policy to a less pushy one on governance aspects, the Community has now engaged in strong efforts to legalise its unlawful practice by attempting to incorporate detailed good governance provisions in newly negotiated cooperation agreements. A controversial example is the set of good governance and corruption provisions in the Cotonou Agreement. Its Article 9(3) qualifies good governance as a 'fundamental element' of the Cotonou Agreement and defines it as:

> the transparent and accountable management of human, natural, economic and financial resources for the purposes of equitable and sustainable development. It entails clear decision-making procedures at the level of public authorities, transparent and accountable institutions, the primacy of law in the management and distribution of resources and capacity building for elaborating and implementing measures aiming in particular at preventing and combating corruption. (Partnership Agreement, 2000)

Despite this broad definition, the enforcement mechanism for the good governance standard is strictly confined to the element of corruption. In case of 'serious cases of corruption', and when the Community is 'a significant partner in terms of financial support to economic and sectoral policies and programmes', 'appropriate measures' may be taken after having exhausted a prescribed consultation procedure (Partnership Agreement, 2000: Article 97). Basically the Community forced its most recent political priority through, and was not open to ACP opposition on this point. This appears clearly from the respective public statements made by both sides after the negotiations had finished. According to the Community, proudly, the newly agreed procedure is:

> a real innovation, both in the EU–ACP context and in international relations. This procedure will be applied not only in cases of corruption involving [European Development Fund] EDF money but also more widely, in any country where the EC is financially involved and where corruption constitutes an obstacle to development. It is thus not confined to EC activities. . . . By adopting such a provision in their partnership agreement, the EU and the ACP States are together

sending a clear and positive signal that will doubtlessly be appreciated by European taxpayers and investors, and by the legitimate beneficiaries of aid. (CEC, 2000b: 3–4)

The ACP, in an unusually strongly worded press release, expressed its dissatisfaction with the course of events and pointed at its attempts to amend the provisions concerned because it:

> found them to be imbalanced as a result of the overemphasis given to EU objectives, particularly political objectives, while those of the ACP – such as development – were often ignored. Some attempt was made to remedy this criticism but the text is still unbalanced with EU objectives not only repeated ad nauseam but often elaborated whilst those of the ACP, such as the arms trade and the EU's role in this, do not merit a mention. (ACP Secretariat, 2000: 2; see also Dludlu, 2000)

The course of affairs concerning the elaboration of good governance provisions in the Cotonou Agreement clearly reveals the European Community's determination to create new ways and means for it to intensify this element of political conditionality. This is likely to be extended further in the future.

Determinants of EU development cooperation policy

The assumption of this book is that there are a number of causal factors in the disappearance of a unique European development policy, which was regularly referred to as a positive model for such a policy. These factors can be found in the internal workings of the European machinery as well as in external circumstances. Very often it is the interplay of the two which brings about shifts in the direction and content of development policy. Chapters 2 to 5 substantiate the position that EU development cooperation lost its uniqueness due to a variety of external explanatory factors.

Chapter 2, by William Brown, focuses on the influence of the World Bank on EU development cooperation policy, with special emphasis on the Lomé Convention. In particular, the chapter explores the extent to which EU policy has followed rather than diverged from that of the World Bank. It shows that the European Union has changed its Lomé policy gradually, for example by including structural adjustment issues and tightening political conditionality of aid. There are strong indications that these changes, which have caused a major and principled shift in the terms underlying ACP–EU cooperation, were instigated by World Bank ideas and practice. Thereby, the Union has compromised its own distinct policy-making identity.

Chapter 3, by Anna K. Dickson, explains the influence of trade liberalisation on EU trade preferences. It seeks to identify the main determinants of EU trade policy in relation to the developing countries. Whereas in 1975 the EU was prepared to challenge the prevailing liberal consensus and sign an innovative trade chapter with the ACP, by the 1990s this was no longer the case. The chapter asks what factors drove the EU decision to liberalise existing trade preferences. The working hypothesis was that the EU committed itself to trade liberalisation in part because the international climate for development cooperation has changed significantly so that preferential agreements are increasingly difficult to justify. In addition, external pressures – for example to reform the Common Agricultural Policy (CAP) – have implications for the trade preferences that the Union can offer to developing countries. The chapter assesses the manner in which the Commission has been influenced by the ideology of global trade liberalisation, and more recently its incarnation in the WTO, and the substantive political interests at stake in reforming the CAP. Specific reference is made to the Banana Protocol of the Lomé Convention, as an example of the EU's waning interest in preferential trade facilities.

Karen Smith, in chapter 4, provides a comparative analysis of the content and direction of the policies developed towards the ACP, the Mediterranean, Asia, Latin America and Eastern Europe. She examines the evolution and content of EU relations with these areas. She argues that the periphery of the European Union has become increasingly important to it. Relations with the traditional developing country partners, such as the ACP, are in the process of being 'normalised' and are beginning to look much more similar to relations with other regions. The signalled changes will be explained through a framework considering internal and external demands for EU action and involvement, the EU's sense of responsibility, economic interest, security considerations and others.

Chapter 5 by Gorm Rye Olsen shows how relevant European concerns have changed from development to security and complex political emergencies. This chapter argues that the developing world in general, and Africa in particular, are symbolic in the context of the European Union's efforts to become a more prominent international player. Since the end of the Cold War and the start of Lomé IV one can identify a change in the EU's external priorities, especially concerning sub-Saharan Africa. The EU has become more concerned with security issues, as reflected in the French–British plans to establish a special African intervention force supported and financed by the Union, and in the overall attention for conflict prevention and crisis management in Africa. The focus on security is partly a reflection of the growth in the number of so-called complex political emergencies which are caused by conflicts and civil wars. The mass media tend to focus on such dramatic events, which has strengthened the tendency in the EU to allocate more money to emergency operations. This put additional pressure on European aid budgets, already threatened by a combination of aid fatigue and a lack of vision for European aid. Also, it strengthened the prospects for stronger linkages between the CFSP and development cooperation policy.

Chapters 6 to 8 provide insight into some significant internal factors that help to explain the changes in EU development cooperation as they occurred over time, particularly since 1990. Karin Arts, in chapter 6, discusses the influence of changing EU membership and of advancing European integration. She first explores the effect on EU development policy of the changing EU membership. The chapter investigates the consequences of the accession of, respectively, the UK, Spain, Portugal, Sweden, Finland and Austria, and the (to be expected) further enlargement of the Union within the next decade, on the geographical scope of, and political priority for, development policy. The chapter then looks into the impact of the ever advancing process of European integration. It explores the impact of current efforts to strengthen the Union's external identity, of new Constituent Treaty mandates, the drive for consistency, and the trend to enhance the Union's accountability, transparency and efficiency. The chapter argues that, as a result of the internal determinants explored in it, the Union's interest in development cooperation with the South has clearly been diluted.

Chapter 7 by Anne-Sophie Claeys analyses the role of France and French interests in EU development policy since 1957. Since 1957, France has been heavily involved in the definition and implementation of European development policy. It has always considered this policy as a way to maintain French interests and influence over Africa, while sharing the costs of such a policy with EU member states. Claeys presents the channels used by France to influence the shaping of EU development policy. She examines the French interests and determinants for exerting such influence. France is now in the process of rethinking its approach, and is reducing its involvement in Africa. This has come about as a result of the end of the Cold War, economic concerns and new priorities in the sphere of security and proximity issues. The French Africa policy is thus in the process of 'normalisation', which in turn might have significant consequences for the European Union's policy.

Chapter 8, by Adrian Hewitt and Kaye Whiteman, looks into the bureaucratic politics of EU aid. Their chapter analyses the role of the Commission in the making of EU development policy. While the EU and the member states together are the largest donor, the impact of EU aid has been insignificant. Some reasons for this can be found in the bureaucratic politics of EU aid. These include issues such as division within and between the various relevant Commission Directorates; staffing; the role of individual Commissioners; and the influence of national governments through their experts.

Chapter 9, the final chapter, looks forward at the progress and changes made to EU development policy since the book was first conceptualised. Thus far, these changes indicate that the trends identified in the book have continued.

Concluding remarks

Development cooperation remains an important component of the EU's external relations policy. Nearly five decades of Community development cooperation have transformed the initial and tentative steps enshrined in the Rome Treaty into a collection of agreements, declarations of intent and actual policies. There is now a dedicated Commission that steers most, if not all, policy concerned with development. Issues of development concern numerous committees, delegations and, governmental and non-governmental organisations (NGOs), within the EU as well as in its constituent member states. Although the Lomé Conventions/Cotonou Agreement have not been widely heard of outside the EU/ACP context, they have arguably transformed the external dimension of EU and ACP relations.

The Lomé Convention has also engendered an institutional dialogue between North and South that is unparalleled in the field. That this dialogue has often been unsatisfactory should not detract from the precedent it set. From Europe's point of view the dialogue is significant because it links Europe with a large number of developing countries and boosts its image in the Third World and beyond. It has been particularly important to France and, to a lesser extent, to the UK. Despite its shortcomings, accession to the Convention was aspired to by many developing countries including, most recently, South Africa and Cuba.

However, in all of these spheres of activity, in the end the EU falls short. Whether it be the duplication of tasks by different member states, the contradictions and inconsistencies between policies created by different commissions, or the lack of a real dialogue between partners, the sum effect is the creation of an ineffective, and perhaps symbolic, development policy. That is to say, ineffective in the realm of producing, encouraging or facilitating development, although effective in creating the image of an actor engaged with the world's poor. The EU is aware of this criticism and has sought to remedy it through reform of the Commission and the decision-making structures of the EU, as well as undergoing a thorough rethinking of the methods by which it seeks to encourage development.

The parameters of the new situation have not yet been firmly decided. The ongoing process of enlargement and external events will challenge the Community's ability to effect the choices it makes as well as limit the options available. The analysis contained in the following chapters identifies and assesses trends in overall patterns of development policy since 1957. While largely critical of emerging trends, it does not preclude the possibility of a less symbolic, more substantive development policy for the future.

Bibliography

ACP Secretariat (2000), 'Press release on the conclusion of the successor agreement to the Lomé Convention', www.acpsec.org/gb/press/037900_e.htm (accessed 23 May 2000), p. 2.

Arts, K. (2000), *Integrating Human Rights into Development Cooperation: The Case of the Lomé Convention*, The Hague/London/Boston: Kluwer Law International.

Bretherton, C. and J. Vogler (1999), *The European Union as a Global Actor*, London: Routledge.
CEC (1992), 'Development Policy in the Run Up to 2000', SEC (92) 915 final, Brussels.
CEC (1997), 'The Green Paper on Relations between the European Union and the ACP Countries on the Eve of the 21st Century', Brussels: CEC.
CEC (2000a), 'Communication on the European Community's Development Policy', COM (2000) 212 final, Brussels.
CEC (2000b), 'The new ACP–EU Agreement', http://europa.eu.int/comm/development/ document/acp_eu_agreement_en.htm (accessed 20 April 2000).
Council of Ministers of the European Communities (1991), 'Resolution on human rights, democracy and development', *Bulletin of the European Communities*, 24:11, pp. 122–3.
Council of Ministers of the European Communities (1997), 'Open meeting of the General Affairs Council on the future of Lomé', Brussels, 10 November.
Cox, A. and J. Chapman (1999), *The European Community External Cooperation Programmes. Policies, Management and Distribution*, Brussels: European Commission.
Dickson, A. (1995), 'The EC and its associates: changing priorities', *Politics*, 15:3, pp. 147–52.
Dickson, A. (2000), 'The demise of the Lomé Protocols: revising European development policy', *European Foreign Affairs Review*, 5:2, pp. 197–214.
Dludlu, J. (2000), 'Governance, immigration bedevil a new Lomé pact', *Business Day*, 2 February.
Edwards, G. and E. Regelsberger (eds) (1990), *Europe's Global Links*, New York: St. Martin's Press.
Faber, G. (1982), *The European Community and Development Cooperation*, Assen: Van Gorcum.
Grilli, E. (1993), *The European Community and the Developing Countries*, Cambridge: Cambridge University Press.
Groux, J. and P. Manin (1985), *The European Communities in the International Order*, Brussels: CEC.
Hill, C. (1993), 'The capability–expectations gap or conceptualising Europe's international role', *Journal of Common Market Studies*, 31:3, pp. 305–28.
Holland, M. (2002), *The European Union and The Third World*, Basingstoke: Palgrave.
Hurt, S. (2003), 'Co-operation and coercion? The Cotonou Agreement between the European Union and ACP states and the end of the Lomé Convention', *Third World Quarterley*, 24:1, pp. 161–76.
Lister, M. (1997), *The European Union and the South*, London: Routledge.
McQueen, M. (1998), 'ACP–EU trade cooperation after 2000: an assessment of reciprocal trade preferences', *Journal of Modern African Studies*, 36:4, pp. 669–92.
Middlemas, K. (1995), *Orchestrating Europe*, London: Fontana.
Parfitt, T. (1996), 'The decline of Eurafrica? Lomé's mid term review', *Review of African Political Economy*, no. 67, pp. 53–66.
Partnership Agreement (2000) between the African, Caribbean and Pacific States of the one part, and the European Community and its Member States, of the other part, signed in Cotonou on 23 June, in *The Courier*, special issue, September.
Peterson, J. (1998), 'The European Union as a global actor', in J. Peterson and H. Sjursen *A Common Foreign Policy for Europe*, London: Routledge.

Raffer, K. (1999), 'More conditions and less money: shifts of aid policies during the 1990s', European Development Policy Study Group, *Discussion Paper* no. 15, September, www.euforic.org/dsa/dp15.htm, section 2.

Watts, P. (1998), 'Losing Lomé: the potential impact of the Commission guidelines on the ACP non-least developed countries', *Review of African Political Economy*, no. 75, pp. 47–51.

White, B. (2001), *Understanding European Foreign Policy*, Basingstoke: Palgrave.

2

From uniqueness to uniformity? An assessment of EU development aid policies

William Brown

Introduction

European Union development cooperation stretches back as far as the EU itself but for many years its most visible and important component was the relationship with the ACP states institutionalised in the Lomé Convention. Right from its inception, the Lomé Convention was claimed to be unique, either because of the formal terms of the agreement, the context in which it was first negotiated or – the focus of this chapter – because of the particular modalities of the aid which it provided for ACP states. None have been keener to trumpet the unique character of the relationship than the partner countries themselves – the EU in order to emphasise the 'special character' of its actions in the international arena and the ACP states in order to try to bolster and protect the more advantageous elements of the relationship. But the Conventions, first signed in 1975, renewed four times and in effect until 2000, existed during a period in which the international arena changed drastically. The relations between North and South at a general level, and the particular policies of the major donors and states towards the developing world, underwent radical and far-reaching changes. Has the claimed unique character of Lomé survived this transformation? And how do we understand the new ACP–EC Partnership Agreement, signed in Cotonou in 2000, in the light of these changes?

This chapter assesses the evolution of EU development policies over this period. It concentrates on the terms on which aid has been delivered to the ACP states as defined by the Lomé Convention and its successor, the Cotonou Agreement. The chapter undertakes a comparative assessment of these changes in the light of wider donor policies towards developing countries. In particular, parallels will be drawn with the policies of the World Bank. The World Bank can rightly claim to be a leading donor institution over this period, both in terms of its role in defining the international development agenda and because of its principal role in forging the changes to donor policies over recent years.

Furthermore, the Bank's policies largely reflect the orientation of the dominant Northern states towards the South, and as such are a good indicator of the wider political and policy environment within which the EU's own development policies have evolved. Throughout, the chapter asks whether the claimed uniqueness of the original relationship with the ACP countries has given way to a more uniform stance among donors. If this is the case, then the *raison d'être* for a separate EU development programme may come into question.

This chapter undertakes this task by assessing three phases in the evolution of EU development cooperation: the development of an EU approach to the support of structural adjustment programmes in the ACP states in Lomé IV; the introduction of 'political conditionality' into Lomé in the 1990s; and the recasting of EU development cooperation in the negotiations for the Cotonou Agreement signed in 2000.

The rise of the Washington consensus: adjustment, conditionality and Lomé IV

EU aid policies claimed a distinctiveness on a number of counts. Some of these related to the rhetoric which infused the signing of Lomé I and included notions of a partnership of equals, of an attempt to rid the EU–ACP relationship of 'neo-colonialism' and, for the ACP at least, of the need to reform the international political economy. Thus the modalities of aid provision in the Convention reflected the political character of EU–ACP relations at the time. Aid was to be administered jointly by the two parties, with the ACP possessing the sole right to propose development projects for EU funding. Aid granted by the EU was on a contractual basis, establishing an ACP country's right to a given amount of aid through the programming procedure. Moreover, much of the aid provided was on very favourable terms, with a large (and over subsequent Conventions, increasing) grant component. Furthermore, in an era of Cold War, Lomé aid was to be non-political in so far as it was to be made available to all ACP states, which covered a wide political and economic spectrum. Indeed, the Convention explicitly recognised ACP sovereignty over internal political and economic matters and that development cooperation would not infringe each ACP state's right to determine development strategies.

Lomé aid thus appeared to avoid some of the more politically motivated and ad hoc arrangements that characterised much bilateral and multilateral aid up to the end of the 1970s. However, the actual record of implementation of these aims often fell far short of the partnership ideal. As such, the Lomé aid relationship established in 1975 reflected a number of key aims that developing countries had pursued in the international arena for some time. For the origins of the Lomé Convention lie in an era in which the South sought to achieve substantial changes to the regulation of the international economy and the terms on which aid was provided. In particular the South sought to reinforce notions of national development and non-interference vis-à-vis the richer states while also demanding increased aid and other economic resources from those states. Importantly, the developing countries claimed that such external support should be provided 'non-conditionally' and that to do otherwise would constitute unwarranted interference in their domestic affairs and would be 'neo-colonial' in character. Although largely unsuccessful at the global level, where Cold War considerations had a particular impact on aid allocations, such demands clearly had an impact in shaping the terms of the Lomé Convention.

However, this relatively unique agreement was to come under mounting pressure and became subject to considerable amendment due to changes in donor–recipient relations at the international level. The first of these changes was the rise of structural adjustment conditionality in aid policies – the demand for developing countries to implement processes of macroeconomic reform as a condition for the provision of aid – in the 1980s. The EU response was to be a key test of the extent to which a unique Lomé aid regime would survive in the face of this radical restructuring of North–South relations.

Debt, adjustment and the Bretton Woods institutions

Structural adjustment conditionality arose in the context of the debt crisis in the early 1980s. In response to a generalised inability of developing countries to service their debt payments, donors moved from funding specific development projects to a greater emphasis on funding programmes of policy reform. The Bretton Woods institutions – the IMF and the World Bank – coordinated and led this change. To an extent, the IMF had always been involved in policy conditionality in this sense, granting short-term balance-of-payments support to countries in return for commitments by the recipient to address the sources of imbalance, particularly through austerity measures. The 1980s saw this role revitalised and generalised with respect to developing countries. For the World Bank the change was more marked, having previously concentrated on large-scale project funding with a strong state-centred focus. However, it was the Bank which first introduced special funds for adjustment in 1979, with loans provided for programmes of economic policy reforms intended to achieve a restructuring of the economies in developing countries (Stevens and Killick, 1989; Mosley et al., 1991). Signalling its new approach and under the influence of the Reagan administration in the US, in 1981 the World Bank published what became known as the 'Berg Report' which argued for a reduction in state intervention, de-nationalisation and the removal of protectionist policies in African countries (World Bank, 1981). The IMF reinforced this shift in donor policy in the 1980s by introducing its 'structural adjustment facility' (SAF) and later the more concessional 'enhanced structural adjustment facility' (ESAF), both conditional upon compliance with Structural Adjustment Programmes (SAPs) (Stevens and Killick, 1989; Mosley et al., 1991). The close relationship that emerged between the two institutions resulted in the so-called 'Washington consensus' over donor policy.

In its essentials the Washington consensus rested on a neo-liberal view of the development process which should, it was argued, be focused on removing barriers to the efficient working of the market, in particular those stemming from over-extended state intervention. Aid and loans for balance-of-payments support thus evolved from relatively short-term attempts to rectify external imbalances into medium- and long-term programmes of economic restructuring. SAPs often differed little between countries, specifying similar sets of reforms in a 'one size fits all' approach and including government expenditure cuts, anti-inflation drives through high interest rates, trade liberalisation, currency devaluation, privatisation and freeing of prices. This posed a challenge to governments, states and development strategies that existed in the South and which had become heavily state centred in the post-colonial period. It also represented a fundamental shift in donor–recipient and North–South relations. Aid became dependent on the adoption of this neo-liberal programme and aid policies shifted decisively against the claims for 'non-conditional' support made by developing countries. This shift was reinforced in turn by the gate-keeping role performed by the Washington institutions. In creating a process of cross-conditionality, bilateral donors made their aid and loans provisional upon agreements between a recipient state and the IMF and World Bank, thus generalising the new aid regime across North–South relations.

Adjustment support, the EU Commission and the Lomé Convention
The rise of adjustment conditionality posed a particular problem for the EU Commission. On the one hand it had fundamentally altered the context in which the EU was funding development projects. Between 1987 and 1989 the IMF and World Bank supported adjustment of some form in over seventy developing countries, thirty of them in sub-Saharan Africa and thirty-nine of them from the ACP group (Krueger, 1995). As the Commission claimed, 'Adjustment has become the daily bread of the vast majority of the countries of Africa and a *sine qua non* of their dialogue with the outside world' (Frisch and Boidin, 1988: 67). There was thus a need to come to terms with the new realities, if only to avoid existing development projects being adversely affected. Indeed, the Commission wished to become more involved in the adjustment process – to influence the process of reform rather than simply cope with the consequences. On the other hand, the very mechanism of conditionality posed a challenge to the existing aid relationship with the ACP states which was theoretically premised on the absence of 'interference' in ACP policies.

The Commission's approach to structural adjustment was defined prior to Lomé IV in a series of papers and Council resolutions. The Commission started from the position that adjustment was unavoidable. The ACP countries could only choose 'either ordered, properly managed adjustment or forced adjustment' (Frisch and Boidin, 1988: 68). The Commission stated that it wished to be involved in the process. Two major concerns came up in this context. The first was that the introduction of adjustment support had to be compatible with its traditional relationship with the ACP countries. The Commission wished to avoid the often conflictual and coercive nature of conditionality as practised by the Bretton Woods institutions, where recalcitrant governments were cajoled into reluctantly signing agreements over economic reform. In particular, it sought to ensure that, as far as conditionality operated, it would be pursued in partnership with the ACP countries. It also wished to assuage ACP concerns that adjustment conditionality should not dominate the whole Lomé process by declaring that 'traditional' aid (project and long-term development aid) would be protected and remain outside of the conditionality relationship.

Secondly, the Commission took what seemed at first to be a different and more moderate approach to the design of adjustment programmes. The first wave of SAPs implemented by the Washington institutions in the early and mid-1980s had come under a barrage of criticism from developing countries, development agencies, NGOs and other observers, most famously in UNICEF's response to adjustment calling for 'adjustment with a human face' (Cornia *et al.*, 1987). There was also a long-running debate over the effectiveness of SAPs in terms of promoting growth (see Parfitt, 1990) and criticisms of the doctrinaire adherence to neo-liberal economic precepts which were applied with little regard for the particularities of the individual country concerned. Some of these criticisms hit home and from 1987 onwards the World Bank funded 'social dimensions of adjustment' (SDA) programmes as additions to adjustment programmes (Engberg-Pederson *et al.*, 1996). The EU Commission claimed that in its funding of adjustment programmes it wanted to avoid some of the worst mistakes of the Bretton Woods institutions.

In a discussion paper published by two leading officials of the Commission and in a subsequent Council resolution, the EU policy on adjustment was defined (Council of Ministers, 1988; Frisch and Boidin, 1988). The Union sought to specify differences between its approach and that of the main external donors in a number of important ways. It claimed that its approach would differentiate between recipient countries and would be less doctrinaire, stating that 'reforms should be conceived and carried out in a pragmatic and differentiated manner, with due respect for economic policy options and taking account of the peculiarities and constraints of each country' (Council of Ministers, 1988). The Commission also argued, in line with the 'humanitarian critique', that adjustment should take account of the position of the poorest and most vulnerable in society and that they should be protected from the worst effects of adjustment. For its part the ACP stated clearly that 'The programme should not be linked to or governed by the conditionalities characteristic of international financial institutions, *but should reflect the appreciations special to our ACP/EEC cooperation*. . . . Clearly, the access to any structural adjustment programme should not require an IMF or World Bank imprimatur' (Greenidge, 1988: 15, emphasis added).

In some respects the Lomé IV agreement, signed in late 1989, reflected these aims. It pledged that adjustment would be 'economically viable and socially and politically bearable' (Lomé IV, 1989: Article 243). It also sought to avoid contradicting the principles on which development cooperation had thus far been practised, stating that adjustment would be 'supportive of the ACP State's [sic] priority development objectives' and would 'take place within the framework of the political and economic model of the ACP State concerned' (Article 244). Furthermore, Lomé IV saw the creation of a special envelope for adjustment support – the SAF – of 1.15 billion ECU within the overall aid package provided by the Convention. Representing over 10 per cent of the total grant aid available, this was a significant sum but allowed the Commission to maintain that the bulk of resources, channelled through the National Indicative Programmes (NIPs), would remain 'non-conditional' and dedicated to long-term development projects and would thus leave in place much of the terms and procedures on which Lomé aid had so far existed. If acted upon, therefore, the EU was potentially embarking on a significant departure from IMF and World Bank orthodoxy and one which could have enhanced the claimed 'uniqueness' of the Lomé relationship.

The reality of EU policy was, however, a different matter. Even though the Commission appeared to be trying to square the conditionality of adjustment support with Lomé principles of partnership, it was severely constrained in achieving this. On the one hand the Commission lacked the financial resources, the technical personnel and the support of member states to challenge World Bank leadership in the field (Stevens and Killick, 1989; Parfitt and Bullock, 1990). On the other hand, the Commission would not have been supported by many EU member states, which agreed with the World Bank approach. As the then British Overseas Development Minister, Chris Patten, claimed: 'It makes no sense to argue one course in Brussels and another in Washington ... close coordination with the Bank will be vital. Indeed the quickest and most effective way to support recipients' macroeconomic reforms is to work alongside the Bank' (Patten, 1988).

Even at the level of policy statements and the wording of the Convention there were a number of caveats. The original Council declaration, while making claims to a flexible and pragmatic route, nevertheless committed the Community to ensure 'effective coordination between the Community, on the one hand, and the World Bank and the IMF, which play a leading role in the dialogue on adjustment, on the other' (Council of Ministers, 1988: 103). And while the Convention stated in principle that all ACP countries were eligible for adjustment support depending on the scope of reforms being undertaken, it also specified that 'ACP States undertaking reform programmes that are acknowledged and supported at least by the principal multilateral donors, or that are agreed with such donors but not necessarily financially supported

Table 2.1 *Adjustment funding from 7th EDF (Lomé IV, Part 1), situation at the end of 1996 in million ECU*

	Total	From SAF	(% of SAF)	From NIPs	% NIP used
Decisions	1,514	1,070	(95.5)	444.2	9.6
Payments	1,298	1,017	(88.0)	282.0	15.8

Sources: adapted from: CEC, 1997a; CEC, 1997b.

by them, shall be treated as having automatically satisfied the requirements for adjustment assistance' (Lomé IV, 1989: Article 246). Given that 'principal multilateral donors' clearly meant the IMF and World Bank, such a policy fell short of ACP demands for autonomy from the Bretton Woods institutions.

This ambiguity at the level of policy statements was further reinforced by the implementation of adjustment support in Lomé IV. By the end of 1996, a total of thirty-seven ACP countries had been allocated money in support of structural adjustment and nearly the whole SAF fund had been allocated (CEC, 1997a: 21). As can be seen from Table 2.1, 95.5 per cent of the SAF had been decided and 88 per cent disbursed compared with 75.3 per cent and 28 per cent respectively for programmed aid (NIP and regional aid).

According to Commission sources, all recipients had arrangements with the Bretton Woods institutions. By the time adjustment support was being implemented, even the Commission admitted that it provided 'de facto support only for World Bank or IMF programmes' (interview, Brussels, 15 May 1993). To the extent that negotiations were conducted with countries not in receipt of World Bank support, the Commission has claimed that it would undertake missions for 'mediation and facilitation to help countries without reform programmes with the Bretton Woods institutions adjust viably and in a coherent and palatable way *that would attract support from the main funders and international institutions*', thus using EU policy to help bring agreement between the recipient country and Bretton Woods institutions (CEC, 1992a: 20, emphasis added). It is not surprising that one commentator concluded that 'EC adjustment support is indistinguishable from that of the [international financial institutions], (Mailafia, 1996: 112).

Furthermore, the other Commission aim of protecting long-term, and nominally non-conditional, aid from the Convention was also only partially realised. The Commission had stated that 'The Community has always insisted that it would be wrong to convert the aid earmarked for long term development... into adjustment support' (CEC, 1992a: 16). However, aid instruments such as Stabex (compensation for falls in export earnings) and aid allocated through the project-dominated NIPs were used for adjustment support. Funds for adjustment support from the structural adjustment facility accounted for around 10.6 per cent of the total aid available under the seventh EDF but have been added to by NIP funds. Of aid decisions, 9.6 per cent of NIP funds were diverted to adjustment support, rising to 15.8 per cent of payments by the end of 1996. If we assess total adjustment funds (the SAF, NIP and regional funds), then they represent 15.7 per cent of the decisions of the total EDF and 23.7 per cent for payments. In addition these figures indicate how much of the total ACP allocation of national and regional funds has been diverted to adjustment support. Given that not all ACP countries receive adjustment support, the amount of diverted funds for individual countries undertaking adjustment is likely to be considerably greater. This was, for example, the case in Zimbabwe, where up to 24 per cent of its NIP from EDF 7 was directed to its adjustment support programme (see Brown, 1999). It therefore suggests that, for those countries undergoing adjustment, the change in balance of use of aid towards adjustment in Lomé IV has been considerably more than the aggregate figures indicate.

In summary, the introduction of policies to support the process of structural adjustment represented an important reorientation of the EU's development policies and one that demonstrated a convergence with the dominant neo-liberal policies of the World Bank. The Commission initially claimed that, even despite this shift, the unique character of the Lomé relationship would endure. In practice there is little or no evidence that this was so. Instead, the introduction of support for structural adjustment has amounted to little more than simply lining up aid resources from the Convention behind IMF- and World Bank-led programmes.

Political conditionality

Almost before the ink was dry on the Lomé IV Convention, and certainly before its new conditionality could be implemented, further fundamental revisions to international donor aid policies were afoot. The changes that were introduced went under the broad heading of 'political conditionality'. In contrast to, or, more accurately, in an extension of, the earlier 'economic conditionality' of structural adjustment, now donors directed attention to more overtly political conditions over the receipt of aid. These conditions cover the distinct but related areas of 'good governance', 'human rights' and 'democracy'. Thus from 1989 to 1991 most major donor nations – such as the US, Britain, France, Germany and Japan – as well as donor institutions (including the World Bank and the EU) all declared an intention to link aid dispersals to recipient countries' domestic political situations, in particular favouring those undergoing 'political reform' (Nelson and Eglington, 1992; Baylies, 1995).

The new aid regime had three general objectives: improvement of governmental and administrative capacity in developing country states; the further spread of respect for universal and fundamental human rights in line with international law and international declarations; and the promotion of democratic structures, particularly multi-party elections. The shift in aid conditionality to these 'political' aims arose in response to a number of broader international factors, including the end of the Cold War, increasing demands for political change from within developing countries and problems entailed in the existing 'economic' conditionality relationship. The precise focus of conditionality (whether on human rights, good governance or democratisation); the thoroughness with which conditionality was applied; and the importance of the different causal factors which lay behind this new aid modality, varied between different donors and at different times. For the World Bank, the focus of political conditions has been on issues of 'good governance' and particularly anti-corruption. In 1989 the Bank argued that adjustment needed to 'go beyond the issues of public finance' and that market reforms 'must go hand in hand with good governance' (World Bank, 1989: foreword, 1). In part this originated from its experience of implementing SAPs, particularly in Africa. In two major reviews of implementation of adjustment in Africa (World Bank, 1989, 1994), the Bank argued that while adjustment worked when properly implemented, too often this was not done either because states reneged on implementing reform programmes or did not implement the more politically difficult measures. The Bank thus argued for the need to improve the ownership of reform programmes in adjusting countries and to 'muster support among the interest groups that have most to gain from reforms' (World Bank, 1994: 15). Enhancing governance was seen as facilitating this process by making the reform measures taken more transparent and reducing the space for non-implementation (transparency would undermine attempts by elements within the states who sought to obstruct reforms). As such, the Bank recognised the continued role needed for a functioning and efficient state simply to carry out what were often very protracted, complex and demanding economic reforms. The earlier emphasis on reducing the scope of state intervention in the economy thus gave way to a concern to create lean and efficient administration. The Bank thus concluded, 'underlying a litany of Africa's development problems is a crisis of governance' (World Bank, 1991: 60).

These concerns have led to a variety of measures to support good governance which have included: support for policy formulation; institutional strengthening; reform of the civil service and reform and privatisation of public enterprises; anti-corruption measures; improvements in accounting, accountability and transparency; and strengthening the rule of law (Crawford, 1995). However, in a more negative vein, the Bank also warned, 'countries cannot expect an increased flow of foreign resources without undertaking the economic reforms necessary . . . and such economic reforms will probably not take place until the conditions for good governance are established' (World Bank, 1994: 15). Thus development assistance would, in the Bank's view, become conditional on commitments to good government.

The wider political issues of human rights and democracy have also been taken on board by the Bank but to a lesser degree. Within the good governance agenda, the Bank's focus has often been on tackling corruption, which not only results in wasted resources but also distorts the policy process. However, this has direct political implications, for not only is corruption seen as bad for citizens' rights and freedoms, but enhancing those rights, and improving openness and accountability, are a key mechanism for reducing corruption. The problem for the Bank is that such actions are in danger of breaching its Charter, which specifies that 'the Bank and its officers shall not interfere in the political affairs of any member' (cited in Gillies, 1996: 120). The Bank's defence has been that its narrow concern with good governance defined as 'efficient administration' is driven by what is necessary for successful economic reforms. Its concern with 'politics' is therefore neutral and a product purely of developmental considerations (Williams and Young, 1994: 86–7; Gillies, 1996: 115–17). Thus, denying the political nature of the Bank, former President Barber Conable felt able to claim: 'Allow me to be blunt: the political uncertainty and arbitrariness in so many parts of sub-Saharan Africa are major constraints on the region's development . . . *I am not advocating a political stance here*, but I am advocating increased transparency, respect for human rights and adherence to the rule of law' (cited in Gillies, 1996: 115, emphasis original).

The Bank has been more circumspect over the issue of democratisation. Here it was donor states, which, in response to the fall of the Berlin Wall, made movement towards multi-party democracy a condition for former Eastern bloc states receiving aid resources. In response also to the rise of internal demands for democratisation in developing countries, the condition quickly spread to development aid. Democracy is an even more contested concept than human rights, the latter having the benefit of codification in several international declarations and treaties. As such, it is even more liable to be ruled out by the Bank's Charter. However, the Bank's 2000/2001 World Development Report, *Attacking Poverty*, noted that, while the relationship between democracy and economic growth was mixed, democracy was nevertheless 'intrinsically valuable for human well-being as a manifestation of human freedom' and that most non-democratic states performed badly in terms of economic growth and poverty reduction (World Bank, 2000: 112–13). Donor states, on the other hand, were more overt in maintaining democratic conditions as a key element of the new political conditionality, however uneven the practice (see Baylies, 1995; Olsen, 1998).

Overall, therefore, the early 1990s further broadened the extent to which aid would be conditional upon 'internal' actions and policies of recipient states. Alongside the existing demand for market-friendly development policies based on neo-liberal SAPs, the newer political conditionality was seeking to extend liberal democratic principles of open accountable administration, respect for the rule of law, respect for human rights and, to an extent, the promotion of democratic forms of governance into aid policies. As with adjustment conditionality, the EU's programme of development cooperation also moved in line with the global trend.

Political conditionality and EU–ACP relations

The rapid emergence of a new aid agenda, and the leading role played by EU member states in defining it, confronted the European Union with something of a problem as far as relations with the ACP countries were concerned. Political conditionality presented the same kind of challenges to the partnership ideals of Lomé as had structural adjustment conditionality. However, this time the new agenda came to the fore when Lomé IV had just been concluded and was in the process of being ratified. This meant that the ability of the Commission to adapt policy was limited by the terms of the new Convention. Furthermore, Lomé IV had a ten-year duration rather than the usual five, with only a limited review planned at the mid-term point. However, the EU was quick to respond to the new orientation of policy and pursued an activist interpretation of the terms of Lomé IV and a much more radical review of the Convention in 1995 than had been envisaged.

The EU's policy on political conditionality was formed in 1991 with a proposed resolution presented by the Commission to the May 1991 Council of Ministers (CEC, 1991). The proposals claimed that a series of changes internationally had enabled a higher profile for democracy and human rights in development policies. The member states, including Britain and France which had been vociferous in supporting the new policy line, approved the Commission's increased attention for the issue. In its meeting of 28 November the Council passed a resolution on 'human rights, democracy and development', the key Community decision on the issue (Council of Ministers, 1991a, 1991b).

The resolution promoted a common EU policy which would give a high priority in development policies to 'positive measures' to support human rights and democratisation, for example through supporting the holding of elections, creating democratic institutions, strengthening legal systems and promoting the role of NGOs (Council of Ministers, 1991b). Alongside this 'positive approach', the resolution also provided for negative sanctions, including suspension of aid to the developing countries concerned. It stated that, 'in the event of grave or persistent human rights violations or the serious interruption of democratic processes, the Community and its member states will consider appropriate responses'. These would include 'confidential or public démarches as well as changes in the content or channels of cooperation programmes and the deferment of necessary signatures or decisions in the cooperation process or, when necessary, the suspension of cooperation with the States concerned' (Council of Ministers, 1991b: 13).

The compatibility of this new line with the existing text of the Lomé agreement was problematic as Lomé contained no explicit statement of political conditions as such. However, Lomé IV did include a new version of Article 5 which stated (for the first time in EU–ACP relations) that development cooperation 'entails respect for and promotion of all human rights' and that 'development policy and cooperation are closely linked with the respect for and enjoyment of fundamental human rights'. Despite its broad terms, the Commission maintained that Article 5 of Lomé IV permitted, in the light of the new Commission policy, a much more active application of human rights and democratic conditions within Lomé (interview, Brussels, 25 May 1993). Indeed the Commission used Article 5 as a reason and justification to act against several ACP countries where it felt human rights or democratic processes had been violated, including the unilateral (and it is claimed, illegal) suspension of aid (see Arts, 2000 for an extended discussion; also, European Research Office, 1994a). In addition, the EU pursued positive measures including support for election processes in seventeen ACP countries and the sending of observer missions from the European Parliament and the ACP–EC Joint Assembly (ACP–EEC Joint Assembly Working Party, 1994; European Research Office, 1994b). It also actively encouraged utilisation of elements of Lomé aid which supported building the 'democratic fabric' in ACP countries, such as decentralised cooperation based on building relations with NGOs and other civil society bodies (Laidler, 1991).

However, the mid-term review of Lomé IV offered the opportunity to specify the new conditionality less equivocally and became the primary objective of the EU in the negotiations. Respect for human rights and democratisation thus became an 'essential element' of cooperation with the ACP in an amendment to the existing Article 5. The Convention could now be suspended 'in part or as a whole' in relation to countries where there were serious human rights violations or interruptions of the democratic process, for 'Respect for human rights, democratic principles and the rule of law . . . shall constitute an essential element of this Convention' (Lomé IV-bis, 1995). The mechanism for suspension of aid provided for consultations prior to any action being taken although it left open the possibility for the EU to act unilaterally if it saw fit (Lomé IV-bis, 1995: Article 366a, 2). The revision of Lomé IV also included a series of measures to promote human rights and democracy, such as promotion of decentralised cooperation, the creation of a special fund or 'incentive envelope' for institutional support for democratisation and good government in the ACP states (worth eighty million ECU) and a new requirement that unelected government officials could only attend the ACP–EU Joint Assembly with the prior agreement of the Assembly (Lomé IV-bis, 1995: Article 32).

The changes to EU development policy constituted a forthright adoption of the new aid agenda. Commissioner for development Manuel Marin underlined this by declaring boldly that, 'In the past we gave support to the likes of Amin, Bokassa or Mobutu. That will never happen again' (*Guardian*, 10 September 1993). Commission policy on adjustment support was at least partly constrained by member states which wished to ensure that the EU did not seriously stray from IMF and World Bank leadership. However, the policy on political conditionality was enthusiastically supported by member states which, at least rhetorically, supported a stronger and more far-reaching conditionality than the World Bank was able to pursue. In fact, both the Commission and member states have been less hesitant in promoting the obviously political aspects of the new aid regime. The shift in policy was also facilitated by the changes underway in the ACP states, many of which were undergoing democratisation processes, giving at least some support to the changes from the ACP side. Furthermore, the principle that conditions could be attached to Lomé aid had already been conceded in the Lomé IV negotiations.

The 1990s therefore saw an extension and entrenchment of the principle of conditionality with a much broader range of criteria that recipient countries had to fulfil in order to receive aid. For the Lomé aid regime, it was a further indication of the extent to which the EU's development policies were becoming intimately bound up with the wider international trends in North–South relations. The differences that were discernible between EU and World Bank policies on political conditionality owed more to the constraints on World Bank policy than to the special character of the EU approach. Furthermore, while adjustment conditionality had been limited in its impact on Lomé aid by leaving in place substantial parts of the 'traditional' aid provision, political conditionality potentially applied to the entire Convention.

Together, the twin objectives of conditionality sought to enhance a process of liberalisation in developing countries. Initially focusing on the economy, adjustment conditionality elevated a market-friendly approach to development and economic policy together with a liberal, law-abiding, non-corrupt and possibly democratic state that respected human rights as a model and basis for all subsequent development efforts. The Lomé Convention encapsulated this well, terming such features 'essential elements' of development cooperation. But donor policies have continued to evolve and have centred on two areas: an ongoing concern with producing what donors see as the necessary 'policy environment' for development, and a revitalised interest in poverty reduction as the goal of aid policies.

A post-Washington consensus era?

The late 1990s saw further and substantial changes in donor policies which affected both the process and aims of development cooperation. In terms of process, the limitations of conditionality as a means by which to get developing countries to create the kind of policy environment that donors wished to see, had become increasingly apparent. In its place donors sought greater developing country ownership of reforms and the formation of relations based on 'partnership'. In terms of aims, donors gave increased attention to poverty reduction as an overriding goal while maintaining an adherence to the liberal market-friendly approach to development and economic growth. The changes in donor policies that resulted led some to talk of a 'post-Washington consensus era'. While we will not address this claim directly, it was in the context of these shifts that the EU and ACP negotiated a new Partnership Agreement to succeed the Lomé Convention. We therefore do need to sketch the major features of change in the general aid picture before again assessing how far the new Partnership Agreement reflects or departs from these wider trends.

In terms of the aims of development aid, the late 1990s saw the emergence of a consensus among many donors on poverty reduction as a, if not the, main goal (OECD, 1996, 1999). Initiatives by the OECD and World Bank built on a series of UN-organised international conferences in the 1990s which created broad-ranging international support for a range of development aims. These included the declarations resulting from the Rio UN Conference on Environment and Development in 1992, the Vienna Conference on Human Rights in 1993, the Cairo Conference on Population in 1994, the Copenhagen Conference on Social Development in 1995, and the Beijing Conference on Women and Development in 1995. A series of international development targets were then defined and outlined by the OECD. They included the aim of a reduction by half of the numbers in extreme poverty by 2015 as well as various targets for health and education provision, removing gender inequality and moving towards sustainable global development (OECD, 1996). The shift was exemplified by the Wolfensohn Presidency of the World Bank from 1995 which forcefully re-emphasised the aim of poverty reduction in Bank policies. Even the IMF, whose focus on financial stability precluded poverty reduction becoming an overarching goal of its policies, nevertheless adopted some of the new agenda, replacing its concessional lending fund – the enhanced structural adjustment facility – with the poverty reduction growth facility (PRGF) in 1999 (IMF, 1999a).

In terms of the process of aid delivery, there was also an attempt to shift away from the confrontational dialogue on aid that adjustment conditionality had often produced. Strict and detailed policy prescriptions agreed to (but not necessarily implemented) in advance of the release of funds had been the basis of both the Bank and Fund lending. As we have seen, these also came to dominate decisions of other donors. Nevertheless, now the Bank claimed starkly that conditionality 'generally does not work' (World Bank, 2000: 10.8). Such claims stemmed from many of the issues that had come to the fore in Bank consideration of the successes and failures of adjustment programmes in the early 1990s (World Bank, 1994). Then it was argued that where adjustment was implemented fully it produced the desired results, but in too many cases and for various reasons adjustment programmes simply were not implemented. As we have seen, factors such as these contributed to the burgeoning focus on governance. However, by the late 1990s the Bank was rejecting the strategy of conditionality as a means of achieving 'good policies'. Instead it was claimed that 'ownership is essential. Countries must be in the driver's seat and set the course' (Wolfensohn, 1999: 9). Also, 'policy conditionality works best where there is robust government ownership of the reform programme' (IMF/World Bank Development Committee, 1999: 20). And, more broadly, 'Development cannot be donor driven . . . We must learn to let go'

(Wolfensohn, 1997: 2). The Bank thus argued for 'partnerships' with developing countries in which the Bank was to facilitate the recipient country in reaching and implementing good policies which they had formed after a process of inclusive and open consultation with internal and external actors (Wolfensohn, 1999: 21–31).

This move towards partnerships was also reflected in the adoption by the Bank of a 'comprehensive development framework' (CDF). The CDF sought to outline a basis for partnership between the various 'actors in development', including donors, recipient states and civil society groups (Wolfensohn, 1999). As such the CDF proposed a matrix within which the aims, arenas of action and actors in the development process could be located. It also envisaged a process whereby 'internal' consultations between government and civil society would lead to recipient-defined development strategies that could then be supported by partnerships with donors. The CDF proposal also emphasised the complementary roles of the IMF and the World Bank, with the Fund taking its traditional responsibility for issues of macroeconomic stability and the Bank's arena of action in social and structural areas (Wolfensohn, 1999). This division of labour between the two organisations, which had become somewhat blurred with the joint funding of adjustment programmes, was pursued in coordination with the IMF and included the specification of responsibility for monitoring different areas of conditionality (IMF, 1999a; IMF/International Development Association, 1999).

Nowhere were the new directions in aid policy more evident than in the adoption of the 'highly indebted poor countries' (HIPC) initiative. The HIPC scheme arose from widespread calls for debt reduction for the poorest countries and covered both the areas of change we have identified; that is, the status of conditionality and the goal of poverty reduction. The scheme was launched in 1996 and entailed debt write-offs for the poorest countries that had proven records of implementing IMF and World Bank adjustment programmes. In the summer of 1999 the HIPC initiative was accelerated when speedier routes to debt relief were agreed by the Group of 8 industrialised countries. In order to ensure that funds released by debt relief contributed to development, and in line with the Bank's twin-track conceptualisation of aid policies, debt relief was conditional upon *both* adherence to macroeconomic stability under IMF guidance and the creation and implementation of programmes through which poverty reduction would be achieved in recipient countries. Debt relief therefore centred on the adoption both of letters of intent in the traditional manner of adjustment programmes and of 'poverty reduction strategy papers' outlining how specific poverty reduction targets would be reached (see IMF, 1999a; IMF/International Development Association, 1999; IMF/World Bank Development Committee, 1999).

By the end of the 1990s, therefore, both the *content* of aid policies and the *process* of allocating aid seemed to have changed. On the former, specific poverty reduction strategies existed alongside more familiar and orthodox macroeconomic policies. On the latter, the aim of partnership replaced the conditionality demands made by donors. As such these shifts represent some serious rethinking of aid policies. However, the change in the Bank's stance remains qualified in a number of ways. Firstly, there are potentially serious conflicts and tensions between the two elements of the new aid policy – macroeconomic stability and poverty reduction. The Bank recognised that while there existed a high degree of donor agreement on the broad parameters of what constituted 'good policies', there remained a host of options over the precise details (World Bank, 2000: 192) and that universal uniformity in development strategies was undesirable (World Bank, 2000: 194). However, both the World Bank and the IMF concurred, in a manner entirely consistent with the earlier neo-liberal stance, that the policies needed to enable broad based growth will generally include measures to ensure macroeconomic stability, appropriate fiscal and exchange rate policies and financial sector development' (IMF/World Bank Development Committee, 1999: 7). The two organisations underscored the need for macroeconomic stability in launching the revitalised HIPC in 1999 (IMF, 1999b). Indeed, adherence to an ESAF (now PRGF) programme is a condition of progressing through the HIPC scheme and has been a major obstacle preventing more countries benefiting from it.

Furthermore, while social sector policies aimed at poverty reduction are conceived as accompanying such adjustment-oriented macroeconomic policies, little attention is given to the tensions that may thus arise. For example, the IMF noted the need to ensure that poverty reduction measures did not have a negative macroeconomic impact, that they would be funded in a non-inflationary way and, in a clear echo of the earlier policy era, that they did not lead to undue 'crowding out' of the private sector (IMF, 1999a, 1999b). Indeed, the new division of responsibilities kept a clear role for the IMF in ensuring that the macroeconomic criteria were met by the recipient in jointly funded programmes (IMF, 1999a). Given that adjustment programmes had in the past often resulted in cutbacks to social policy areas which are now seen as more important (e.g. education, health, social safety nets), there is clearly a potential danger that poverty reduction will become an add-on to macroeconomic reform and will be pursued only where the macroeconomic situation allows. Indeed, there is some evidence that on the ground poverty reduction aims are less important to the Bank than in its central policy pronouncements (OECD, 1999).

Similar tensions arise with respect to the purported move away from conditionality. While the Bank wished to get away from cajoling reluctant governments to adopt policy measures that they did not like, rightly recognising the limitations of such a relationship, it is definitely not proposing non-conditional aid. In its World Development Report of 2000/2001, *Attacking Poverty*, the Bank argued that in a context of declining aid flows and the rising importance of private capital flows to the richer developing countries, development aid should be concentrated on countries with high rates of poverty and effective policies and institutions (World Bank, 2000). The mechanism for ensuring this was to be found in an *increased* emphasis on selectivity of aid allocations based on the policy choices of recipient governments (World Bank, 2000). To a large extent, however, this is simply wishing away the problem of conditionality which consists of some divergence in views between the donor and recipient as to what constitutes good policy. As the OECD noted, 'A key constraint [to the proposed partnerships] is the shortage of governments or even sectoral ministries with both the commitment and the capacity to move into "the driver's seat"' (OECD, 1999: xxiv). Granted, some states in the developing world, including the 'star performers' such as Uganda, have taken on board Bank-approved 'good policy' stances relatively wholeheartedly and have either faced little internal opposition or overcome it. But even the Bank recognises that some may continue to decide not to choose 'pro-poor policies' (World Bank, 2000). Here selectivity – the focus of development aid on those that have chosen good policies – comes in as a way to ensure good money is not sent after bad into a 'poor policy environment'. However, given that donor preferences are known, and given a certain amount of fiscal desperation on the part of developing countries (see Harrison, 2000), governments may 'voluntarily' choose policies that they know will meet donor approval and the appearance of developing country ownership may in fact hide a more familiar picture of conditionality. As Hanlon (2000) identified in Mozambique, the desire to remain on board the HIPC train has impacted significantly on internal government policy and decisions taken by the national Parliament have been in conflict with detailed policy prescriptions of the Bank and Fund. Indeed, the HIPC initiative is explicit in stating that while there may be a need for long-term aid support, 'this does not mean non-conditional pre-committing of resources but it does imply a long-term framework for consistent graduated support to countries based on the level of policy effort' (IMF/World Bank Development Committee, 1999: 18–19). Therefore, in some ways, underlying the argument that conditionality does not work is in fact a rigorous conditionality that requires the demonstration of good policies and the realisation of output and impact targets *before* donor funding. This strategy is clearest in the HIPC initiative, where several years of adjustment and the agreement and implementation of a programme of poverty reduction are required before debt is reduced (IMF/World Bank Development Committee, 1999).

To summarise, the changes in Bank policies (and those of donors more generally) entail an expansion of the policies desired of recipient countries to include poverty reduction aims alongside more familiar macroeconomic and good governance goals. In addition it is hoped that these can be pursued in partnership with recipients which wholeheartedly support such aims. As we have noted, these attempts to move beyond the Washington consensus are complex and problematic. Such changes also have important implications for the EU's relationship with the ACP countries and the Lomé Convention itself was due for renewal in 2000. We now need to ask to what extent this evolving aid policy environment is reflected in the Cotonou Partnership Agreement with the ACP countries.

The ACP–EC Partnership Agreement

As we have seen, EU development cooperation underwent substantial changes during the lifetime of Lomé IV which resulted in a much closer alignment of the EU's development policies towards the ACP countries with the wider trends in donor–recipient relations, in particular as defined by the World Bank. Nevertheless, by the time Lomé IV was due to expire in 2000, the EU sought a more thorough reorientation of development cooperation. Indeed, the impression that the Commission had saddled itself with a Convention whose time had passed had been around for some time. As early as 1992 a Commission document on the future of development cooperation argued that 'the Convention's machinery is only partially suitable for the type of negotiations with governments which now seem to be necessary' (CEC, 1992b: 73). And substantial though they were, the changes introduced in 1995 did not go as far as the Commission had hoped. In launching a consultation process prior to the renegotiation of the ACP relationship, the Commission made it clear that a simple renewal of the Convention was not on the table and even raised the possibility of an end to the ACP as a unified group, an end to Lomé trade relations, a new political relationship and a fundamentally reordered aid relationship (CEC, 1997c). The further shifts in World Bank and donor policies that we have detailed above merely added to the Commission's and member states' desire to yet again recast relations with the ACP countries. A new agreement was struck with the ACP states in February 2000 and signed in Cotonou, Benin in June (Partnership Agreement, 2000).

The Cotonou Agreement is based on four areas of change: restatement of the political principles of the relationship; agreement and definition of the central aims and objectives of development cooperation; new aid procedures; and a new trade relationship. In each area, the changes introduced further demonstrate the closeness of approach of the EU and World Bank in the twenty-first century. We will survey the first three of these areas. The fourth, trade, will be analysed in the next chapter.

From an early stage the EU was intent on establishing key political principles as the basis for future cooperation with the ACP countries. In its consultation paper on the future agreement, the Commission stated: 'The colonial and post-colonial period are behind us and a more politically open international environment enables us to lay down the responsibilities of each partner less ambiguously' (CEC, 1997c: vi). The new Partnership Agreement thus restates and reinforces the political conditionality present in the revised Lomé IV: 'Respect for human rights, democratic principles and the rule of law, which underpin the ACP–EU Partnership, shall underpin the domestic and international policies of the Parties and constitute the essential elements of this Agreement' (Partnership Agreement, 2000: Article 9). Serious breach of any of these would constitute grounds for suspension of cooperation. The vaguely worded clause allowing 'appropriate measures to be taken' (Article 96) leaves open the possibility of unilateral suspension of the agreement by the EU. In an extension of the political conditions on cooperation, a new commitment to good governance and anti-corruption was also included, much against the ACP's wishes. In defining good governance, the emphasis is on anti-corruption as a central issue. While Cotonou specifies good governance as a 'fundamental element' rather than an 'essential element', it leaves open the possibility of suspension of cooperation by the EU in cases of serious corruption (Articles 9 and 97). While much of this agenda had been central to ACP–EU relations through the 1990s, as we have seen, the re-emphasis on political conditions and the new and controversial extension to include specific targeting of corruption are clearly in line with the World Bank's central concerns.

Secondly, the Cotonou Partnership Agreement also follows the wider trends that were highlighted above in its specification of the aims of development cooperation. As with the World Bank and other donors, the reduction of poverty is defined as the 'central objective of ACP–EC cooperation' (Article 19). The Agreement also makes specific reference to the various UN conferences and the international development targets detailed above (Preamble and Article 19). In addition, the new agreement incorporates the EU's own development aims (which originated in the Maastricht Treaty) of integration of developing countries into the world economy, reducing poverty and the political principles detailed above. Thus, although the declaration that ACP states have the right to define their own development priorities 'in all sovereignty' remains (Article 2), this now exists alongside, and it is implicitly assumed by the agreement to be in accord with, the wider consensus on the aims of development cooperation.

As with the Bank's commitment to poverty reduction, the Cotonou Agreement also posits this new emphasis on poverty reduction alongside the by now well-established funding of adjustment and macroeconomic reform. As with Lomé IV practice, such funding is to be granted automatically to ACP states undertaking reforms that are 'supported by the principal multilateral donors' (Article 67). However, in an indication of the extent to which macroeconomic reform has come to dominate aid programmes, there is no separate financial envelope for adjustment, the funds for which can now be drawn from the aid package as a whole. It is worth remembering that at the time of Lomé IV, the Commission was at pains to claim that 'long-term development aid' was kept separate from adjustment support. In the Cotonou Agreement, the whole aid budget is referred to as 'the envelope to support long-term development' (Annex I) and in principle virtually all of it may be used, if so desired, to support adjustment programmes. Also like the Bank and Fund stance, potential tensions exist between the aims of poverty reduction and the more orthodox and familiar aims of macroeconomic stability, the latter defined as 'disciplined fiscal and monetary policies that result in the reduction of inflation and improve external and fiscal balances' (Article 22). Again, whether these aims have priority over, or are assumed to be serving, the newer aims of poverty reduction will be a key test as to whether the EU too has moved beyond the Washington consensus.

Finally, the Cotonou Agreement parallels the Bank over the issue of aid process. As we saw above, the Bank was trying to move beyond conditionality towards partnerships and selectivity in deciding allocations of aid. Here Cotonou makes significant changes from past practice. Previously (until the revision of Lomé IV) the Commission would announce the allocations to each individual ACP state from the overall aid budget and that amount (the National Indicative Programme) represented a contractual agreement of funding. This was modified slightly in the revised Lomé IV so that only 70 per cent of aid resources were thus allocated and the remaining 30 per cent would be allocated depending on the performance of each ACP state in utilising the first tranche. The Cotonou Agreement extends this change by introducing a new aid procedure (Annex IV). In a manner reminiscent of the poverty reduction strategies of the HIPC initiative, the aid process begins with the definition of a 'country support strategy' (CSS) to which the EU will allocate an initial aid amount. The progress of this will be reviewed in a two-yearly cycle with future allocations dependent on the 'performance' of the recipient state in implementing the CSS. Also like the Bank's new approach to ensuring good policies, EU aid will be allocated selectively, rewarding those ACP countries that most clearly demonstrate adherence to the newly defined priorities and implicitly penalising those that do not. In this the Commission sought to increase the ACP ownership of development cooperation and 'put an end to the cynical and basically dishonest behaviour of countries which respect the letter of conditions imposed in their adjustment programmes in order to get their hands on the money while refraining from any real, in depth reform' (CEC, 1996: 43). Again as with the Bank, the extent to which this really does move beyond conditionality is a moot point. The OECD noted that 'Selectivity is seen as affording some leverage over policies through the gentler and more effective means of on-going dialogue about implementing shared principles' (OECD, 1999: xxiii) but the reality may still be the release and withholding of funding dependent on the policies adopted by recipient governments. As with the Bank's general stance and the HIPC initiative in particular, it thus, if anything, makes conditionality tougher by rewarding policy performance rather than policy promises.

This new aid agenda is almost certainly going to have a significant impact on the provision of aid under Cotonou. Even before the Agreement, the World Bank's Poverty Reduction Stately Paper (PRSP) had impacted on the Commission's support for adjustment programmes. Now, in the words of Commissioner for Development Poul Nielson: 'support for endorsed PRSPs should over time become the central focus of Commission country strategies' (Nielson, 2000). While such an intent, and the focus on a rolling programme and policy performance, indeed demonstrate very clearly the extent to which the Partnership Agreement has been formulated with the new aid agenda in mind, the issue may pose some familiar problems for the Commission. For while the Commission and Bank are if anything closer in terms of their rhetoric (a comparison of the Partnership Agreement and the Bank's *Attacking Poverty* report shows a shared emphasis on partnership, policy performance, poverty reduction, recipient ownership of reforms, and so on), the World Bank routinely fails to live up to its rhetoric in practice. Indeed, Commission assessments of PRSPs note a series of problems with the design and practice of particular PRSPs. Some of these relate to the operation of the HIPC scheme itself in terms of the criteria for decisions about which countries qualify and which do not (and which PRSPs are endorsed and which are not). However, it also recognises that the Bank still often operates in terms of the old agenda of prescribing detailed policies to recipient governments which undermine any aim of recipient ownership, tend to prioritise old-style macroeconomic reforms and sideline any consultations which may have taken place between a government and its civil society (CEC, 2000). Indeed, the Commission notes how consultations between the government and civil society in the formation of an 'endorsed' PRSP in Burkina Faso involved one seventy-five-minute meeting between government and NGOs (CEC, 2000). The problem for the Commission is what it will do when support for an endorsed PRSP means support for a PRSP that it sees as seriously flawed. Will it, as it did with adjustment programmes, ultimately defer to World Bank leadership? Or will it have the where-with-all and political support from member states to influence the implementation of the HIPC scheme and the formation of PRSPs in ACP states? The answer will be a crucial test of the uniqueness of the aid provided under the Cotonou Partnership Agreement.

Conclusion

This chapter has sought to outline the parallels between the EU's development policy in its relationship with the ACP countries and the wider trends in donor aid policies, those of the World Bank in particular. We have seen how the development cooperation agreements with the ACP countries have been periodically modified since the mid-1980s. These changes resulted in the undermining of the claims of the EU or ACP to have a unique development cooperation relationship. First with adjustment conditionality, then with political conditions, and most recently with the definition of new aims and processes for aid, the ACP–EU relationship has moved towards an ever closer uniformity with the wider aid policy environment, particularly as embodied in the policies of the World Bank.

For the EU's development policy this poses some key problems. For many years, there was both the political space and the political will on the part of the EU to engage in a relationship with the ACP states that departed from the more general North–South relationship in limited but important ways. The experience of change in that relationship detailed above has shown this to be no longer the case. While in some ways it is inescapable for the EU's development programme to have to respond to changes in this wider, international picture and, given its importance, to the specific policies of the World Bank, there appears to have been little initiative to do this in any way that departs significantly from Bank practice. The claim to provide an alternative approach to adjustment conditionality in the 1980s amounted to little in practice, as we have seen. In part this reflected constraints on the Commission as an aid donor in terms of limits of personnel, policy-making capacity and financial clout. But it also reflected the more significant political limitations imposed by member states. Since the original Lomé I agreement they have given little support to the further development of a unique EU relationship with the South. Given that many member states are both key proponents of the kinds of policy that have been pursued at the global level, and are important and influential members of the World Bank, this is not surprising. However, if the EU's relationship with the ACP countries offers nothing significant that is distinctive from other multilateral and bilateral sources, then it does beg the question as to the purpose and rationale for such an elaborate and extensive development cooperation programme.

Bibliography

ACP–EEC Joint Assembly Working Party (1994), 'Interim report on the second phase of Lomé IV', Rapporteur Margaret Daly MEP (unpublished).

Arts, K. (2000), *Integrating Human Rights into Development Cooperation: The Case of the Lomé Convention*, The Hague: Kluwer Law International.

Baylies, C. (1995), 'Political conditionality and democratisation', *Review of African Political Economy*, 22:65, pp. 321–37.

Brown, W. (1999), 'The EU and structural adjustment: the case of Lomé IV and Zimbabwe', *Review of African Political Economy*, 26:79, pp.75–91.

CEC (1991), 'Draft communication from the Commission to the Council and Parliament: human rights democracy and development policy', Brussels, 9 January (internal).

CEC (1992a), *The Role of the Community in Supporting Structural Adjustment in ACP States*, Luxembourg: Office of the Official Publications of the European Community (OOPEC).

CEC (1992b), 'Communication from the Commission to the Council and Parliament: development policy in the run up to 2000', SEC (92) 915 final/2, Brussels, 16 September (internal).

CEC (1996), *EU–ACP Cooperation in 1995: What Form of Structural Adjustment?*, Brussels: CEC DGVIII.

CEC (1997a), *EU-ACP Cooperation in 1996: The Fight Against Poverty*, Brussels: CEC DGVIII.

CEC (1997b), *Financial Cooperation Under the Lomé Conventions: Aid Situation at the End of 1996*, DE 92, Brussels: OOPEC.

CEC (1997c), 'Green Paper on Relations between the European Union and the ACP Countries on the Eve of the 21st Century: Challenges and Options for a New Partnership', Brussels: CEC DGVIII.

CEC (1997d), 'Communication from the Commission to the Council and Parliament: Guidelines for the Negotiation of New Cooperation Agreements with the African, Caribbean and Pacific (ACP) Countries', COM (97) 537 final, Brussels.

CEC (2000), 'Note to heads of delegation, heads of unit and desk officers: poverty reduction strategy papers: guidance notes', B2(00)D/4371, source: http://europa.euint/comm/development/sector/poverty_reduction/index.htm.

Cornia, A., R. Jolly and F. Stewart (eds) (1987), *Adjustment With a Human Face*, Oxford: Clarendon Press.

Council of Ministers (1988), 'Resolution of 31 May 1988 on the economic situation and adjustment process in Sub-Saharan Africa', in Council of the European Communities, *Compilation of Texts Adopted by the Council*, Brussels: OOPEC.

Council of Ministers (1991a), press release 6379/91 (Presse 73), 1409th Council Meeting–Development Co-operation–Brussels, 27 May.

Council of Ministers (1991b), 'Council resolution on human rights, democracy and development', press release 9555/91 (Presse 217), Brussels, 28 November.

Crawford, G. (1995), *Aid and Political Reform: A Comparative Study of the Development Cooperation Policies of Four Northern Donors*, Leeds: University of Leeds.

Engberg-Pedersen, P., P. Gibbon, P. Raikes and Udsholt (eds) (1996), *Limits of Adjustment in Africa: The Effects of Economic Liberalisation 1986–1994*, Copenhagen and Oxford: Centre for Development Research in Association with James Currey.

European Research Office (1994a), 'Issues arising from the 1993 Court of Auditors report: grant refunds on past loan financing and un-allocated programmable resources', *Reflections on the MTR Proposals Series*.

European Research Office (1994b), 'The mid-term review: human rights and democracy', *Lomé IV Mid-Term Review Positions Series*, extract from ACP–EEC Joint Assembly Working Party.

Frisch, D. and J. C. Boidin (1988), 'Adjustment, development and equity', *The Courier*, no. 111, pp. 67–72.

Gillies, D. (1996), 'Human rights, democracy and good governance: stretching the World Bank's policy frontiers', in J. M. Griesgraber and B. G. Gunter (eds), *The World Bank: Lending on a Global Scale*, London: Pluto Press.

Greenidge, C. B. (1988), 'Statement by the President of the Council of ACP Ministers Honorable Carl B. Greenidge on the occasion of the opening of the negotiations for a fourth ACP/EEC Convention', Luxembourg, 12 October (unpublished).

Hanlon, J. (2000), 'Power without responsibility: the World Bank and Mozambiquan cashew nuts', *Review of African Political Economy*, 27:83, pp. 29–45.

Harrison, G. (2000), 'Administering market friendly growth? Liberal populism and the World Bank's involvement in administrative reform in Sub-Saharan Africa', paper presented at ROAPE Millennium Conference *Africa Capturing the Future*, University of Leeds, 29 April.

IMF (1999a), 'The Poverty Reduction Growth Facility (PRGF): operational issues', Washington, 13 December.

IMF (1999b), 'Concluding remarks by the chairman of the IMF's executive board: poverty reduction strategy papers – operational issues and poverty reduction growth

facility – operational issues', Executive Board Meeting 99/136, Washington, 21 December.
IMF/International Development Association (1999), 'The Poverty Reduction Strategy Papers (PRSP): operational issues Washington' 10 December.
IMF/World Bank Development Committee (1999), 'Building poverty reduction strategies in developing countries', Joint Ministerial Committee of the Boards of Governors of the Bank and Fund on the Transfer of Real Resources to Developing Countries, DC/99–29, Washington, 22 September.
Krueger, A. O. (1995), *Political Economy of Policy Reform in Developing Countries*, Cambridge, Massachusetts: MIT Press.
Laidler, M. (1991), 'Programming Lomé IV', *The Courier*, no. 128, pp. 8–10.
Lomé IV (1989), 'Fourth ACP–EEC Convention signed in Lomé, Togo on 15 December 1989', *The Courier* (1990), no. 120.
Lomé IV-bis (1995), 'Fourth ACP–EC Convention of Lomé as revised by the agreement signed in Mauritius on 4 November 1995', in *The Courier* (1996), no. 155.
Mailafia, O. (1996), *Europe and Economic Reform in Africa*, London: Routledge.
Mosley, P., J. Harigan and J. Toye (1991), *Aid and Power: The World Bank and Policy Based Lending*, Volume One: *Analysis and Policy Proposals*, London: Routledge.
Nelson, J. and S. Eglington (1992), *Encouraging Democracy: What Role for Conditioned Aid?*, Washington: Overseas Development Council.
Nielson, P. (2000), 'Letter to Michel Camdessus, Managing Director IMF', B2(00)D/2999, http://europa.eu.int/comm/development/sector/poverty_reduction/index.htm.
OECD (1996), *Shaping the 21st Century: The Contribution of Development Cooperation*, Paris: OECD.
OECD (1999), *DAC Scoping Study of Donor Poverty Reduction Policies and Practices*, Paris: OECD.
Olsen, G. R. (1998), 'Europe and the promotion of democracy in post-cold war Africa: how serious is Europe and for what reasons?', *African Affairs*, 97:388, pp. 343–367.
Parfitt, T. W. (1990), 'Lies, damned lies and statistics: the World Bank/Economic Commission for Africa structural adjustment controversy', *Review of African Political Economy*, 17:47, pp. 128–41.
Parfitt, T. W. and S. Bullock (1990), 'The prospects for a new Lomé Convention: structural adjustment or structural transformation?', *Review of African Political Economy*, 17:47, pp. 104–16.
Partnership Agreement (2000) between the African, Caribbean and Pacific States of the one part, and the European Community and its Member States, of the other part, signed in Cotonou on 23 June, in *The Courier*, special issue, September.
Patten, C. (1988), 'Improving the impact of European Community aid', Speech by Mr Christopher Patten MP, Minister for Overseas Development, London, Royal Commonwealth Society, 3 May (unpublished).
Stevens, C. and T. Killick (1989), 'Development cooperation and structural adjustment: the issues for Lomé IV', report prepared for discussion at the Conference *Structural Adjustment and Lomé IV*, Brussels, 21 April.
Williams, D. and T. Young (1994), 'Governance, the World Bank and liberal theory', *Political Studies*, 42:1, pp. 84–100.
Wolfensohn, J. (1997), 'The challenge of inclusion', Annual Meeting Address, Hong Kong, 23 September.

Wolfensohn, J. (1999), *A Proposal for a Comprehensive Development Framework*, Discussion Draft, Washington: World Bank.

World Bank (1981), *Towards Accelerated Development in Sub-Saharan Africa: An Agenda for Action*, Washington: World Bank.

World Bank (1989), *Sub-Saharan Africa: From Crisis to Sustainable Growth*, Washington: World Bank.

World Bank (1991), *World Development Report: The Challenge of Development*, Oxford: Oxford University Press.

World Bank (1994), *Adjustment in Africa: Reforms, Results and the Road Ahead*, Oxford: Oxford University Press.

World Bank (2000), *World Development Report 2000/01: Attacking Poverty*, Washington: World Bank.

3

The unimportance of trade preferences

Anna K. Dickson

In 1975 the EU operated a pyramid of preference in terms of market access and disbursement of development assistance to non-member states. The ACP countries were at the top of this pyramid, enjoying the most preferred status in the EU market for their exports, including duty free access for all industrial products and 80 per cent of agricultural exports. In addition there were special Protocols for bananas, sugar, beef and rum which guaranteed access to the EU market for specific quotas of these products.

It is now argued that the ACP no longer occupies this position, or at least that the pyramid has changed shape. Hill, for example, argued that there are now concentric circles of favoured nations rather than a pyramid (1993: 324). Other partners are being offered virtually the same level of preferences, and tariffs have in general been gradually lowered throughout the period. For example, the Community has offered a GSP scheme since 1971, which allows preferential access for industrial exports (and limited agricultural exports) from all developing countries. Extension and enhancement of the GSP meant that the tariff difference between Lomé and the GSP became only 2 per cent (Dickson, 2000). Many ACP states will have their preferences further reduced under the Cotonou Agreement and will probably enter new reciprocal regional or sub-regional agreements by 2008. Thus the comparative advantage which the ACP states had in 1975 has been significantly eroded.

This chapter seeks to identify the main determinants of EU trade policy in relation to the developing countries. It asks why the EU has adopted trade liberalisation (and the conclusion of regional and sub-regional partnership agreements) rather than any other option for the future of its relations with the ACP, and in stark contrast to previous policies. The working hypothesis is that the EU has committed itself publicly to trade liberalisation for a number of reasons. In part this occurred as a result of external pressures – for example to reform the CAP – which increased during the Uruguay Round of GATT negotiations. The Commission is keen to be seen to be moving in the right direction in order not to draw too much attention to its own illiberal policies. In addition, the Lomé preferences are seen not to have worked and, in the context of external pressure, no alternative option has been considered viable. Finally, overlying these two factors, the end of the Cold War has provided the opportunity to reassess development cooperation in general and the ideological climate of development policy has shifted significantly since 1989. This has obvious implications for future agreements with developing countries.

The first part of this chapter looks at the general policy environment in which EU policy towards the Lomé countries has been made. Whereas in 1975 the EU was prepared to go against the prevailing norms of the international system, by 1990 this was no longer the case. The following section then looks at the trade-related directorates and their contribution and response to the phenomenon referred to here in shorthand as 'trade liberalisation'. This includes trends towards the removal or elimination of trade preferences and the ideology underlying this which is reflected in and created by the GATT/WTO.

The trade-related directorates within the European Commission have been the driving force behind the changes in the nature of the Lomé agreement. Their view is that the goal of integrating developing countries into the world economy will not be achieved by continued preferences, except for the poorest, but by the gradual introduction of reciprocity within regional or sub-regional agreements and, above all, WTO compatibility. Along with the assumption that the existing preferences have not been successful in their developmental objectives, the Commission now seeks to change the basis of cooperation between the two groups (CEC, 1997).

The Commission has presented these changes to the ACP as though no other alternative exists. One point made in this chapter is that the choice is a political one and is by no means inevitable. The chapter provides an analysis of the political interests at stake in the trade liberalisation debate. In particular it identifies the CAP as the centrepiece of a significant political debate about how best to protect domestic interests from the vagaries of the world market while subscribing to the principles of economic liberalism.

Finally, a case study of the Banana Protocol is offered as an example of the type of choice with which the EU is faced. The experience of the banana dispute in the WTO is symbolic as it demonstrates that the substantive interests at stake in the CAP and the commitment to trade liberalisation override concerns about development and the socioeconomic costs of losing trade preferences for the ACP.

The dominance of the market economy and the influence of the neo-liberal economic agenda in the EU

The 1975 Lomé Convention represented a particular way of thinking about trade and development which went against the post-war liberal consensus on the conduct of international affairs. In particular it challenged the norms of reciprocity in trade and the most favoured nation (MFN) principle which the GATT upheld. Lomé embodied the idea that special measures need to be put in place in order for the more economically disadvantaged countries to benefit from the international system. Not only was special and differential treatment accorded to the ACP, but programmes of compensation for commodity price fluctuations (Stabex and later Sysmin) were put in place along with guaranteed access to the European market for key products, in the case of sugar at EU support prices. In stark contrast to Lomé's predecessors, the Yaoundé Conventions, the preferences were non-reciprocal.

One might reasonably ask why such a unique programme of assistance was agreed to when it was clearly in contradiction to the prevailing norm in the international system. There are two main reasons. First, the Lomé Convention was concluded at a time when the call for a NIEO placed the North–South debate at the forefront of world attention. While the NIEO demands largely went unheeded by the North, the EEC tried to respond collectively and positively. It interpreted the demands in terms of providing exemptions from long-established rules of the world economy and increasing trade and aid. Lomé was, in many ways, a response by the EEC to that debate. Furthermore, the negotiating position of the ACP states was enhanced by extensive commodity shortages, exemplified by OPEC, which facilitated the conclusion of a trade chapter that guaranteed the continuation of traditional trade preferences and non-reciprocity in new preferences.

Nevertheless, there were also important historical antecedents to the Lomé Convention. These lay in specific agreements between Britain and France and their former colonies which both member states wished to prolong. The Yaoundé Conventions are often regarded as French creations while the UK accession was predicated on the inclusion of an association agreement for the non-Asian developing Commonwealth (Dickson, 1995). However, when Lomé I was signed the European Community was a mere nine member states. It has since become fifteen, with future enlargement on the agenda. It follows that the interests of the EU will have changed as membership has grown. In particular, whereas French and British interests could prevail upon the Community in the 1970s this is no longer consistently the case.

The assumptions embodied in Lomé subsequently became unpopular with the EU for all but the least developed states. Part of the reason for this is that since the 1980s there has been a dramatic shift in development thinking in both North and South. Neo-liberalism emerged in the North in response to the crisis of welfare capitalism in the 1970s. According to this perspective, the way forward was to dismantle the welfare state and embrace the global market. Neo-liberalism also impacted upon development studies in what John Toye has called the 'counter-revolution' in development economics by which Third World states were advised to liberalise their economies and find their comparative advantage (Toye, 1987). The inability of dependency theory to explain the rise of the newly industrialisation countries (NICs), and the failure of most socialist and inward-oriented industrialisation experiments, made protectionism unfashionable. Instead, the success of the NICs was viewed as a green light for market-oriented policies, while the debt crisis and the lost development decade (the 1980s), in which the real incomes of many Third World states decreased, constituted a further case against state-led development.

Neo-liberalism argues against two important assumptions of development theory: that the Third World constitutes a special case and should therefore be offered special concessions, and that the state should play a major role in economic development (Slater et al., 1993). This paradigm became the dominant one in the World Bank and the IMF through the 1980s and 1990s: 'the new vision of growth is that markets and incentives can work in developing countries. But they are filtered through government policies and agencies, which, if inappropriate, can reduce or even negate the possible benefits' (Toye, 1987: 48). Thus poor development performance is due not to a hostile international system, as dependency proclaimed, but to incorrect government policies in developing countries. In 1996 the IMF proclaimed that 'the robust growth in many developing countries [mostly in Asia] was seen as having been associated with increased openness and greater integration into the global economy ... Strong and consistent reform and stabilisation efforts had promoted increased openness' (IMF, 1996: 26). The practical implications of this view manifest themselves in World Bank and IMF policies of structural adjustment (SAPs; see chapter 2).

This debate has not bypassed the European Union. In 1990 support for structural adjustment was introduced in Lomé IV. The conclusion of Lomé IV negotiations coincided with the collapse of the Berlin Wall and the dramatic events in Eastern Europe. The so-called 'triumph of democracy' added fodder to the belief that more emphasis should be placed on democracy and market-based economies. Subsequently, in the revised Lomé IV a new clause on the essential nature of democracy was added, along with the possibility of suspension from the Convention if sufficient progress towards democracy or human rights observance was not achieved.

In 1992 the TEU set out for the first time the objectives of a common development cooperation policy designed to harmonise relations with all developing countries. These are: to foster sustainable economic and social development, the gradual integration of developing countries into the world economy and the alleviation of poverty. In addition it is declared that Community policy should contribute to the general objective of developing and consolidating democracy, the rule of law and the observance of human rights (TEU, Title XVII, Article. 130u). As objectives they are not exceptional, rather they are more or less universally acceptable and in line with the development policy objectives of the member states and the wider donor community. These objectives apply to relations with all third parties. They are part of an ongoing process to make development policy more consistent. In so doing they effectively begin to end the special status accorded to the ACP states. It is ironic that in this long awaited declaration of common objectives for development policy the EU ceases to be unique as a donor.

The campaign against poverty is a declared priority for Community development policy and of the new Cotonou Agreement. However, the nature of the link between anti-poverty policies and trade policy is not self-evident. The Community views integration into the world economy as the chief means by which poverty and exclusion can begin to be alleviated. To this end the economies of the developing countries should be made more liberal and the Community will assist in establishing the appropriate institutional framework to achieve this. Trade preferences, which are seen not to have worked, will be granted according to need and phased out when that need is judged to exist no longer (CEC, 1994).

Regional cooperation, along with the creation of regional and sub-regional groups within the ACP, is another means by which integration into the world economy will be promoted (McQueen, 1998; Oden, 1999). Regionalism is viewed by the EU as a way of bolstering structural transformation in the ACP states. That is, any regional agreements entered into must be consistent with globalisation and will probably reinforce the implementation of structural adjustment policies. As yet it is unclear whether the proposed regional agreements will substantially benefit the developmental goals of the ACP although the EU will benefit from access to new markets (McQueen, 1998).

The priorities outlined in the TEU translated more or less directly into the negotiations for a successor to the Lomé Convention which began in 1988. In relation to trade the EU entered the post-Lomé negotiations with three objectives. Firstly, to create an agreement which was more effective at promoting trade than the existing Lomé preferences had been. The general feeling in the Community was that the preferences had not been as successful as intended. ACP states have not fared as well as states without similar levels of preferences. The ACP share of the world market fell from 20.8 per cent in 1975 to 9.7 per cent in 1995. The ACP share in the EU market also fell, from 7 per cent in 1975 to 3.7 per cent in 1992 and 2.8 per cent in 1995. However, certain key products take up a large percentage of the EU market, including coffee, where the ACP share of the EU market was 38 per cent in 1993, and cocoa, where the ACP share was 79 per cent in 1993. In addition, the ACP share of EU developing country imports fell from 14 per cent in 1990 to 9 per cent in 1995, even though the ACP accounted for 40 per cent of developing countries. In contrast, non-ACP developing countries increased their share of EU imports from 9.4 per cent in 1974 to 17.1 per cent in 1989 (Grilli, 1993: 162). These generally pessimistic results are seen to confirm 'the unimportance of being preferred' and have led to a disenchantment with trade preferences as a means of assisting developing countries (Davenport, 1992).

However, it is not clear that preferences *per se* have failed and indeed there are some declared success stories among the ACP group, including Mauritius,

Zimbabwe, Côte d'Ivoire, Botswana, Fiji and Jamaica. Stevens (1994) argues that the case against trade preferences has been overstated. The poor performance of the ACP in EU markets is more a reflection of the fact that ACP exports are heavily concentrated in the commodity sector where international demand is stagnant and prices, in particular for oil, have declined. The revision of Lomé IV in 1995 sought to address the unsatisfactory position of the ACP in non-agricultural products. More emphasis was placed on industrial transformation and diversification as well as on the creation of an enabling environment.

There has also been a decline in the relative value of preferences over time, both absolutely (reduced support prices) and in relation to other groups of developing countries (the extension of the GSP). It is the more developed countries (such as Kuwait, China, India, Brazil and Singapore) which have been best able to take advantage of this scheme because of the strict rules of origin criteria. Thus analysts have concluded that the GSP scheme has in fact diverted trade away from the least developed countries (Heidensohn, 1995: 145). Interestingly, while the Community is arguing that preferences have not worked it is still prepared to offer them to the poorest countries.

The EU was keen to make any new trade agreement effective in promoting trade. This objective was bound by the second declared objective, which was that all new or revised agreements and preferences must be made WTO compatible. The EU faced external manifestations of global liberalism which supported and justified this new orientation in development policy. The trend towards trade liberalisation which began in the mid 1980s gathered pace with the start of the Uruguay Round in 1986. The establishment of the WTO in 1995 reflected and reinforced this trend. There is now a contradiction between the desire to meet obligations to the ACP and a commitment to economic liberalism. This contradiction was played out most vocally in the banana dispute between the EU and the US in the WTO (McMahon, 1998). The conflict was resolved in favour of economic liberalism.

Lomé-type preferences are said to be in breach of Article XXIV of the GATT, which states that all trade agreements must be based on reciprocity. Any non-reciprocal trade agreements can exist only by the granting of a waiver. Furthermore, special trade concessions for developing countries are permissible only if they are granted to all developing countries (again, unless there is a waiver) according to Part IV of the GATT (otherwise known as the enabling clause of 1979). The Lomé Convention as a whole had a WTO waiver until 2000. The EU and ACP are in the process of obtaining a waiver to cover the transition period until the start of the new agreement(s) in 2008.

Thirdly, the EU also claimed that it had no wish to dissolve a partnership of over twenty-five years but that the partnership would nevertheless change in orientation. In particular, the EU stated that there are limits to preferences in an environment concerned with trade liberalisation. However, trade liberalisation should be seen primarily as a political phenomenon; that is, one which is driven by political processes and requires political will to implement. Thus EU policy both accommodates liberalisation and helps to create the rules and regulatory framework for it. In this sense the EU is inseparable from the development of the broader world trade system, particularly as the world's largest trader. The EU on the one hand may defend its particular interests, such as the CAP, or indeed sometimes the ACP, but also benefits from upholding the multilateral system which it wishes to strengthen. The remainder of this chapter explores the manifestations of this tension in relation to the post-Lomé debates and the new Cotonou Agreement.

Trade-related directorates: the bureaucratic level

The Commission is the chief initiator of policy and, as such, is a key actor in the policy network and a main target for external lobbying activities by actors such as NGOs, private corporations and third parties. In the WTO the EU is formally represented by the Commission although each member state is also a member. Trade policy thus has many overlapping layers, including the relationship between member states and the Commission, the institutional politics of the Commission and external influences.

In the Commission there are a number of directorates which deal with what may loosely be called external relations with third countries and groups of countries. The chief one for development is DG Development; however, DG Trade has responsibility for negotiating the trade component of external agreements. In addition there is the DG for external (mainly political/security) relations DG Enlargement, along with the European Community Humanitarian Office (ECHO) and the newly created EUROPE AID, both of which deal with the allocation, disbursement and assessment of aid to third countries. The various external relations commissioners meet regularly to coordinate Commission positions.

In 1996 the Commission produced a discussion paper on the future of ACP–EU relations. Commonly referred to as 'the Green Paper' (CEC, 1997), the text marked the start of a fundamental shift in the Commission position on Lomé from a partnership based on contractuality towards a neo-liberal approach which is not dissimilar to that which guides the Bretton Woods institutions. Of course, in 1990 the EU had already introduced structural adjustment in Lomé IV and in 1995 political conditionality was strengthened in Lomé IV *bis*, but the main trade features of the Convention had remained intact. The Green Paper argued that the Community still had an important role to play in the field of development. However, the changing international context plus the fact that preferences have not been as successful as intended, meant that this role must change. In relation to trade the paper argued that

> a broader approach to trade cooperation, linked to operations to support structural adjustment and the private sector and reflecting the ACP countries' need

to create political and institutional conditions conducive to foreign investment, should help improve their ability to take advantage of trade preferences and, moreover, to diversify their external economic relations. (CEC, 1997: 12)

The Green Paper put forward a number of options for the future trade relations between the two groups. These included the principle of differentiated reciprocity between the EU and regional groups of ACP countries. The introduction of the principle of reciprocity signalled the beginning of the end of the preferences that made Lomé unique. The proposed regional agreements reflect the growing importance of free trade agreements in the post-Uruguay Round period. Various authors heralded a 'new regionalism' in international trade (Hettne et al., 1999). This proposal became codified in the idea of Regional Economic Partnership Agreements (REPAs) during the subsequent EU–ACP negotiations.

Following the Green Paper there were a number of discussions in Europe and the ACP states. In these discussions the Commission repeatedly stressed the need for any new agreement to be WTO compatible. Nevertheless, it is possible to discern a shallow u-turn in the Commission between the publication of the Green Paper (1996–97) and the eventual recommendations (1998), where more emphasis was placed on the social dimension of development (Elstrom, 2000; interviews DG VIII, 1998). In addition, any suggestion that the ACP group should be disbanded was clearly rebuffed by the affirmation of the group at the ACP Conference of Ministers in Libreville in December 1997. Subsequently the EU proclaimed its desire to maintain a 'special relationship' with the ACP in the negotiating mandate.

The final Commission negotiating mandate stressed the importance of integration into the world economy. The assumption is that preferences are exceptions rather than the rule and that the ACP must become competitive in the world market. Thus the Cotonou Agreement provides for the setting up of new trade arrangements 'characterised by the progressive abolition of obstacles to trade between the parties, in accordance with WTO rules' (Goulongana, 2000: 5). The implications of this for the ACP are that only the least developed states, defined according to per capita income rather than structural considerations, will be eligible for preferences. In 2002 all other ACP states are supposed to enter into negotiations for new regionally based agreements which are to enter into force in 2008.

Furthermore the Community's GSP scheme will be enhanced for those LDCs not participant to a REPA. The 'super-GSP' will thus give to non-ACP least developed countries benefits equivalent to those of Lomé. 'The Council and the Commission will start by the year 2000 a process which by 2005 will allow duty free access for essentially all products from all LDCs building on the level of existing trade provisions of the Lomé Convention' (CEC, 1999 2:2). This process then brought forth a Commission proposal for the EU to grant tariff-free and quota-free market access for 'everything but arms' exported by LDCs

(CLONG, 2000: 19). In extending the benefits of Lomé to all developing countries, the development policy of the EU becomes more WTO compatible. Nevertheless it should be noted that most LDCs are already members of the ACP and so the extension of the GSP and of the 'everything but arms' proposal only serves to include nine additional LDCs.

In the Commission, and the external relations directorates in particular, there has been a clear shift in ideology since the end of the 1980s. The traditional pyramid of preference approach by which the ACP was granted the most preferred status has been replaced with an approach designed to treat all third parties equally, in line with WTO regulations. The twin principles of non-discrimination and reciprocity are interpreted in such a way as to leave little room to dispute the notion that more free trade is necessarily better for all developing economies. Nevertheless there remain different emphases between the external relations directorates.

DG Trade is a key player in terms of the importance and benefits of free trade and negotiates the trade component of the post-Lomé agreements. It stated that, 'the rule-based, open, multilateral international trade system is the key factor in EU and global prosperity' (CEC, 2000a). It would like to see the advantages of this system extended and is keen to promote a new round of trade negotiations which should entail concrete benefits for LDCs, including improved market access and measures to address supply-side constraints facing developing countries. To this end the Community adopted the Everything but Arms Initiative in February 2001. This provides duty-free entry for all exports (except arms) from LDCs into the EU market. The value of preferences for developing countries, on the other hand, will decrease over time as MFN rates are cut. In order to provide some special and differential treatment, the EU will provide greater certainty and predictability that those reductions will be progressive (CEC, 2001a, 2001b).

The new Partnership Agreements with the ACP are designed to enable the ACP states to manage the challenge of globalisation and adapt progressively to the new conditions of international trade, thereby facilitating their gradual integration into the world economy. As such, in the new agreement there is an eight-year preparation period during which barriers to trade will progressively be removed and cooperation in trade-related areas will increase. Consequently the Stabex and Sysmin compensatory schemes have not been renewed. The Sugar and Beef Protocols are maintained provisionally although they will be re-examined in the context of the new trade agreements. The Rum Protocol has not been renewed and there is a new Banana Protocol.

DG Development presents a slightly modified approach to trade liberalisation, with greater emphasis on poverty reduction. Speaking to the World Bank development Committee in April 2000, Commissioner Nielson said that the objective was 'globalisation with a human face'. He went on to say that 'while there is no alternative to an open and liberal world economy, this is not an end in itself. Political action is required to harness not only the potential and opportunities offered by the global economy, but also to limit the transition costs and ensure benefits accrue to the poor'. Furthermore, he argued, the EU is 'actively following this [World Bank] approach in the framework of the country strategy papers for developing countries' (CEC, 2000b).

The main difference between the old Lomé and the Cotonou Agreement is, according to the Commission, the view that aid is a leverage for trade. The emphasis will therefore not be on new or novel trade facilities, but rather will lie in aid designed to facilitate the objective of integrating developing countries into the world economy. Aid will be concentrated on the poorest countries, while those countries where poverty is declining will be encouraged to pursue WTO-compatible integration into the world economy and greater links with the private sector. Thus, according to the Commission, 'the fight against poverty requires markets to deliver growth and policies to deliver equity' (CEC, 2000b).

The politics of trade preferences and the CAP

While trade has historically been a central component of the EU's relationship with the South, the Lomé trade preferences were relatively risk free for the EU. They were offered primarily to poorer or small economies which could not make significant incursions into the EU domestic market. In addition there were safeguard clauses which could resolve any problem, for example a significant increase in the export of any product to the EC, should it arise (Edwards and Regelsberger, 1990).

The preferences have therefore not been economically costly to the EU. Where costs exist, they have been political. Such costs lie partly in the maintenance of a system which is attractive to only a few member states. The main proponents and defenders of Lomé have historically been Britain and France, which have also historically been influential players in the EU, but which are no longer capable of overriding the concerns of a larger number of states with no particular colonial ties and no interest in perpetuating what is now viewed as an outdated basis for cooperation. This is exacerbated by the fact that British and French interests are no longer so clearly aligned with their ex-colonies.

The changing hierarchy in trade preferences indicates another political cost. The member states have become increasingly interested in the southern Mediterranean and north African countries in recent years. In particular they acknowledge that poverty in the region, coupled with high fertility rates, will lead to migration into Europe, legally or illegally. In 1990 the Commission declared that 'the most important way to improve the economies of the north African countries is to increase economic cooperation, that is, aid and investments, and, especially to radically reduce restrictions on imports of goods' (Nedergaard, 1993: 36). There are also political concerns to safeguard market reforms in Eastern Europe and significant steps have been taken towards trade liberalisation with Eastern Europe in this regard.

Importantly, the EU is 'a key player in world trade negotiations and the principal driving force behind the proposal to establish the WTO' (Cameron, 1998: 19). The hypothesis here is that the end of preferences has its substantive cause in the external pressure from the GATT/WTO to reform internal policies such as the CAP. That is, the Community is now being asked to justify these preferences to third parties, such as the USA and indeed the WTO Dispute Settlement Body, and in the process having its very own system of protecting farmers and farm incomes questioned. When faced with a choice between fighting to maintain preferences to third parties and defending domestic preferences, the Community would rather do the latter.

The Common Agricultural Policy is symbolic of the values upon which the EU was founded. It has among its objectives the maintenance of reasonable farm incomes, the raising of agricultural productivity and the stabilisation of markets (demand and supply) as well as the abolition of barriers to trade (Treaty of Rome, Article 36). In short, it is welfare state institution, designed to provide the EU with a certain level of food security and to secure rural livelihoods. Yet despite being the original 'common' policy of the EU, the CAP is also the means by which member states defend national agricultural policies. It is a means by which member states attempt to reduce the impact of unstable agricultural markets on their own domestic constituencies – in particular, the strong and well-organised agricultural producer groups in France and Germany (historically consumer groups have not been as strong or as well organised). Thus national political interests play a key role in the determination and extent of CAP reform within Europe (Grant, 1997).

In the GATT/WTO it is the Commission which has competence over agricultural negotiations, although of course there continues to be tension between the Commission and Council, as exemplified during the Uruguay Round negotiations (Woolcock and Hodges, 1996: 302). Importantly the Commission championed the creation of a new multilateral trade organisation (which became the WTO) and the principle of globalism by which the whole agreement, rather than select parts of it, must come into effect. This reflected not only a desire to discipline the US, but also a willingness to accept multilateral discipline over its own internal agricultural policies (Woolcock and Hodges, 1996: 311).

Although the CAP has been subject to successive challenges in the GATT, it remains important to the EU, and to member states and the Commission's DG Agriculture in particular. The current Commissioner for Agriculture, Frans Fischler, maintains that the EU is not prepared to sacrifice the European model of agriculture on the altar of liberalisation. Although it is keen to have a new round of negotiations, the Union wants a balance between progressive reductions in support, protection and non-trade concerns (CEC, 2000c). This position is indicative of an ongoing dilemma within the EU and many Northern states. On the one hand, there is a desire to promote a rule-based, open trading system. On the other hand, while pressing the developing countries to open their markets the EU wants to protect its own strategic markets such as agriculture. This dilemma is obvious in the case of the banana trade war discussed below.

The banana trade war, 1993–99[1]

It is in the context of trade liberalisation that the banana trade has risen to prominence in recent years. In particular there is an ongoing trade dispute between the EU and the United States through the GATT, and more recently the WTO, over the Community's banana regime. Through this system, imports of the fruit into the EU are strictly controlled by quotas and tariffs. The rationale behind the regime is to protect former European colonies and the French Overseas Department within the structure of the international banana market. The ACP states have been granted preferential status for the export of bananas into the EU since Lomé I. While fears of commodity shortage have now subsided, there is still arguably some sense within the EU that the ACP countries deserve some support for historical and developmental reasons (Coote and LeQuesne, 1996).

The economic reason for preferential treatment lies in the dramatically different modes of production utilised in the Caribbean and Latin America. In the Caribbean most farmers grow their fruit on farms of five acres or less. Furthermore, because of the topology of the islands, the plots are often steep and the ground unsuitable for any crops other than the versatile banana plant. In contrast, Latin American or 'dollar bananas' are grown on large plantations which accrue significant economies of scale; production costs in the Caribbean are, consequently higher (Godfrey, 1998).

In addition, three giant transnational corporations dominate the production of bananas in Latin America, from where 83 per cent of the bananas on the world market originate (Caribbean Bananas Exporters' Association (CBEA), 2000), and consequently world trade. Chiquita Brands and Dole Food Company (both based in the United States) each have about 25 per cent of international trade. Del Monte Fresh Produce, a company now owned by a Chilean conglomerate and with its capital based in the United Arab Emirates, has about 15 per cent of the market. The dominance of the companies in the region is such that they can influence government policy directly, in order to keep down wages and minimise social and environmental requirements. In contrast, productivity in the Caribbean is much lower. But because most farmsteads are operated by their owners and employ a small number of people, the working conditions are better while chemical use is lower.

The Windward Islands are particularly dependent on banana production. Bananas make up 91 per cent of St Lucia's foreign exchange earnings, 71 per cent for Dominica, 28 per cent for St Vincent and 13 per cent for Grenada. Fifty per cent of jobs in St Vincent and 30 per cent in St Lucia are banana related (Coote and LeQuesne, 1996: 121). The percentage of GDP which is gained from bananas is 14.3 in the Windwards as a whole. However, the output of these countries is remarkably small in comparison to that of Latin America: the entire output of the ACP countries is equivalent to 10 per cent of Chiquita's sales.

The historical basis for the Banana Protocol lies in specific agreements between Britain, France and Italy and their former colonies. Until 1992 other Community members controlled their own banana imports. The creation of the single market posed problems for the Banana Protocol as common export tariffs were needed. Some states, such as Germany, were used to buying cheaper dollar bananas from Latin America. The question of how to extend the banana preferences to the whole of the EC, when some member states opposed such a move, was compounded by the fact that the stakes were high: the EU represents the second largest market in the world, with an average annual consumption of ten kilograms of bananas per person. A more important question was how to reconcile the regime with trade liberalisation as agreed in the GATT and the preferences offered to the ACP under the Lomé Convention.

An agreement was reached in 1993 whereby Latin American producers paid ECU 100 per tonne tariff quota on the first 2 million tonnes they imported into the EU, with a prohibitive ECU 850 per tonne thereafter. ACP imports were free from tariffs. Maximum quotas were applied to each country but these were more than the maximum capacity. The solution was designed to allow the ACP to maintain their advantage primarily in the UK and French markets, while also allowing Latin American countries to continue exporting the same share of the market but making expansion of that share costly. However, the Latin Americans wanted their quota to be raised to 2.5 million tonnes and their tariffs reduced and filed a complaint with the GATT. The EU managed to reach an agreement with four of the Latin American countries in return for them dropping the GATT complaint. In turn this led the US-based trading companies to raise the issue in November 1994 under Section 301 of US trading law (the so-called 'super 301'), saying that the signatories to the agreement with the EU were being favoured contrary to GATT regulations. The US government supported their position strongly and threatened retaliatory action.

In January 1995 a World Bank report criticised the EU agreement, stating that: the costs to the European consumer had risen by $700 million to $2.3 billion since the introduction of a Europe-wide regime; the main beneficiaries were not the ACP producers, who only received $300 million, but European trading firms; and that the regime distorted the world market and raised prices. A report for CBEA claimed that the costs to the European consumer had actually decreased under the new regime, and that any reform of it in line with US proposals would spell economic and social disaster for the Windward Islands (Pantin et al., 1999; see also Godfrey, 1998).

In 1996 the US and the Latin American governments took the issue to the newly formed WTO. WTO disputes panel decisions operate in the opposite way to those of its predecessor, needing a unanimous vote to override them instead of a unanimous vote of support. The US government stated that its quarrel was with the EU and not the ACP producers, because the regime was denying the US companies legitimate business. In May 1997 the dispute panel found that the EU regime violated WTO rules on nineteen counts. However – its report did not condemn tariff preferences *per se*, but the licensing system that the regime employed to allocate import rights. After an appeals panel upheld the decision in September 1997, the EU was given until January 1999 to reform its regime (Chambron, 2000).

In 1998 the EU abolished individual quotas for ACP countries and allocated 857,000 tonnes, tariff free, to the ACP countries, which allowed for about 100,000 tonnes of expansion on existing trade levels. In contrast, the other producers were allocated 2.553 million tonnes at a tariff of ECU 75 per tonne. Beyond these limits ACP imports were to be subject to a tariff of ECU 537 per tonne, while other bananas were to have a tariff of ECU 737 per tonne (Chambron, 2000). The US government was furious about the new proposals, accusing the EU of knowingly creating another unsatisfactory arrangement in order to stall for time over the lengthy WTO proceedings. The US Trade Representative stated: 'The implications of the European Union's actions go far beyond this dispute, threatening the effectiveness of the multilateral trading system as a whole' (US Trade Representative, 1999: 8). The issue had assumed a new level of symbolic significance in a power struggle between the world's two largest economic powers. In January 1999 Ecuador called for a new disputes panel to investigate the new regime. However, in March 1999 the United States unilaterally imposed 100 per cent import tariffs on a number of high-value EU exports to the US. The targeting of unrelated and innocent industries in the EU was perceived as a cynical new twist to the story.

The WTO ruling of April 1998 found the EU regime to be at fault and allowed the US to impose sanctions of an equivalent amount. The Commission stated that it would not challenge the WTO ruling (CEC, 1999b). The problem is that while the US is a far more significant trading partner than the ACP banana producers, the Caribbean countries are very susceptible to any change in the EU regime. The effects of losing the Protocol will be felt all over the Eastern Caribbean because of the shared currency, and in the wider Caribbean community because of their close trading links (Chambron, 2000). The alternatives facing Caribbean farmers are migration to towns contributing to urban unemployment, emigration abroad or illegal drug cultivation – all consequences that ironically the US will suffer from due to its geographical proximity to the region. The second Banana Protocol (Protocol 5) is a much shortened and less ambitious agreement recognising the importance of bananas to the region and agreeing to improve conditions for the production and marketing of bananas. No banana quotas are allocated by it. In November 2001 the WTO granted a waiver for Article I of the Protocol, which allows for continued tariff preferences for ACP imports, and Article XIII permitting the reservation of the C quota for ACP bananas.

A new regulation was adopted in January 2001 to cover the period up to 2006 and in April 2001 the EU reached agreement with the US and Ecuador on how to manage tariff quotas during that period. The agreement allows for a two-phase reduction. Phase one, from July 2001, preserves existing tariffs and quotas based on historical allocation of licences. Phase two, from January 2002, decreases the ACP quota by 100,000 tonnes. These 100,000 tonnes move to the B quota which is available to all suppliers. This is intended to finally lift the US sanctions against EU luxury goods. In January 2006 the regime will shift to a tariff-only system and the ACP will have to compete against dollar bananas, unless they qualify for the Everything but Arms Initiative (CEC, 2001c).

The challenge to the Banana Protocol of the Lomé Convention has become an important event in the history of EU–ACP relations. It could be regarded as a litmus test of the EU's political will to defend the interests of the ACP against those of the USA and Latin American banana producers. The changes to the Banana Protocol are on the one hand a response to specific challenges made to the Lomé Convention by the Latin American banana producers and US government. However, this is a simplification of the situation. The EU also faces external pressure within the WTO to reform its own agricultural sector and this is impacting on its willingness to uphold agreements with third parties which have been declared WTO incompatible.

Conclusions

This chapter asked why the EU has chosen trade liberalisation over any other theoretically possible option. On the one hand, external pressure, evident most obviously in the banana dispute, is a key factor in changing the trade preferences offered by Lomé. However, the changes began long before the banana dispute surfaced. They have their origins in the perceived failure of existing preferences, along with changes in the international environment since the 1980s, which make the continuation of such preferences difficult. The combined consequence of these factors has meant that the Commission, as initiator of policy, has pushed for an agenda in which trade liberalisation becomes an objective of development cooperation.

There is more to the story than this. On the one hand the EU has declared the Lomé preferences largely unsuccessful, without fully acknowledging the impact of the CAP on wider markets which made it difficult for ACP agricultural exporting states to benefit sufficiently from the preferences. The WTO ruling on bananas also does not appear to take account of the vulnerability of small island economies, such as the Windward Islands. Instead it takes a limited view of the 'special and differential' treatment permitted under WTO rules. On the other hand the EU faces external pressure to reform its own agricultural policy while facing internal pressure to maintain a socially acceptable policy. Having agreed to place agriculture on the GATT/WTO agenda, and in so doing reduce the influence of national politics, the EU is less keen to defend preferences to third parties.

The effect of this is that trade liberalisation is now firmly entrenched on the European development agenda precisely because the EU has made WTO compatibility such a key factor in the new negotiations. Furthermore, the EU, in not challenging the WTO interpretation, has contributed to the likely increase in poverty of the affected ACP countries and to regional instability despite its declared commitment to do otherwise. As the world's largest trading bloc, it seems unlikely that the EU did not have the capacity to alter or adjust the interpretation of WTO rules to benefit more developing countries. It seems that political will was lacking.

Note

1   This section has been prepared with the research assistance of Mark Ewing, MA candidate 1999–2000, University of Durham, UK.

References

Cameron, F. (1998), 'The EU as a global actor: far from pushing its political weight around', in C. Rhodes (ed.), *The EU in the World Community*, Boulder, Colorado: Lynne Rienner.

Caribbean Bananas Exporters' Association (CBEA) (2000), www.cbea.org (accessed 17 May 2000).

CEC (1994), 'Integration of Developing Countries into the International Trading System: Role of GSP, 1995–2004', COM (94) 212 final, Brussels: CEC.

CEC (1997), 'Green Paper on Relations between the European Union and the ACP Countries on the Eve of the 21st Century: Challenges and Options for a New Partnership', Brussels: CEC.

CEC (1999a), 'Consequences for ACP Countries of Applying to the GSP, Joint Analysis by EU and ACP Experts', CE/TFN/GCE3/29-EU, Brussels: CEC.

CEC (1999b), *The Week in Europe*, London, 12 April.

CEC (2000a), http://europa.eu.int/comm/trade/2000_round/index_en.htm (accessed 12 May 2000).

CEC (2000b), http://europa.eu.int/comm/trade/whats_new/development_en.htm (accessed 12 May 2000).

CEC (2000c), http://europa.eu.int/comm/trade/2000_round/Fischler_en.htm (accessed 12 May 2000).

CEC (2001a), 'EC position in relation to the development dimension of a new round of multilateral trade negotiations', memo, europa.eu.int/comm/trade (accessed 24 January 2002).

CEC (2001b), 'Special session of the Committee on Agriculture: tariff preferences for developing countries 3–5 December 2001', http://europa.eu.int/comm/agriculture (accessed 24 January 2002).

CEC (2001c), 'Commission welcomes decision on final step to settle banana trade dispute', Brussels, December 2001, http://europa.eu.int/comm/trade (accessed 24 January 2002).
Chambron, A. M. (2000), 'Straightening the bent world of the banana', http://bananalink.org.uk (accessed 17 May 2000).
CLONG (Liaison Committee of Non-governmental Organisations) (2000), Liaison News, no. 10, Brussels.
Coote, B. and C. LeQuesne (1996), The Trade Trap: Poverty and the Global Commodity Markets, Oxford: Oxfam.
Davenport, M. (1992), 'Africa and the unimportance of being preferred', Journal of Common Market Studies, 30:2, pp. 233–51.
Dickson, A. (1995), 'The EC and its associates: changing priorities', Politics, 15:3, pp. 147–52.
Dickson, A. (2000), 'Bridging the gap: great expectations for EU development co-operation policies', Current Politics and Economics in Europe, 9:3, pp. 275–96.
Edwards, G. and E. Regelsberger (eds) (1990), Europe's Global Links, New York: St. Martin's Press.
Elstrom, O. (2000), 'Lomé and post-Lomé: asymmetric negotiations and the impact of norms', paper presented at the 5th UACES Conference, 8 April, Budapest.
Godfrey, C. (1998), A Future for Caribbean Bananas: The Importance of Europe's Banana Market to the Caribbean, Oxford: Oxfam.
Goulongana, J.-R. (2000), 'Together we must take up the challenges of the Cotonou Agreement', The Courier, Special Issue, September.
Grant, W. (1997), The Common Agricultural Policy, London: Macmillan.
Grilli, E. (1993), The European Community and the Developing Countries, Cambridge: Cambridge University Press.
Heidensohn, K. (1995), Europe and World Trade, London: Pinter.
Hettne, B., A. Inotai and O. Sunkel (eds) (1999), Globalism and the New Regionalism, Basingstoke: Macmillan.
Hill, C. (1993), 'The capability–expectations gap or conceptualising Europe's international role', Journal of Common Market Studies, 31:3, pp. 305–28.
IMF (1996), Annual Report, Washington: IMF.
Lister, M. (1997), The European Union and the South, London: Routledge.
McMahon, J. (1998), 'The EC banana regime, the WTO ruling and the ACP', Journal of World Trade, 32, pp. 101–14.
McQueen, M. (1998), 'ACP–EU trade cooperation after 2000: an assessment of reciprocal trade preferences', Journal of Modern African Studies, 36:4, pp. 669–92.
Nedergaard, O. (1993), 'The end of special interests? The political economy of EC trade policy changes in the 1990s', in O. Norgaard, T. Pederson and N. Peterson (eds), The European Community in World Politics, London: Pinter.
Oden, B. (1999), 'New regionalism in southern Africa: part of or alternative to the globalisation of the world economy', in B. Hettne, A. Inotai and O. Sunkel (eds), Globalism and the New Regionalism, Basingstoke: Macmillan.
Pantin, D., W. Sandiford and M. Henry (1999), Cake, Mama Coca or? Alternatives Facing the Caribbean Banana Industry in the Light of the April 1999 WTO Ruling on the EU Banana Regime, Commissioned by the Caribbean Policy Development Centre and the Windward Island Farmers' Association.

Slater, R., B. Schutz and S. Dorr (1993), *Global Transformation and the Third World*, Boulder: Lynne Rienner.
Stevens, C. (1994), 'Europe and the south in the 1990s', in L. Swatuk and T. Shaw (eds), *The South at the End of the 20th Century*, Basingstoke: Macmillan.
Toye, J. (1987), *Dilemmas of Development*, Oxford: Blackwell.
United States Trade Representative (1999), 'United States Response to the EU banana import regime', December 1998, from *House of Commons Research Paper* 99/28, 'The trade dispute between the EU and the USA over bananas'.
Woolcock, S. and M. Hodges (1996), 'EU policy in the Uruguay Round', in H. Wallace and W. Wallace (eds), *Policy Making in the EU*, Oxford: Oxford University Press.

4

The ACP in the European Union's network of regional relationships: still unique or just one in the crowd?

Karen E. Smith

This chapter analyses the European Union's relations with five broad regional groupings: the ACP countries, the Mediterranean, Asia, Latin America and Eastern Europe. The Union prefers to deal with third countries collectively. It lays out regional strategies, sets up aid programmes on a regional basis and concludes specific kinds of agreement with countries in a particular region. The EU has important bilateral relationships with industrialised countries (notably the United States), but most of the developing countries that the EU deals with fall into one of the five groupings considered here.

This regional focus dates from the Community's beginnings and its relations with the African associates and ex-colonies. The African emphasis was unsuccessfully opposed by 'globalist' member states (Germany and the Netherlands), which supported a wider network of development cooperation centred on the poorest countries (Grilli, 1993: 335–6). With enlargement to the UK in particular, the African focus grew into the Lomé partnership with African, Caribbean and Pacific states. The Community later added countries to its network of relations, but always following the regional approach originally set out in the Yaoundé and Lomé Conventions.

Relations with the ACP as a regional grouping thus formed the model for the Community's relations with other countries. Furthermore, the basic building blocks of the EC–ACP relationship – trade preferences, aid and institutionalised dialogue – were extended, on a more limited basis, to other regions. Throughout the Cold War period, the ACP countries were at the top of the Community's 'pyramid of privileges' (see Grilli, 1993: 150–1). Other groups of countries (the Mediterranean, Latin America, Asia) appeared further down, while the Eastern European countries were not even on the pyramid.

The pyramid of privileges has since shifted such that it is almost unrecognisable: the regions closer geographically to the Union have risen in importance. The ACP countries are no longer privileged to the extent they once were. The globalists have won the argument in that there is a wider EU role in the world, although the regionalist legacy remains in the EU's preference to deal with third countries collectively.

The EU–ACP relationship is also no longer as unique as it once was. From serving as the model on which the Community's development cooperation relations were based, the EU–ACP relationship is now catching up with more recent policies towards other regions. Most notably, it is becoming 'politicised', in that political objectives such as the protection of human rights and conflict prevention assume much greater significance, and the EU's policy is now 'intended to shape the political complexion and policy preferences of recipient governments' (Bretherton and Vogler, 1999: 136). Politicisation really began in earnest with respect to Central and Eastern Europe at the end of the Cold War, where the EU's main aim was support for political and economic reforms. Politicisation reflects the view that sustainable development can take place only in a context of security, democracy and freedom (Council of Ministers, 1991; Arts, 2000: 21–50, 118–21). Implementation of this view is closely related to the Union's developing status as an international actor. Since the end of the Cold War, the Union has been trying to project a more united stance in international relations.

The EU's growing international status has another implication for the ACP countries. Its relations with third countries develop as a result of various political and economic driving forces. The old colonial ties to the ACP countries are no longer enough to keep them high up on the pyramid of privileges. To explore why the EU–ACP relationship is losing its uniqueness, this chapter examines the evolution of the Union's policies towards the five regions. Firstly it notes the expansion of the Union's commitments, globally and in the EU's neighbourhood, and sets out the key reasons behind this expansion. It then analyses why and how there has been change in the Union's relations with each of the five regions.

The end of the Cold War: geography as determinant of foreign policy?

In 1973 the Community member states took offence when Henry Kissinger, in his infamous 'Year of Europe' speech (Nuttall, 1992: 86), implied that the Europeans, working within their new framework of European Political Co-operation (EPC), could only have regional interests (that is, close to Europe), in contrast to the global interests and reach of the US. Ironically, although at the time EPC was concentrating on the Conference on Security and Cooperation in Europe and the conflict in the Middle East, the Community's most extensive network of external relations lay in Africa and could not really extend to the European neighbourhood, given Cold War realities. Now there are fears that the African dimension is fading, as the Union strengthens relations with countries closer to home – such that Africa has been described as the 'forgotten continent' (Harding 1999).

The end of the Cold War has been a crucial turning point. Suddenly, relations with countries that once lay behind the Iron Curtain became, first of all, *possible* and, as a result, the Community's European neighbours became larger and larger recipients of aid (as well as of other policy initiatives, such as association agreements and, eventually, the offer of membership). Between 1976 and 1997, Africa was still the largest recipient of EU aid, and aid to Africa even increased over this period, but by the mid-1990s it was clearly no longer the privileged aid recipient. Aid to other regions, notably Central and Eastern Europe, North Africa and the Middle East, grew considerably, particularly in the 1990s. For example, in 1986 44.7 per cent of EU aid was committed to the ACP countries, and none at all to the Central and Eastern European countries. In 1997, 33.1 per cent of EU aid went to the ACP, while 18.4 per cent went to the Central and Eastern European countries (Cox and Chapman, 1999: 2–4). Furthermore, the ACP has virtually disappeared from the list of top recipients of EU aid. In 1970–74, thirteen of the top fifteen aid recipients were ACP countries. In 1996–97, only two were. The others had been replaced by countries in Europe (Russia, some Central and Eastern European countries, some former Yugoslav republics) and countries around the Mediterranean (Cox and Chapman, 1999: 3). More recently, Africa has indeed dropped below the Central and Eastern European countries. Under the new European Development Fund (June 2000) the member states pledged 13.5 billion Euro in new grants for seventy-six ACP countries over the next seven years. This equals 1.93 billion Euro per year. In addition to grants, the European Investment Bank will lend the ACP countries up to 1.7 billion Euro over seven years. An additional 9.9 billion Euro of previous EDF resources remains uncommitted. The total for the ACP is thus 3.5 billion Euro per year. But the ACP are falling behind the Central and Eastern European countries on new commitments (not even considering per capita or per country commitments): the grant commitment to the ten Central and Eastern European countries for 2000–6 will top 3 billion Euro per year.

The emphasis on the neighbourhood came through in several key documents in the 1990s which consider where the Union should concentrate its energy and resources. In June 1992, the Foreign Ministers submitted a report to the Lisbon European Council on potential areas for CFSP Joint Actions vis-à-vis particular countries or groups of countries (Council of Ministers, 1992). The report specified three priority areas for EU foreign policy. All are neighbours: Central and Eastern Europe, including the Commonwealth of Independent States and the Balkans; the Mediterranean, especially the Maghreb; and the Middle East. Under the Amsterdam Treaty, the EU may resort to 'Common Strategies' under the CFSP in fields where the member states have important common interests. In December 1998, the Vienna European Council decided that the first CFSP Common Strategies would target Russia, Ukraine, the Western Balkans and the Mediterranean/Middle East. Again, the emphasis was clearly placed on the neighbourhood.

The post-Cold War foreign policy priorities of the Union have thus been defined as 'regional' in the sense of the European region. Certainly the substance of policy seems to bear this out: the enlargement project, the huge aid commitments to the Balkans, the recent attempts to reinvigorate the Euro-Mediterranean partnership. But is this the whole picture? Christopher Piening, the author of a book notably entitled *Global Europe*, maintains that the EU has assumed 'the status of an emerging global power' and he aims to 'show just how wide-ranging the EU's international role has become, both geographically and substantively' (Piening, 1997: 1, 11). The end of the Cold War boosted the EU's global role. It is in fact now *expected* to act internationally by outsiders, EU policy makers and the public. Its freedom of manoeuvre to do so has expanded since the end of bipolarity made room for an actor such as the EU. Firstly, the member states could act together for their collective interests, as superpower competition no longer set the limits of autonomous action. For example, the extent to which the EU has encroached on the traditional US sphere of influence in Latin America would have been inconceivable during the Cold War. While the Community was active in Central America in the 1980s, it is unlikely that the member states would ever have effectively countered American policy there (assuming they would have been able to muster the resources to do so). The transatlantic relationship was far too important to put at such risk. And secondly, the instruments that the EU can wield – predominantly civilian – have acquired more influence in a world of countries seeking to reform their political and economic systems.

The EU is certainly becoming a global player. It gives more aid to more countries around the world than it has ever done before. It has concluded trade and cooperation or association agreements with virtually every country or regional grouping in the world. It is engaged in political dialogues with numerous countries: in 1998, there were 156 meetings between the EU (presidency, troika or full Council) and third countries or regional groupings (Cameron, 1999: 34). In 1999 and 2000, the EU held high-profile summits with Latin American countries and with African countries. It has been trying to build a partnership with Asian countries, through the Asia–Europe meeting (ASEM). The EU is not limiting its ambitions to a regional role. Its global ambitions are even officially declared: under Article B of the Maastricht Treaty, one of the EU's objectives is 'to assert its identity on the international scene'.

Whence the pressures for involvement?

The end of the Cold War provided the opportunity and necessity to prioritise relations with the neighbours, as well as the opportunity for a stronger global role. But within this context, more concrete reasons for EU involvement internationally need to be identified. What is driving the expansion of the EU's international relations? Several reasons can be identified: external pressures, member state interests and European interests. Some of these contribute more to setting the regional priorities of the EU, others more to fuelling the EU's global extension. But a mix of most, if not all, of these reasons has contributed to the EU's involvement in the five regions.

External demands

The expectations of outsiders that the EU will pay them some attention have grown exponentially as the EU has evolved. These expectations may be unrealistic, and they may stand no chance of being adequately addressed. But the EU has certainly been under considerable external pressure to respond to the many demands on it for political dialogue, aid, trade agreements, association, membership, and so on. External demands grew particularly with the completion of the single European market (which sparked fears of a 'fortress Europe') and have not diminished. Several writers (Schmitter, 1969; Ginsberg, 1999) have termed this 'externalisation': development of the internal market generates outsiders' pressure for compensation, to which the member states must respond collectively.

But external demands are not just related to the international effects of the internal market. There are high expectations that the EU will spread peace, security and prosperity. These demands are considerably stronger from neighbouring countries, and from the US and other outsiders who clearly expect the EU to take responsibility for its European neighbours. Why and how the EU responds specifically to such expectations reflect the other factors below.

Member state interests

One or more member states (acting together) may also lead a concerted push for the EU to become involved with a region. Although the Commission has often made proposals for strengthening relations with regions, it is usually acting within a context already receptive to stronger relations because of member state pressure.

Member states push for EU action either because the EU will 'add value' to, or supplement, their own activities (it may have more appropriate or even more potentially influential policy instruments), or because unilateral action is considered ineffective or impossible. Individually, the member states could not make much of a global impact (as some of them did in bygone days) but together they can. The member states recognise that there is a 'politics of scale'. They will 'carry more weight in certain areas when they act together as a bloc than when they act separately' (Ginsberg, 1999: 438). The European level is often seen as appropriate for pursuing economic or security interests. Enhancing trading and investment opportunities or ensuring access to natural resources are motivations for the member states to press for EU involvement with a particular region or third country. The EU's policy instruments (aid, trade, diplomacy) are suitable for dealing with the new security threats, including ethnic disputes, violations of human rights, economic deprivation and international crime, which may affect one or more member states in particular. This does not mean that the member states are always eager for EU action. As intergovernmentalists would remind us, member states often block collective action because they view it as inimical to their own interests. But on occasion, the logic of the politics of scale can prevail.

European interests

Many observers might doubt that the European Union itself could have foreign policy interests. As David Allen has argued, foreign policy is intrinsically linked to the 'idea of a state with a set of interests identified by a government' (1996: 303). But the member states and EU institutions do seem to share a number of objectives and interests. These can be considered 'European interests', which 'reflect an indigenous and unique European quality' (Ginsberg, 1999: 439) and help to explain why the EU has expanded its international reach. These interests include a sense of EU responsibility, security, countering US hegemony, and promoting human rights and democracy.

Sense of EU responsibility Outsiders' demands are more likely to be met with greater attention the more they invoke or resonate with the EU's 'historical' responsibility to deal with them. The oldest of these historical responsibilities is towards the ex-colonies. More recently, the member states seem to share a very powerful sense of responsibility towards Eastern Europe – and it cannot be shirked easily, precisely because of geographic proximity. The Cologne European Council noted in June 1999:

> The six months since the Vienna meeting [European Council, December 1998] have, in various ways, again clearly brought out the importance of all these regions [Russia, Ukraine, the Western Balkans and the Mediterranean/Middle East] to the European Union not only as partners in its external relations but also for the stability and security of our continent and its immediate neighbourhood. The European Union both has a special responsibility and is in a special position to work in close partnership with all of its neighbours to achieve these objectives.

Security In the post-Cold War period, a number of violent conflicts have broken out on the EU's periphery – in the former Soviet Union, south-eastern Europe and Algeria. The EU has not dealt with these crises very well. Its civilian policy instruments are inappropriate for handling conflicts. But some involvement usually follows because the EU and the member states cannot afford to ignore the situation (because of geographical proximity), or because the EU is expected by others (such as the US) to become involved. The member states share common interests in the neighbouring regions because the political and economic stability of these areas is important for the Union, and because direct threats to the security of the Union could arise there.

Security is thus one factor that would clearly encourage the EU to concentrate resources and energy on its neighbourhood. But mopping up after conflicts and trying to prevent further ones is a task that the EU seems to be better at, and it has the appropriate civilian instruments for it. This is one distinctive way in which it can play a leading role internationally. Conflict prevention has become a key EU objective – especially in Africa (see chapter 5).

Counter US hegemony On several occasions, the EU has become involved in a region in an explicit or implicit attempt to balance the US. During the Cold War, US policy was perceived to be potentially dangerous, as in Central America, because it could lead to superpower clashes or simply exacerbate instability or insecurity within the region. The member states considered it imperative to express a different Western voice. Since the end of the Cold War there has been competition with the US to support various regional schemes (in Asia and Latin America) – a competition clearly related to securing economic advantages (see M. Smith, 1998). These driving forces led the EU to cast its net further afield than the neighbourhood.

Respect for human rights, democratic principles and the market economy, and efforts for regional integration Since the end of the Cold War, the EU has pursued the objectives of promoting human rights, democratic principles and the principles of the market economy with notable, though not always consistent, vigour. Promotion of human rights and democracy has become an increasingly visible aspect of its international identity. It is a key CFSP objective as well as an official development policy objective (Articles 11 and 177, consolidated Treaty on European Union). A human rights clause is now to be included in every formal agreement that the Union concludes with third countries. This would allow the agreement to be suspended if one of the parties violates human rights or democratic principles (agreements with other European countries include principles of the market economy). Aid is to be suspended in case of violations, and is to be increased to countries that have good or improving human rights and democratic records. Countries trying to reform their economies are also supposed to be given special help, while those that are not could receive less assistance.

To this one could also add 'propensity to cooperate within regional schemes'. The existence of a regional cooperation framework is likely to gather EU support, and all the more so if that framework is well functioning. There are economies of scale in dealing with groupings of countries, and groupings often share problems that it makes sense to deal with collectively. But more importantly, the EU – as a regional bloc itself – has sought to spread the message of regional cooperation. The export of the Community model is believed to provide the basis for peace and stability, economic development and prosperity (Edwards and Regelsberger, 1990). These (putative) guiding principles of EU foreign policy contribute to both its neighbourhood and international roles.

All of the above are positive reasons for EU involvement with a particular region, further from and closer to the EU itself. The implications for the ACP countries are clear: these forces dilute their privileged status.

A cautionary note about the EU's capacities to act on these forces must be introduced at this stage. Beyond the obviously crucial need for the member states to agree to act collectively vis-à-vis a given region in the first place, there are two reasons why the EU might be unable to translate its ambitions into effective international action.

Overstretch

Christopher Hill (1993) has pointed to the danger of raising expectations that the Union cannot possibly meet, given its limited capabilities and institutional shortcomings. The EU does not have unlimited resources. In fact, its budgetary resources are quite modest. They cannot be spread around indefinitely without jeopardising the resources promised already. Not only have the member states been unwilling to increase the Community budget (the ceiling remains 1.27 per cent of EU GNP), they have also been unwilling to consider significantly increasing the portion of the budget (around 7 per cent) devoted to external action. Thus the temptation has been to reduce assistance to some regions (the Mediterranean) and transfer those resources to others, notably the Balkans.

Nor is the 'attention span' of the EU unlimited. Foreign ministers and Commission officials cannot be expected to deal adequately with an ever increasing list of responsibilities. Already the General Affairs Council is so overloaded that it is virtually paralysed, unable to coordinate policy (Working Party, 1999).

Frustration

Outsiders do not have unlimited influence, and the EU in particular has had a difficult time translating its capabilities into real influence. Conflicts are never easily resolved by outsiders – and the continuing conflicts in the Middle East and Africa make it very difficult for the Union to exercise influence. If countries or regions persistently fail to respect human rights, democratise, implement market economic reforms or cooperate, then the EU's attention could easily shift elsewhere.

Neither of these two negative factors would necessarily lead to a privileging of neighbouring regions over further-flung areas including the ACP. But they do point to the difficulties that the EU faces in following through on its declared international ambitions, and could lead to readjustments or even a contraction of those ambitions.

The next section of this chapter explores the extent to which the Union's policies towards the five regions have evolved, and why. It begins with the ACP countries, the oldest of the EU's regional relationships.

The EU's regional relationships

The ACP

The Lomé Convention, which linked the Union and seventy-one African, Caribbean and Pacific countries was, in Christopher Piening's words, 'the centrepiece of the EU's efforts to provide help to the Third World' (Piening, 1997: 169). The Convention was so central because of the strength of former colonial ties (mainly with France) and the clear sense of historical responsibility shared (more or less enthusiastically) by the member states. With the dissipation of those factors – through enlargement and the addition of other areas of responsibility as well as a lessening of French interest (see chapter 7) – the EU–ACP relationship has diminished in relative importance and acquired a much more 'normal' aspect.

According to the first Article of Lomé IV (1990–2000), the Convention was to promote and expedite the economic, cultural and social development of ACP states, and to consolidate and diversify their relations in a spirit of solidarity and mutual interest. The instruments used to reach these objectives included trade preferences, aid and institutionalised dialogue. Under Lomé, 99 per cent of ACP exports entered the EC duty free, with no reciprocity for Community exports. This preferential system, however, did not improve the ACP trading position. The relative value of trading preferences has been decreasing as world trade is liberalised and other countries benefit from better access to the Community market. The WTO is pressing for the elimination of trade preferences (see chapter 3). Thus what was originally one of the unique instruments in EU–ACP relations has fast lost its appeal.

Development assistance to the ACP countries is provided primarily through the European Development Fund. Uniquely, this is not funded by the EC budget but is instead pledged by the member states separately. However, in other ways aid to the ACP countries is becoming similar to other aid programmes, in that it is now conditional. In the early 1990s, political conditionality was imported from other aid programmes, notably Central and Eastern Europe, where it first appeared.

Conditionality – necessarily an imposition of donor views – represents a shift in another of Lomé's principles, that of the 'partnership of equals'. The partnership was embodied in an innovative institutional structure for cooperation and dialogue between the two parties, which involved an EU–ACP Council of Ministers, a committee of ambassadors and a consultative EU–ACP joint assembly. The institutional structure is now less obviously unique, as the EU has set up institutionalised relations with other regions. The EU–ACP joint assembly remains distinctive, although the European Parliament is engaged extensively in dialogue with parliamentarians in many other third countries (see in particular Piening, 1997).

The Cotonou Partnership Agreement (2000) revises many of Lomé's key provisions, and looks remarkably similar to other frameworks for cooperation between the EU and third countries/regional groupings. It has three main components: political dialogue, support for development, and economic and trade cooperation. Political dialogue assumes a more central role, and is to emphasise the consolidation of democracy, respect for human rights, and measures to ensure peace and security. The Community's aid programmes are to be reformed to increase their effectiveness, and conditionality has expanded to include good governance. As set out in chapter 3, the new trading regime has been designed to comply (eventually) with WTO regulations and reflects concerns that trading preferences have not improved the ACP countries' trade positions. All but the least developed countries (which will be given special GSP treatment) are to form regional sub-groupings, and a series of economic partnership agreements, creating free trade areas, are to be negotiated with these sub-groupings. These agreements would be implemented by 2008 at the latest.

The ACP grouping is the largest grouping with which the EU deals. The economic partnership agreements will likely loosen the ACP grouping, which is considered too big to cooperate effectively and efficiently. In this way, too, the ACP will become more 'normal'.

Contemporaneously, the EU has directed more attention to Africa outside of the Lomé framework. The spread of conflicts in Africa has prompted the EU to launch initiatives to try to prevent or manage conflicts there, as Gorm Rye Olsen elaborates on in chapter 5. In May 1998, the Council approved a CFSP Common Position on 'human rights, democratic principles, rule of law and good governance in Africa', which clearly links the CFSP and the Community's aid programmes (Council of Ministers, 1998). The extent to which the EU's relations with Africa, in particular, have become wide ranging was obvious at the first EU–Africa summit, held in Cairo in April 2000. The summit covered, among other issues: regional economic cooperation, trade, private sector development, investment, research and technology, human rights, refugees, peace building, terrorism, food security, health, education and the environment. Yet it also produced few achievements and tellingly did not set up a regular schedule of further meetings at ministerial or senior official levels, although a second summit is to take place in 2003. This contrasts with commitments made to some other regional groupings.

The ACP countries, and Africa in particular, are still of concern to the EU and there is still a lingering sense of responsibility for the former colonies. As Marjorie Lister points out, it is highly unlikely that the long-established EU–ACP relationship would simply be wound up: institutional inertia', if anything, would keep it going, and EU aspirations for a global role could hardly be taken seriously if the ACP countries were left off the map (Lister, 1997: 149–54). But there is clearly frustration with the failure of the EU's policy instruments to lift the African economies and, more recently, to consolidate democracy and respect for human rights and prevent conflicts. What is happening, though, is not a shift *away* from the ACP states, or at least African states, but a normalisation of relations with them, in that those relations are becoming more like the EU's relations with other regions: more political and encompassing a wider range of concerns.

Mediterranean non-member countries

Before the end of the Cold War, more attention was paid to the Mediterranean than to most other non-ACP countries. In the 1960s, limited commercial agreements were concluded with some Mediterranean states, while association agreements linked the Community with Greece and Turkey. In the 1970s, the Community tried to establish a 'Global Mediterranean Policy', but it involved little more than upgrading or concluding individual agreements with the Mediterranean countries (see Gomez, 1998: 137–9). The member states also sought to formulate common positions in EPC with regards to the Middle East conflict, although this went little beyond declaratory diplomacy. The Euro-Arab dialogue began in 1974, between EPC and the Arab League, although it fizzled out after the Camp David accords and Egypt's expulsion from the Arab League.

This situation changed radically in the early 1990s, largely as a result of internal pressures from southern member states (whose number had increased with the 1986 accession of Spain and Portugal). These member states were vociferous in their concerns that the region was being neglected compared with Central and Eastern Europe and yet posed as much, if not more, of a political and security challenge to the Union. The 'eastern dimension' had to be balanced by a 'southern' one (see Barbé, 1998). Security concerns included risks to stability from religious fundamentalism and underdevelopment – whose direct impact on the EU would be via increased illegal immigration – as well as harder security concerns such as the spread of chemical and biological weapons. The Commission was also active – prodded by the Commissioners in charge of Mediterranean policy, the Spaniards Abel Matutes and then Manuel Marin. In addition, the Mediterranean countries feared that the single European market and the events in Eastern Europe would further isolate them, and pressed for closer ties.

In June 1992, in their Lisbon report, the Foreign Ministers considered the Mediterranean and the Middle East to be priority areas for the CFSP. The Commission then published a number of proposals for strengthening relations. The culmination of these activities was the Euro-Mediterranean Partnership, launched by a high-level conference in Barcelona in November 1995, under the auspices of the Spanish presidency. The Barcelona conference brought together the Foreign Ministers of the EU member states and twelve Mediterranean countries (Jordan included, as well as the Palestinian Authority but not Libya). The conference agreed on a detailed work programme on the basis of three pillars: strengthened and regular political dialogue, the development of economic and financial cooperation, and greater emphasis on the social, cultural and human dimension (Euro-Mediterranean Conference, 1995). These objectives are to be implemented by concluding Euro-Mediterranean association agreements, setting up a Euro-Mediterranean Assistance Programme (MEDA) and engaging in regular dialogue. The Barcelona conference also adopted an extraordinary (non-binding) declaration of principles, including respect for democratic principles and human rights, the peaceful settlement of disputes, and the prevention of terrorism and drug trafficking. A Charter of Stability to implement these principles has still not been agreed.

Three Euro-Med countries are also EU membership candidates: Cyprus, Malta and Turkey. The first two have already started negotiations; Turkey was told by the December 1999 Helsinki European Council that it could open negotiations once it fulfilled the political conditions (democracy and protection of human rights). The three already had concluded association agreements and will not sign Euro-Med agreements. They are included in the MEDA programme.

The Euro-Mediterranean agreements provide for: institutionalised political dialogue; the establishment of a free trade area by 2010; economic, social, cultural and financial cooperation; and a human rights clause. Agreements have thus far been signed with Israel, Jordan, Morocco, the PLO (for the Palestinian Authority), Tunisia, Algeria and Lebanon.

MEDA is to promote socioeconomic development, regional cooperation and the Middle East peace process. As agreed at the Cannes European Council in June 1995, the MEDA I (1995–99) programme had a budget of 4.685 billion ECU – which represented a considerable increase on previous aid levels to the region, and began to redress the imbalance in comparison with aid to Central and Eastern Europe. The ratio of aid to the Mediterranean compared with that to Central and Eastern Europe went from 1:5 to 3.5:5. The Commission proposed cutting MEDA's budget (perhaps even by 25 per cent), officially because aid allocations had not been fully utilised, but also because the EU needs to find all the funding it can to fulfil its commitments in south-eastern Europe (CEC, 2000). The member states, however, agreed to allocate 5.35 billion Euro to MEDA for the 2000–2006 period. This will make it more difficult for the EU to meet its commitments elsewhere (the familiar problem of overstretch).

The political dialogue set up by the Barcelona declaration involves regular meetings of the foreign ministers, the Euro-Mediterranean committee of senior officials, and parliamentarians and local authorities. And since Barcelona, there have been numerous conferences and meetings to discuss various aspects of the partnership. The overall objective is to encourage the Mediterranean partners to cooperate among themselves, as well as to strengthen links with the EU.

However, there have been serious problems in fulfilling the promise of the Euro-Mediterranean partnership, as the region is torn by internal and external conflicts. It has been stymied particularly by the lack of progress in the Middle East peace process; this has overshadowed Euro-Mediterranean meetings and blocked the development of the relationship. There are periodic attempts to revive the partnership. The June 2000 Lisbon European Council issued a Common Strategy on the Mediterranean, which merely restated current policy (European Council, 2000). But the collapse of the Middle East peace process in late 2000 is making it very difficult to strengthen the partnership; external events are frustrating the EU's strategy.

Asia

Of the five regions covered here, Asia is the most diverse. It encompasses some of the richest economies in the world (Japan, South Korea) and some of the poorest (Cambodia, Laos). Disputes and conflicts divide the region's countries (India–Pakistan and China–Taiwan, to name but two). As a result, devising a strategy for all of Asia is difficult, but the Union still locates its assistance programme under one 'Asia' heading. The Union's relations have developed on a bloc-to-bloc basis with ASEAN and on a bilateral basis with the remaining countries. The ASEAN relationship is the strongest of these although, as noted below, it is not free of problems. It reflects the importance of bloc-to-bloc ties, as well as the challenges of dealing with other individual partners (China, Japan) or not, as the case may be (Burma, North Korea).

After the Mediterranean, Asia was the next big area where the Community began to make inroads, attracted to another relatively successful regional cooperation scheme, ASEAN. Political dialogue with ASEAN dates from 1978. The foreign ministers meet every two years to discuss political, economic and development issues. Senior officials meet in the alternate years. In 1980, the Community concluded an economic cooperation agreement with ASEAN, which then consisted of Indonesia, Malaysia, the Philippines, Singapore and Thailand. The agreement provided for commercial cooperation economic cooperation, and development cooperation, and a regular dialogue at senior official level.

In its 1994 'Asia Strategy' the Commission argued that the Union must strengthen its economic presence in Asia if it wished to maintain its leading role in the world economy (Piening, 1997: 143). Yet political considerations have caused considerable tension in relations with ASEAN. ASEAN's membership has since expanded to Brunei, Vietnam and Burma/Myanmar. But the EU has imposed diplomatic and economic sanctions on Burma over its lack of democracy and respect for human rights. It has refused to allow Burma to accede to the EC–ASEAN cooperation agreement and the political dialogue has been troubled as a result. In addition, since the massacre of protesters in Dili, East Timor, in November 1991, Portugal (the former colonial power in East Timor) has blocked the conclusion of a revised EC–ASEAN cooperation agreement. With agreement on East Timorese autonomy and elections in Indonesia, the EU–ASEAN relationship could be revitalised. To that end, the Union has minimized the Burmese issue. It agreed to resume ministerial meetings with ASEAN – suspended in 1997 when Burma joined ASEAN – even if they include Burma.

In 1996, the Union also launched ASEM. This is clearly the EU's answer to the US-sponsored Asia–Pacific Economic Cooperation forum. It includes all of the EU and ASEAN member states (with the exception of Burma), Japan, China and South Korea. A summit is held every two years to discuss matters of foreign affairs, economic cooperation and other issues of interest to the participants. ASEM thus draws other (large and/or rich) Asian countries into a regional relationship with the EU.

Of the EU's aid to Asia, the South Asian countries receive the highest share (Cox and Chapman, 1999: 88). This reflects mostly the extent of poverty in the region rather than their importance to the EU. Relations with the South Asian countries (Bangladesh, Bhutan, India, Maldives, Nepal, Pakistan and Sri Lanka) are bilateral, even though these countries set up the South Asian Association for Regional Cooperation (SAARC) in 1985. SAARC is much less of a success at regional cooperation than ASEAN, so the EU prefers to deal with certain individual countries. The EU holds regular foreign ministerial meetings with India and, less regularly, with Pakistan. In June 2000, the EU held its first summit with India. According to diplomats, this indicates the EU's awareness of India's 'economic and political clout' (Islam, 2000).

Latin America

Until the 1990s, there was very little Community involvement with Latin America. Authoritarian regimes governed in many Latin American countries, the US was the dominant external presence in the region, regional cooperation schemes were ineffective, and the Community had no security interests there (Piening, 1997: 120–1). This began to change with enlargement to Spain and Portugal, the former colonial powers, but slowly. Even in 1993, Enzo Grilli (1993: 225) could write that 'the region has remained a marginal concern for the Community'.

The exception to this lack of involvement was Central America. In 1984, the Community/EPC launched the San José process, to try to resolve conflicts in Central America. The European approach contrasted with that of the US, which was seeking a military solution to the conflicts there. US involvement was also considered dangerous, in that it could spark superpower confrontation. The Community member states instead considered economic development and regional cooperation to be the most appropriate means for stabilising the region. The San José process is a political dialogue, originally aimed at supporting peace processes in Central America. As part of it, the Community signed a trade and cooperation agreement with the Central American countries (Costa Rica, El Salvador, Guatemala, Honduras, Nicaragua and Panama) in 1985, which was revised in 1993. The new agreement provides for trade preferences for certain exports to the EC, and economic and development cooperation in a wide range of areas (including environment and the fight against illegal drugs). It sets up an institutionalised dialogue, with ministerial meetings held every two years (Piening, 1997: 128).

With democratisation in Latin America, the establishment or reinvigoration of regional cooperation schemes, and an increasing awareness within the EU of the economic importance of Latin America, the EU in the 1990s began to strengthen its relations with the region. There was a distinct fear that if the EU did not act to boost trade, it would be shut out of the region by the US, which has promoted the North American Free Trade Agreement (NAFTA) and proposed a Free Trade Area of the Americas. Hazel Smith (1998: 166) has argued: 'The EU's impetus to closer links with Latin America derives from global structural economic changes. It was also partly a response to the economic interventionism of the Clinton administration. The designated beneficiaries of the EU's policy are European business and, more intangibly, the European global political presence.' Countering the soft security threat of the illegal drugs trade has also, however, contributed to efforts to strengthen relations with Latin America.

Aid is not the most important of the EU's policy instruments in this relationship. Of the five regions covered here, Latin America receives the lowest share of EU aid, reflecting the relative economic strength of many of its countries (and perhaps a reticence to grant assistance to countries that compete with the EU in the global economy, particularly in the agricultural sector). More important is the institutionalisation of EU–Latin American relations through regular political dialogue and the reaching of extensive trade and cooperation agreements.

The EU has dealt with Latin American countries primarily on a regional basis, although its biggest success thus far involves a single country, Mexico. In November 1999, the EU and Mexico concluded a free trade agreement. This quite remarkable agreement is clearly a response to NAFTA and rather a challenge to US foreign economic policy in its own backyard.

In 1990, the EC member states began a political dialogue with the Rio Group (Argentina, Bolivia, Brazil, Chile, Columbia, Ecuador, Mexico, Panama, Paraguay, Peru, Uruguay and Venezuela). Foreign ministers from both sides meet annually and discuss issues of mutual relevance, including the debt problem and drug trafficking. In 1993, the Community concluded a trade and cooperation agreement with the Andean Pact (Bolivia, Columbia, Ecuador, Peru and Venezuela). Talks with MERCOSUR (Argentina, Brazil, Paraguay and Uruguay) led to an inter-regional framework agreement in 1995 and an association agreement in 1996.

In June 1999, an EU–Latin America summit was held in Rio de Janeiro, with thirty-three Latin American and Caribbean countries (including Cuba). The leaders adopted a wide-ranging declaration, including points on human rights and opposing the trade in illegal drugs. As a result of the summit, the EU opened talks with Mercosur on a free trade agreement. Cooperation with Latin America is increasing quite rapidly now, although the EU's reluctance to open its agricultural markets and the general problems of overstretch could slow these developments.

Eastern Europe

Until the late 1980s, the Community had hardly any dealings with the communist countries behind the Iron Curtain. The collapse of communism changed all this and several former communist countries are now set to join the EU in the first decade of the twenty-first century. The extent to which the EU shares a sense of responsibility towards its eastern neighbours is impressive. While there have been key actors pushing for enlargement (Germany, the Commission, the UK), all of the member states have agreed collectively to enlargement. Enlargement poses serious challenges to the EU, which have certainly not been dealt with swiftly or even adequately (causing consternation in the aspiring new member states), but the commitment to enlarge is arguably the EU's most important promise. The basic rationale for enlargement is to spread security and prosperity, by consolidating and guaranteeing democracy, the protection of human rights, market economy principles and good-neighbourliness in the east.

Ten countries from Central and Eastern Europe are in the EU's membership queue: Bulgaria, Czech Republic, Estonia, Hungary, Latvia, Lithuania, Poland, Romania, Slovakia and Slovenia. Relations with these countries have been political right from the beginning. From 1988, the Community hoped to encourage its eastern neighbours to carry out political and economic reforms by making trade and cooperation agreements, aid, association agreements and finally EU membership conditional on satisfying certain criteria, including democracy, the rule of law, human rights, and respect for and protection of minorities. Fulfilment of the conditions was considered necessary to ensure stability and security in Europe, a traditional liberal internationalist view (and one that reflects the West European experience). The EU was willing to use both carrots and sticks to achieve these goals (see Smith, 1999). Political conditionality in this regional relationship has served as a model for other regional relationships.

The intensity of relations with the Central and Eastern European countries is matched by ever increasing assistance commitments. From a PHARE aid programme budget of 500 million ECU in 1990, the total amount of pre-accession aid has risen to 3.120 billion Euro per year from 2000 to 2006. This dwarfs the new aid commitments to the ACP.

The Union's commitment to the former Soviet republics (bar the Baltic republics, which are on their way to EU membership) has been less intense. In 1992, following the collapse of the Soviet Union, the Community decided to regulate relations with the new states by special Partnership and Cooperation Agreements (PCAs). These do not set up as intensive a trading or political relationship as a Europe Agreement. PCAs have entered into force with nine countries, including Russia, Ukraine and the three Caucasian states. Belarus, Turkmenistan and Tajikistan do not yet meet the political conditions for a PCA. The former Soviet republics receive aid under the TACIS (Technical Assistance to the Commonwealth of Independent States) programme. The TACIS budget for the 2000–6 period is approximately 4 billion Euro.

The Union has made no promises to enlarge eventually to the former Soviet republics, although several countries (Ukraine, Georgia, even Russia) have expressed their interest in joining. Russia and Ukraine, however, are singled out for special attention. Each was the subject of a Common Strategy: Russia in June 1999 and Ukraine in December 1999. There are obvious reasons for this. Russia is a crucial power, especially in Europe, and Ukraine's independence needs support. Within the EU, Finland has also been pushing for a comprehensive EU strategy on the northern dimension – encompassing relations with Norway, the three Baltic republics and Russia. The December 1998 Vienna European Council endorsed the idea, but the Kosovo war and the Chechen crisis led to a cooling of relations between Russia and the EU. By mid-2000 relations began to recover, reflecting the EU's reluctance to isolate Russia.

While the Union's record in the conflicts that have wracked the Balkans is rightly judged to have been inadequate, it has made more of a contribution by trying to consolidate peace. In fact, the Union is expected to lead the rehabilitation of south-eastern Europe. For example, in June 1999 the Cologne European Council declared that the EU would 'take a leading role in the reconstruction efforts in Kosovo' and reaffirmed the EU's readiness 'to draw the countries of this region closer to the prospect of full integration into its structures' (European Council, 1999: paragraphs 65 and 72).

After the 1995 Dayton peace agreement, the Union set up a special aid programme (OBNOVA), which has been updated since the Kosovo war and renamed CARDS (Community Assistance for Reconstruction, Development and Stabilisation). The Union has pledged a great deal of money for the programme: 5.5 billion Euro for 2000–6. Some of this money will come from resources redeployed from other programmes but a large sum (1.8 billion Euro) has still not been provided (CEC, 2000).

The Union is sponsoring the Stability Pact for south-eastern Europe to encourage stability and good-neighbourliness in the region. This is a framework for cooperation among the countries of the region (including Albania), in which special roundtables are to draw up proposals for measures on democracy and human rights, reconstruction and security issues, which will be funded primarily by the Union. The EU has also offered trade relations and other benefits, such as new Stabilisation and Association Agreements, to countries that protect minority rights, are ready to engage in cross-border cooperation and comply with the Dayton peace process. The only countries that have thus far met the conditions are the Former Yugoslav Republic of Macedonia and Croatia.

All of the Union's various initiatives are to be wrapped up in a Common Strategy on the Western Balkans – and one sign of the confusion and lack of coordination among them is the delay in agreeing it. Nonetheless, the responsibilities that the Union has tried to assume are very large indeed.

Conclusion

The periphery of the Union has become increasingly more important relative to more far-flung areas. The reasons for this include: greater pressures for EU action from its neighbours; more member states are concerned with developments closer to home; there is a growing sense of responsibility by the Union for its periphery; there are stronger economic interests there; and security concerns there are of more direct and immediate interest to the Union. Promoting human rights, democracy and the market economy among the EU's neighbours forms part of a strategy to spread stability and prosperity, thus ensuring the security of the Union as well.

But the EU is not retreating to the homefront, as is clear from its attempts to build stronger relations with Asian and Latin American countries. What is disappearing is a unique emphasis on the ACP grouping. The EU's relations with the ACP countries – and particularly Africa – are beginning to look much more like its relations with other regions. The policy objectives are similar, as are the policy instruments: dialogue, (conditional) financial and technical assistance, and institutionalised trade. The ACP will be more subject to the other forces driving the EU's global extension besides the sense of EU responsibility for the former colonies – just as other regions are. It will also be subject to the contrary forces of overstretch and frustration.

Whether the EU can actually fulfil the expectations stemming from its increasing commitments around the world is, of course, quite another matter. There are distinct signs of overstretch, which affects relations even with countries on the EU's periphery. Correcting this will require a willingness on the part of the member states to increase quite substantially the resources available to the EU for external relations. This challenge will co-exist uneasily with the forces favouring a 'global Europe' for some time to come. The periphery may, as a result, assume an ever greater importance. Globalists – including those now arguing for a strong EU–ACP relationship – will still have their work cut out for them.

References

Allen, D. (1996), 'The European rescue of national foreign policy?', in C. Hill (ed.), *The Actors in Europe's Foreign Policy*, London: Routledge.

Arts, K. (2000), *Integrating Human Rights into Development Cooperation: The Case of the Lomé Convention*, The Hague: Kluwer Law International.

Barbé, E. (1998), 'Balancing Europe's eastern and southern dimensions', in J. Zielonka (ed.), *Paradoxes of Europe's Foreign Policy*, The Hague: Kluwer Law International.

Bretherton, C. and J. Vogler (1999), *The European Union as a Global Actor*, London: Routledge.

Cameron, F. (1999), *The Foreign and Security Policy of the European Union*, Sheffield: Sheffield Academic Press.

CEC (2000), 'Commission proposes financial guarantees for assistance for the Balkans in the financial programming for 2001–2006', http://europa.eu.int/comm/externalrelations/news/0500/ip00435.htm, press release, 4 May, Brussels.

Council of Ministers (1991), 'Resolution of the Council and of the member states meeting in the Council on human rights, democracy and development', *EC Bulletin*, 24:11, item 1.3.67.

Council of Ministers (1992), 'Report to the European Council in Lisbon on the likely development of the Common Foreign and Security Policy (CFSP) with a view to identifying areas open to Joint Action vis-à-vis particular countries or groups of countries', Annex to the Conclusions of the Presidency, Lisbon European Council, 26–27 June, 25 *EC Bulletin*, no. 6.

Council of Ministers (1998), 'Common Position on human rights, democratic principles, the rule of law and good governance in Africa', *European Foreign Policy Bulletin online*, Document no. 98/078, Florence: European University Institute.

Cox, A. and J. Chapman (1999), *The European Community External Cooperation Programmes: Policies, Management and Distribution*, London and Brussels: Overseas Development Institute and European Commission.

Edwards, G. and E. Regelsberger (eds) (1990), *Europe's Global Links: The European Community and Inter-regional Cooperation*, London: Pinter.

Euro-Mediterranean Conference (1995), 'Barcelona Declaration', 28 *EU Bulletin*, no. 11.

European Council (1999), 'Presidency Conclusions, Cologne, 3–4 June', *European Foreign Policy Bulletin Online*, Document no. 99/099, Florence: European University Institute.

European Council (2000), 'Presidency Conclusions, Santa Maria de Feira, 19–20 June', http://ue.eu.int/en/info/eurocouncil/index.htm.

Ginsberg, R. (1999), 'Conceptualizing the European Union as an international actor', *Journal of Common Market Studies*, 37:3, pp. 429–54.

Gomez, R. (1998), 'The EU's Mediterranean policy: common foreign policy by the back door?', in J. Peterson and H. Sjursen (eds), *A Common Foreign Policy for Europe?*, London: Routledge.

Grilli, E. (1993), *The European Community and the Developing Countries*, Cambridge: Cambridge University Press.

Harding, G. (1999), 'Leaders aim to put "forgotten continent" top of the agenda', *European Voice*, 29 July–4 August.

Hill, C. (1993), 'The capability–expectations gap, or conceptualising Europe's international role', *Journal of Common Market Studies*, 31:3, pp. 305–28.

Islam, S. (2000), 'EU's efforts to rebuild ties with Asia risk losing momentum', *European Voice*, 6–12 April.

Lister, M. (1997), *The European Union and the South*, London: Routledge.

Nuttall, S. (1992), *European Political Cooperation*, Oxford: Clarendon Press.

Piening, C. (1997), *Global Europe: The European Union in World Affairs*, London: Lynne Rienner.

Schmitter, P. (1969), 'Three neofunctional hypotheses about international integration', *International Organization*, 33:2, pp. 161–6.

Smith, H. (1998), 'Actually existing foreign policy – or not? The EU in Latin and Central America', in J. Peterson and H. Sjursen (eds), *A Common Foreign Policy for Europe?*, London: Routledge.

Smith, K.E. (1999), *The Making of EU Foreign Policy: The Case of Eastern Europe*, London: Macmillan.
Smith, M. (1998), 'Competitive cooperation and EU–US relations: can the EU be a strategic partner for the United States in the world political economy?', *Journal of European Public Policy*, 5:4, pp. 561–77.
Working Party set up by the Secretary-General of the Council (1999), 'Operation of the Council with an enlarged Union in prospect' (Trumpf/Piris Report), 10 March, Brussels.

5

Changing European concerns: security and complex political emergencies instead of development[1]

Gorm Rye Olsen

Introduction

In February 2000, the High Representative for the Common Foreign and Security Policy of the European Union, Javier Solana, declared:

> The European Union is the only institution in the world which has all the instruments to cover all aspects of crisis management – both the military and the civilian ones. We can handle humanitarian missions, economic aid, trade initiatives, police deployments and military actions and when everything has fallen into place, we will be the most complete organisation for crisis management. (Solana, 2000a: 13)

And, Mr Solana continued: 'the EU has at its disposal crucial instruments for conducting a credible foreign policy in the field of economics and trade. Now it wants to be able to develop these instruments if and when it is necessary, with the possibility to use force where its vital interests are at stake' (Solana, 2000: 14). The EU CFSP High Representative is no unimportant person. Recalling that Mr Solana is directly appointed by the Council of Ministers, it seems likely that when he airs his opinion on the potential international role of the European Union, he probably expresses the prevailing views found among the most prominent European politicians engaged in foreign policy making. Based on his remarks as quoted above, there cannot be much doubt that the European Union strongly seeks to establish itself as an important international player in its own right. The Helsinki Summit of December 1999 contributed considerably to speeding up the process of giving the Union a much stronger international role.

The ambition to develop 'Europe' into a significant foreign policy actor has existed ever since the start of the European Community (Cafruny and Peters, 1998: 1ff; Cameron, in Rhodes, 1998: 20). The possibilities for realising this aim have increased considerably due to the ending of the Cold War and not least because of what happened in the Balkans during the 1990s, including the events in Kosovo in 1999. It is often forgotten that the Community's development policy was actually one of the first common policies which had consequences for the position of the EC as an international actor. From the late 1950s until the early 1980s, it was even considered as one of the 'cornerstones' of European integration (Lister, 1997: 22). As late as 1996, the Commission described the Lomé Convention as 'one of the most important facets of the European Union's external activities' (CEC, 1996: 1). Even though the Lomé Conventions and the more recent Cotonou Agreement cover countries in Africa, the Caribbean and the Pacific, there is no doubt that Sub-Saharan Africa is the most important of the three regions for the EU. This is reflected in the holding of the first joint EU–Africa Summit which took place in Cairo in April 2000.

This chapter argues that the Third World in general, and Africa in particular, are becoming more and more important components in the EU's efforts to develop into a significant international player. This does not mean that Africa *per se* has moved up the list of foreign policy priorities of the Union. It only implies that Africa is becoming instrumental to another, and partly new, set of European interests which have been strengthened by the recent crucial changes in the Union's external environment, especially the dissolution of the bipolar international system and the Balkan crises of the 1990s. The changes in European interests in the developing world during the 1990s are manifested in a shift in Europe's policy towards Africa, from the initial focus on development issues towards increasing concern with so-called 'complex political emergencies'. As a consequence of the latter concern, the Europeans have reflected more and more on conflict prevention and crisis management in Africa. It is hardly a coincidence that the Portuguese Presidency in January 2000 issued a so-called 'Reflection paper' which stressed that:

> development priorities should also be thought of in the context of ongoing European dynamics, namely those related to the reorganisation of external relations (in the Commission) and the building of a European CFSP [Common Foreign and Security Policy]. Being realistic about development means thinking in an integrated manner about politics, security and trade as well as development aid itself. (Cardoso *et al.*, 2000: 12)

The fundamental argument of this chapter is that it is possible to identify a change in Europe's Africa policy from development towards emergencies and conflict. To substantiate this position, it is necessary to analyse the shifts in Europe's development aid policy, to look into the issue of European humanitarian assistance, and to reflect on crises and conflicts in Africa. Therefore, the chapter is structured around these supposedly important dimensions of Europe's policy towards Africa. Firstly, it looks into the changes which took place in the volume of aid which was channelled to Africa during the 1990s. Secondly, the issue of humanitarian aid in emergency situations is scrutinised.

This section includes a separate discussion of the role of the mass media because the media are supposed to play a unique role in encouraging political reactions to humanitarian emergencies. The third section deals with aspects of the foreign and security policy that relate to development and crisis management.

In order to have a framework for interpreting Europe's Africa policy of the 1990s, apart from a short description of the Union's foreign policy sion-making structure, the next section contains a brief general presentation of some theoretical reflections on policy making within the European Union, and some remarks on the role of the European Union as an international actor.

European interests and policy making on international issues

The focus on three more or less separate policy fields (development cooperation, emergency aid and foreign policy) makes a thorough analysis of the European Union's policy towards Africa quite comprehensive. The analysis necessarily has to take into account that different interests and different actors are involved in each of these policy fields. Roy Ginsberg argued that decisions are brought about by different elites, both national ones and those based in Brussels, who are engaged in 'bureaucratic politics' (Ginsberg, 1989). Characteristics of bureaucratic politics are that 'the decision is formulated through bargaining and compromise', and that 'numerous individuals and organizations, with varying interests, are involved for any single issue, without the predominance of any participant' (Rosati, 1981: 238; see also Ginsberg, 1989; Peters, 1992 and Peters, 1997). Apart from the bargaining among a large number of actors, there are at least two other relevant and characteristic features of European decision making. On the one hand there is 'an apparent fragmentation . . . of policy making within the Commission'. On the other hand there are 'increased linkages of the components of the Commission to the components of national bureaucracies' (Peters, 1992: 76–7).

In spite of the considerable changes during the 1990s with the Maastricht and the Amsterdam Treaties, decision making on EU external relations is still based on the principle of intergovernmentalism. The CFSP continues to be clearly intergovernmental and thus open to separate actions from individual EU member states parallel to the common or multilateral policies. According to the Maastricht Treaty (Title V, Article J), the CFSP is mainly a matter for the Presidency of the Council. The Treaty does not describe an explicit role for the Commission. Irrespective of this, the Commission has become more and more involved in day-to-day foreign policy making, and has actually developed an institutional role that is not sanctioned by the different Treaties (Peters, in Cafruny and Peters, 1998: 11–33). So, the Maastricht Treaty established a dual structure among the EU institutions involved in external affairs. It created formal predominance of the Council vis-à-vis the Commission, which previously had an important role and expertise in this field.

The Union Treaty sets out the general objectives for development policy; that is, for the Commission, which has the competence to implement its own development programmes. However, this competence is complementary to that of the member states, which all have their own bilateral development aid programmes. Within this framework of dual competence, the Treaty sets out a number of objectives, which include the aim to achieve more coordination with the member states' programmes, greater coherence between different policies carried out by the Community, and effective complementarity between the Community's and the member states' bilateral programmes.

The organisation of Europe's humanitarian assistance is no less complicated as this kind of aid comes from three sources: first, some assistance is channelled through 'ECHO', the Union's own special branch for humanitarian assistance. Secondly, humanitarian aid is also financed by so-called 'other Commissions' (which in the past referred to different Directorates-General, such as DG I and DG VIII). Thirdly, humanitarian assistance is disbursed bilaterally by the member states.

The institutional structure for European Union policy making on external affairs consists of the Council and the Commission, plus, to some extent, the European Parliament. Until the spring of 1999, no less than four Commissioners plus the President of the Commission were involved in European foreign policy making (Peters, 1997: 25). There was pronounced competition between the different Commissioners, and thus between the individual Directorates-General, which all had their own ambitions and their own agendas. This can be understood as an example of the notion of 'bureaucratic politics', as referred to above (Peters, 1992: 75–122; Peters, 1997: 22–36). In addition, the national bureaucracies of the fifteen member states are also common European institutional actors. In most cases they are split into several government departments which either take care of development issues or foreign policy, with the consequent problems of coordination.

This chapter understands the external actions of the Union as the outcome of a number of bargaining and decision-making processes, which take place both in the individual member states and in Brussels. This is sometimes called 'two-tier bargaining' (Ginsberg, 1999: 442–3) or a 'two-level game' (Moravcsik, 1993: 473–524). The notion of two-tier bargaining raises the question of which interests are involved at the different levels of decision making, and also whether these interests are in conflict. This chapter assumes that a thorough understanding of Europe's Africa policy has to be founded on an analysis of the national interests of individual member states. Based on the realist assumption that states have some more or less well-perceived national interests and preferences, it is argued that the bilateral Africa policies of the member states are basically determined by a more or less clear conception of what is the national interest of each individual country. The conception of the national interest is the result of a domestic bargaining and negotiation process which involves coalition building among local political actors. The individual national interests are then carried on to the European Union level, where there is yet another round of negotiations, bargaining and coalition building before a European position is reached. As Andrew Moravcsik pointed out, however, such a common agreement requires that the 'interests of dominant domestic groups in different countries converge' (Moravcsik, 1993: 487).

The chapter's understanding of decision making within the European Union is basically in agreement with Moravcsik's 'liberal intergovernmentalist approach', which argues that the EC/EU can be analysed as an intergovernmental regime (Moravcsik, 1993). This approach is in line with Thomas Riesse-Kappen, according to whom the individual member states are still the dominant actors in Europe's foreign policy, and therefore their interests and preferences to a large extent influence European foreign and international actions (Riesse-Kappen, 1996). Christopher Hill found that European foreign policy is the result of a bargaining process of the dominant states within the Community (Hill, 1993; Hill and Wallace, 1996), implying that the actual policy has to be understood as the outcome of the different interests and positions of the dominant states. Finally, a slightly different position is found with Cafruny and Peters, who argue that the policy preferences of the EC/EU are the result of a hybrid process reflecting different types of interest, which diverge depending on the specific issue which is to be decided upon (Cafruny and Peters, 1998: 16ff).

Irrespective of the minor differences between these authors, here it is maintained, as for Andrew Moravcsik, that it is both possible and fruitful to understand European interests as something different from the result of a bargaining process among the fifteen member states. Thus it is argued that it is possible to talk about 'European' interests, meaning common interests which might very well be different from the interests of the individual member states. So, on the one hand there are the national interests of the fifteen member states, which might very well differ from the interests of the European Union. Special 'European' interests are supposed to be related to the idea that, based on values, Europe has a special role to play in the world (Hill and Wallace, 1996: 9). According to Roy Ginsberg (1999: 436), such principles and values are 'democracy, soft-edged capitalism, a zone of peace among members, and diplomatic mediation between third parties to undercut the causes of major conflict'. In order to pursue such aims, cooperation among the member states and common policy initiatives achieve a value in themselves, as they might promote the creation of common interests and eventually also the establishment of a common identity in world politics.

Based on these reflections, it is the hypothesis of this chapter that the attempts to form a common European policy towards Africa have a dual purpose. First, they seek to take care of the special 'European' global interests. Secondly, they achieve a value in themselves, as such endeavours might contribute to the creation of a common European identity. As a consequence of both these purposes, European foreign policy initiatives towards Africa in reality would become symbolic policy.

European development aid to Africa

As outlined above, development aid is the first of three important dimensions to be analysed. This section presents the main changes in EU aid to Africa during the 1990s. As a starting point, there is no doubt that development aid was the most important policy instrument in Europe's relations with the ACP countries in general and with Africa in particular (Riddell, 1999: 309). France is the only EU member state where foreign aid has had a similarly unique position in its relations with Africa. This has to be explained by the remarkably high priority of the region in the overall foreign policy strategy of France (Brüne, 1995; Marchal, 1998; Martin, 1995). Irrespective of this high foreign policy priority, or maybe exactly because of this position, French aid to Africa has been conspicuous as far as the absolute amount of aid is concerned. Thus in the 1990s French aid was greater than that from all European donors, including the EU itself (OECD, 1997).

During the 1990s, EU aid to the ACP countries underwent considerable changes. First and most manifest, the real value of the available financial envelope decreased. This occurred both in 1995, in connection with the so-called 'mid-term review', and in 2000 by the financial protocol of the Cotonou Agreement (Crawford, 1996; *Financial Times*, 10 December 1999; interviews, November and December 1999, Brussels). The decline in the real value of aid allocated under the Lomé and Cotonou arrangements becomes even more conspicuous when compared with the growing percentage of total EU development aid that went to other regions. Lomé's relative share of total EU development aid went down from 66.3 per cent in 1989/90 to 42.8 per cent in 1996/97, whereas aid to other areas grew from 33.7 per cent to 57.2 per cent during the same period (OECD, 1996; OECD, 1998). The reductions in Lomé aid become even more striking against the background that in January 1995 three affluent countries, Sweden, Austria and Finland, joined the European Union.

Secondly, and just as important, during the 1990s a growing number of conditionalities were added to the Lomé aid package, such as structural adjustment, adherence to democracy and human rights, and anti-corruption. These conditions were combined with a number of explicit control measures, such as trenching of the downpayments agreed upon. Finally there was the 'political dialogue', which to a large extent was equivalent to giving the EU an institutional possibility for continuing critique of the ACP countries for lack of adherence to the principles of good governance.

The apparent strong scepticism towards giving aid to the ACP countries, especially to Africa, under the Lomé treaty was also manifested in the bilateral aid policies of the fifteen EU member states. Thus the total net disbursements to sub-Saharan Africa fell from 50.7 per cent of the members' total aid budgets in 1986/87 to 43.9 per cent in 1996/97 (OECD, 1998: table 33). The cuts were particularly remarkable for the big donors, which reduced both their aid budgets measured as a share of GNP and the share of their budgets directed towards Africa. France, the biggest European donor, reduced its total Official Development Assistance (ODA)/GNP aid commitment from 0.63 per cent in 1992 to 0.41 per cent in 1998 (DAC, 1999). Measured at 1996 prices and exchange rates, the share of the shrinking French ODA going to Africa was reduced from 49.6 per cent in 1993 to 45.4 per cent in 1997 (OECD, 1998: table 29). Accordingly, Africa received less and less aid from France during the 1990s. Measured at 1996 prices and exchange rates, it fell from 3,496 million US dollars in 1993 to 2,450 million dollars in 1997. Germany, the second biggest European aid donor, reduced its ODA as a percentage of GNP from 0.38 per cent in 1992 to 0.26 per cent in 1998 (DAC, 1999). At the same time, the share of German aid to Africa fell from 28.9 per cent in 1993 to 25.4 per cent in 1997 (OECD, 1998: table 29). The same picture appears as with France, namely shrinking net disbursements to Africa, which fell from 1,514 million US dollars in 1993 to 1,057 million in 1997. The British ODA as a percentage of GNP came down from 0.31 per cent in 1992 to 0.27 per cent in 1998, while the share of British ODA going to Africa remained more or less stable at around 32 per cent of the total budget.

Some of the smaller European donors, such as the Netherlands and Denmark, did not reduce their ODA as a percentage of GNP during the 1990s, even though both countries reduced the share of their total aid going to Africa, which is important for this discussion. The slight reduction in the relative share of Dutch aid to Africa was outweighed by the growth of the general aid budget, resulting in a minor growth in the net disbursements of the Netherlands to the region from 588 million US dollars in 1993, compared with 644 million in 1997. The same picture is repeated in the case of Denmark, with a slightly higher amount of aid going to Africa, in spite of a relative decline in the share of its ODA to Africa that was reduced from 45.7 per cent in 1993 to 38.2 per cent in 1997 (OECD, 1998: table 29). For the purposes of this chapter the relative decline is the most interesting change to note. The aggregate result of these changes, and especially of the reductions in most European aid budgets during the 1990s, is that net disbursements to Africa declined markedly. Measured at 1996 prices and exchange rates, the total bilateral aid from the fifteen EU members went down from 8.609 million US dollars in 1993 to 6.816 million dollars in 1997. While the fall in the total amount of aid was significant, for the future of the aid relationship between Europe and Africa it might be more significant that, apart from the UK, all bilateral donors mentioned here reduced the shares of their aid budgets that were allocated to Africa.

It is obvious that the reluctance to finance development aid for the ACP cannot be isolated from trends in individual EU member states' aid policies. Within the framework of interpretation of this chapter, it points to shrinking national interests in most EU member countries engaging in development aid. The decreasing national interests are also clearly manifested in the reductions of the common European aid programme. This can hardly be seen in isolation from other developments in the 1990s, where scepticism increased among donors as regards the effectiveness of aid to promote social and economic development in Africa, which has been perceived as a particularly difficult case (Riddel, 1999; Walle, 1999; Thérien and Lloyd, 2000).

European humanitarian assistance to Africa in the 1990s

The end of the Cold War, and especially the frustration over the lack of a European capability to deliver efficient humanitarian assistance during and after the crisis following the war liberating Kuwait in 1991, led to initiatives to establish an EC office with special responsibility for humanitarian assistance. The organisation became known under the name of ECHO. There were at least three motives for establishing this specialised European unit with such responsibilities. One was simply for the Community to have such an organisation within this particular field. The second aim was to put the organisation into a position to coordinate better and more efficiently the bilateral European humanitarian contributions. Both purposes aimed to fulfil a third motive, which had nothing to do with the sufferings of the victims in the numerous emergency situations. It was to give the European Community much more international visibility in a policy field that is very often in the focus of the media (interview, Brussels, 16 November 1999).

The combined resources from ECHO and other Commission and bilateral contributions made 'Europe' the biggest provider of humanitarian assistance in the 1990s as it accounted for 53–4 per cent of global humanitarian aid on average (ECHO, 1998: 29). ECHO as a separate donor accounted for around one-third of this amount (ECHO, 1998: 29). It is worth noting that, during the 1990s, the bilateral contributions from the EU member states apparently grew, compared with the allocations to ECHO. Thus in 1996 the member states contributed 45 per cent of total European humanitarian aid, while their share had grown to 54 per cent in 1998. The aid of ECHO from 1996 to 1998 fell from 55 per cent to 46 per cent of total humanitarian assistance (ECHO, 1998: 29).

For the purposes of this chapter it is of particular importance to establish a trend in European humanitarian disbursements during the 1990s. Based on the available figures, the total amount of humanitarian aid financed by ECHO clearly reached a peak in 1994. Since then, there has been a downward movement where the amount seems to stabilise at a lower level than the peak year of 1994. Thus, in the second half of the 1990s, the share tended to stabilise at around 14 per cent of total EU aid (i.e. development aid and humanitarian assistance combined) (OECD, 1998: table 14). Still, compared with the 1980s, the amount of European humanitarian aid in the second half of the 1990s was considerably higher. It reached a peak in 1999 because of the massive aid to Kosovo.

Within the total amount disbursed by ECHO, Africa received roughly 40 per cent in the first half of the 1990s. In the second half of the decade, the relative allocations to Africa were, however, somewhat lower. They were reduced to around 30 per cent in 1996 and 1998, to reach an absolute low point in 1999 with a share of 17 per cent. No doubt, the year 1999 was in a number of respects an exception from the general picture of the 1990s because of the massive European preoccupation with the situation in Kosovo and in the Balkans in general. No less than 55 per cent of total ECHO aid went to 'former Yugoslavia'. This necessarily had to show in the statistics for the total aid to Africa (ECHO, 1994, 1995, 1996, 1998).

The 1999 situation underlines a general point about humanitarian assistance, which is that it is virtually impossible to predict where the next human disaster will happen. Therefore, it is impossible to predict how the mass media will react in such situations, and consequently it is difficult to predict what kind of pressure there will be on the European authorities to act. The situation in the Balkans in 1999 illustrates that humanitarian emergencies close to the EU countries attract much media attention and thus much popular attention. This may subsequently lead to more humanitarian assistance than for emergencies in, for example, Africa. On the other hand, it is not to be forgotten that during the 1990s in general there was considerable European willingness to contribute humanitarian aid to Africa.

Complex political emergencies and the mass media

This readiness to give emergency assistance no doubt had its background in a public which was clearly in favour of this kind of involvement in Africa in the 1990s. Because of the strong emotions involved when the TV shows human sufferings on a massive scale, there was a popular expectation and thus pressure on the European governments to act. Here, there is no doubt that to European policy makers the symbolic value of emergency aid has been particularly important, not least because of the massive media coverage which a number of the complex emergency situations have received.

During the 1990s, considerable focus was on the possible influence of the electronic media in relation to international crisis situations, and to the decisions which were taken during such events (Shaw, 1996). It is a common assumption that the media play a crucial role in such situations. The phenomenon has become known as the 'CNN effect', which is expected to explain the course of development in a number of international crisis situations (Robinson, 1999). Among the frequently quoted examples of the CNN effect are the international intervention in Iraqi Kurdistan in the spring of 1991 and the US intervention in the Somali famine in December 1992.

However, it is an open question whether the relationship between media coverage and political decision making is as simple as the CNN effect indicates. At least, the issue of the possible influence of the mass media on humanitarian emergencies involves a whole range of other questions. First of all, is it correct that European reactions to humanitarian emergencies depend on media coverage? And secondly, does this mean that if there is no media attention to an emergency situation, there will be no humanitarian assistance to such a crisis?

Concerning the claim that the media have immense influence on the foreign policy agenda in Western societies, and thus indirectly on the political initiatives of these countries, there is no firm basis for arguing that such a CNN effect exists in general. The state of knowledge concerning media influence on international events claims that the media only have an effect in situations where governments lack a clear policy (Gowing, 1994; Robinson, 1999). On the other hand, in situations where governments have a policy, the media do not have such an influence. Rather, there is a tendency of politicians and governments turning the media into their 'servants', communicating the message of the government to the public (Robinson, 1999).

This is the situation in general, but if the focus is on humanitarian emergencies and the possible influence of the media in such cases, it might very well be different. Thus Lionel Rosenblatt claimed that 'in a narrowly focused situation such as humanitarian emergencies, the media play a decisive role in informing the public and stimulating action' (Rosenblatt, in Rothberg and Weiss, 1996: 140, 139). There is general support for the point that media coverage is important for promoting political action in relation to humanitarian emergencies (Rothberg and Weiss, 1996). Nevertheless, it is not to be forgotten that Piers Robinson claims that the existing research on media influence in humanitarian disaster situations fails 'to clarify the significance of media impact on humanitarian intervention decisions' (Robinson, 1999: 308).

If media coverage is important as far as securing humanitarian assistance from Europe is concerned, what then is required to ensure that the press is on the spot when a crisis arises? One precondition is geographical accessibility, which means airfields, roads, and so on. If logistical difficulties in reaching disaster areas are too big, there will be no or only very limited media coverage. A classic example of geographical accessibility is Somalia in 1992, and a case of the opposite is Sudan over most of the years of civil war. A second precondition for media coverage has to do with the personal security of the reporting journalists, who for obvious reasons are hesitant to report from emergency situations that involve considerable personal security risks. Sudan, Liberia and Sierra Leone are cases in point. A third precondition, and probably the most important one, is that an emergency has to be 'news'. Basically, it is no news if Africa experiences yet another humanitarian disaster. At least that seems to be the most important media-related explanation for the limited news reporting on the civil wars of Sudan and Angola, which have both dragged on for decades. It is simply no news that Africans kill Africans. Furthermore, the African crises also have to compete with emergencies in other parts of the world. This last point has to do with what is sometimes called the 'news attention cycle' or the 'issue attention cycle', which argues that some issues, particularly distant ones that do not directly affect people, invariably receive attention on a cyclical basis. That is what is sometimes formulated in more popular expressions such as 'the world does not have an appetite for more than one crisis at a time' (Livingston, in Rothberg and Weiss, 1996: 83–4). This statement implies that if complex emergencies in Africa are to receive media attention, and thus subsequently hope for emergency assistance from Europe, they either have to contain an element of news or, as a minimum, a 'new' angle to the 'traditional' negative stories from Africa. Somalia in 1992 got media attention, among other reasons because it was a unique case where a society was falling apart. Likewise, the Kosovo crisis of 1999 contained an element of news combined with a strong element of self-interest because of geographical proximity to the EU.

If an emergency situation contains no news, it has to be framed in the right way in order to create a public opinion for action (Robinson, 1999; Girardet, in Rothberg and Weiss 1996: 58). The need for framing is connected with the fact that 'media reports do not objectively report on humanitarian crises. Rather, they report crises in particular, and often very different ways' (Robinson, 1999: 306). Sometimes they tend to advocate action, and in other instances the media do not advocate action. The differences in media framing can explain why the Western powers acted in the cases of Kurdistan and Somalia. It was because the media simply presented it as a necessity. Most importantly, framing may also explain the lack of action towards a number of humanitarian crises in Africa, such as those in Rwanda, Liberia and Sierra Leone during the 1990s. These countries, and what happened there, were largely pictured as the 'Heart of Darkness' (Robinson, 1999). Therefore, there were no reasons nor advocacy to react. The tremendous international support for Mozambique in March 2000 can likewise be explained by framing and not necessarily by the magnitude of the disaster. The framing in the Mozambique case related to images of South African helicopters rescuing people who had sought refuge in the treetops.

In summary, media coverage is crucial to promote political initiatives in Europe towards humanitarian emergencies. But putting an emergency situation on the agenda is one thing. Making sure that public awareness leads to political action is quite another thing. Because the topic is so emotional and so dependent on media coverage, public opinion is crucial in this context. There are no indications that European public opinion has changed from its traditional values, which evolve around the feeling of humanitarian responsibility to help people in dire need. As Ian Smilie put it: 'Little has changed since the conclusion reached in 1983 . . . on the subject of public opinion and development assistance: the rationale for aid in the public mind was and remains emergency relief' (Smilie, 1996: 28). Furthermore, there seem to be indications that 'humanitarian appeals' from NGOs in disaster situations did not lose ground in the 1990s, stressing the point that there is a widespread humanitarian attitude in all, or at least in most, European countries (Smilie, 1996: 32).

Common Foreign and Security Policy

This chapter assumes that the relationship between the ACP countries in general and Africa in particular cannot solely be understood on the basis of an analysis of (humanitarian) aid policy. A thorough understanding of the priority of Africa within Europe's external relations is necessary too. However, it is not possible to make a sharp distinction between foreign policy and development aid/humanitarian aid. Therefore, this section is structured along a rather arbitrary line, which first looks into what happened within the Commission during the 1990s on issues related to conflicts and conflict prevention. Then, the changes and developments in the CFSP, with special reference to Africa, are analysed. Because the development of the CFSP is mainly the responsibility of the Council of Ministers, the Council has to be analysed, too.

Kjell Eliassen argued that the end of the Cold War changed the security framework of Europe in fundamental ways, as new and 'softer' security issues moved to the top of the agenda for foreign policy and security thinking in Western Europe (Eliassen, 1998). Interlinking economic, political and security issues became the order of the day, which created a pressure to find new roles and new responsibilities for the Community in ways which 'approximated to "real" foreign policy' (Smith, 1996: 250ff; Eliassen, 1998: 5). The new security environment also stressed the need for a 'new' European policy which, with civilian means, could take into account the non-military threats and challenges which characterised the post-Cold War situation in Europe (Schirm, in Rhodes, 1998: 76). This intertwining of the old civilian agenda of the European Community and the new high politics of peace and security was particularly outspoken in the 1990s (Smith, 1996: 253). This new momentum in Europe's foreign relations was not only manifest in relation to the near-abroad. For most of the 1990s, the European Union was concerned with the issue of violent conflicts in developing countries, not least in Africa, as former EU Commissioner for development aid Joao de Deus Pinheiro stated (Pinheiro, 1999).

In spite of the reluctance of many member states to give too much power to the CFSP (Cafruny and Peters, 1998: 299; Rhodes, 1998), the Union Treaty introduced a new element in European foreign policy making with the system of 'joint actions'. This opened a door to closer cooperation by creating a possibility of common European foreign policies on selected issues and in areas where the member states share important interests. The important point about joint actions is that, once agreed upon within the Union, the member states are bound by them and have to ensure that their own policies accord with them (Piening, 1997: 40–2). For the purposes of this chapter, it is worth mentioning that the only out-of-area joint action adopted in 1993 was directed towards Africa, namely South Africa (Holland, 1997: 174).

The issues of crisis management and conflict prevention in Africa have been treated differently by the EU Commission and by the Council of Ministers. The institutional division was particularly pronounced in the second half of the 1990s when the establishment of the CFSP was speeded up, and conflict prevention became an important element in this endeavour of the Council. At the same time, and parallel to this exercise, work continued within the Commission to stress the potential key role of development aid and related instruments for peace building and conflict prevention. In spite of this split between the two European institutions, during the 1990s European perceptions on conflict prevention and foreign policy changed, and the EU was pushed towards taking a much more coherent approach to these issues. It is hardly a coincidence that the Portuguese Presidency in January 2000 issued a so-called 'Reflection Paper', which stressed that

> development priorities should also be thought of in the context of ongoing European dynamics, namely those related to the reorganisation of external relations (in the Commission) and the building of a European CFSP. Being realistic about development means thinking in an integrated manner about politics, security and trade as well as development aid itself. (Cardoso et al., 2000: 12)

It is interesting that the reflections on conflicts and conflict prevention in Africa started early in the 1990s within the Commission, and that they took place before most other development organisations acknowledged the significance of the issue. At the time, the initiative to focus on conflict prevention came specifically from the Directorate-General for Development, DG VIII. For example, Martin Landgraf pointed out that the first EC initiative on 'peace-building, conflict prevention and resolution in Africa' can be traced back to early 1993, which was before the real growth in the number of violent internal conflicts became part of the general perception of Africa (Landgraf, 1998: 103). Therefore, it seems reasonable to accept the point of view that the focus on conflict and conflict prevention had its roots in the good governance debate, which was triggered off by the 1989 publication of the World Bank Report on *Sub-Saharan Africa. From Crisis to Sustainable Growth* (World Bank, 1989; interview, Brussels, 15 November 1999).

Viewed from this perspective, it is also worth noting that the debate within the Commission was intimately related to the issue of development aid. Parallel to the focus on development aid and conflict prevention, DG VIII also aimed at strengthening the African capability for conflict management. This was manifested in a number of initiatives to develop closer relations between the EU and the Organisation of African Unity (OAU). From the very start, the main theme of the dialogue with the OAU was that conflict prevention and conflict resolution were primarily the responsibility of Africans themselves. Therefore, the EU Summit in Essen in December 1994 called for 'an intensive political dialogue between the EU and OAU in particular regarding conflict prevention in Africa' (Landgraf, 1998: 105).

In March 1996 the Commission issued a Communication on conflict and conflict prevention in Africa, which stressed that the use of development aid and related instruments was considered important by the European Union. In June 1997 a Common Position on these issues was issued, clarifying that conflict prevention was a priority of the EU. The Common Position also contained a reference to 'implementation of the defence implications of EU actions within the initiative on conflict prevention by the WEU' (Landgraf, 1998: 110). A few days later, the Council of Development Ministers agreed upon a resolution that clearly signalled that conflict prevention, which until then had been discussed within the framework of the CFSP, was now a main concern of the European Community in general (Landgraf, 1998: 110). However, there were considerable problems in defining which activities could be considered as peace building and conflict prevention. According to the Commission, 'every project or policy measure is a peace-building measure' if it is designed and implemented in such a way that it 'addresses the root-causes of violent conflicts in a targeted manner' (Landgraf, 1998: 114). In line with this understanding, the Commission took a number of initiatives in order to implement the guidelines and declarations. Firstly, it tried to identify potential trouble areas. Secondly, the Commission established the research and fact-finding Conflict Prevention Network. Thirdly, it secured the elaboration of a whole series of practical conflict prevention instruments (Landgraf, 1998: 114). This exercise resulted in a publication that, in a quite detailed way, discussed topics such as: why do violent conflicts occur?; what could be possible EU measures?; are they viable?, and so on (Lund and Mehler, 1999).

It can be argued that the debate on good governance and democracy, which was highly profiled as early as 1991, signalled the beginning of a serious European commitment to the (soft) security problems of Africa. Nevertheless, it was not until the end of 1995 at the European Union Summit in Madrid that the Heads of State and Prime Ministers made the security problems of Africa a public concern of Europe, too. It has to be noted, however, that the declaration on African security problems was not part of the main text from the Summit. The texts related to Africa and Africa's security were placed in a special annex (Conclusions, 1995). In spite of the low public and political awareness with regard to these issues, it is worth noting that back in 1995 and parallel to the Madrid Summit declaration, the Western European Union (WEU) started to identify national forces which could be made available for preventive operations in Africa, and for supportive actions. Since then, the WEU has sought to establish some kind of multinational military formation, together with an adequate command structure (Lenzi, in Khüne *et al.*, 1995: 48).

Apart from these minor initiatives, it was not until the end of 1998 that a real change in the European attitudes towards conflict prevention in Africa took place. The first step, which was a rather indirect one, came with the declaration at the EU Summit in Cologne in 1999. That declaration made the formal decision to transfer to the EU the right of the WEU to carry out peacekeeping operations. The Cologne decision meant that the European Union acquired the right to make decisions on the so-called 'Petersberg tasks', which include 'humanitarian and rescue tasks, peacekeeping tasks, [and] tasks of combat forces in crisis management, including peacemaking' (Lenzi, in Khüne *et al.*, 1995: 48). According to Guido Lenzi, sub-Saharan Africa was important because the region 'is an area for Petersberg missions'. And, on the other hand, it is important because it can contribute to 'a global affirmation of the European Security and Defence identity' (Lenzi, in Khüne *et al.*, 1995: 64, 63).

An important step towards developing a CFSP with relevance for Africa came at the French–British Summit in St Malo, France, in December 1998. Here, the crucial decision was the open British support for the plans to establish a so-called European defence dimension. Closely related to the decisions on the CFSP was the recognition by both France and Britain that the time had come to end the contest for influence in Africa between the two old colonial powers (*Financial Times*, 10 March 1999). That the two former colonial powers were serious about their intentions to leave behind the past became clear in March 1999, when the French Minister of Foreign Affairs, Hubert Védrine, and the British Foreign Minister, Robin Cook, made a historical trip to Africa. Together, the two Ministers visited both Ghana and the Ivory Coast, which was seen as an expression of their strong wish to create a 'historic new partnership with Africa . . . Mr. Cook said that the two countries acting together could help Africa to boost trade, reduce debt and find solutions to its conflicts' (*Independent*, 12 March 1999). Africa's potential function as an element in the ambition to establish a CFSP was also pointed out by Ian Black, who noted that 'Africa provides a handy platform for high-profile cooperation between Europe's biggest military powers at a time' (*Guardian*, 12 March 1999). This statement is basically in agreement with the remarks of Guido Lenzi, which were made four years earlier.

It is interesting that the two old rivals suddenly took steps towards having common positions on Africa, and also that they took a bilateral rather than a common European approach. One of the reasons for this seems to lie in the hands of technocrats, who were suspicious of sharing influence with countries with little or no history on the continent (*Financial Times*, 10 March 1999). Also, an important common goal for Paris and London was to control, or at least to have the upper hand in, the multilateral policy of the EU towards sub-Saharan Africa. Thus closer cooperation between the two countries was perceived as a precondition to overcome the traditional reservations of important European actors such as Germany and Italy. A final and partly idealistic motive might have been to avoid a total marginalisation of sub-Saharan Africa vis-à-vis Eastern Europe and North Africa. The risk of total marginalisation of sub-Saharan Africa vis-à-vis Europe and the rest of the world was definitely imminent in the 1990s. First of all, there was a strong focus on the dramatic changes in Eastern and Central Europe and in the former Soviet Union. Then came the violent wars and armed conflicts in the Balkans. The widespread political and social instability combined with population growth in North Africa forced European foreign policy to give some priority to these geographical areas (interviews, Brussels, 15 November 1999). The combination of these circumstances would almost inevitably lead to a situation where Africa south of the Sahara would receive less and less attention from Europe.

In summary, by the end of the twentieth century there were a number of signs that Africa had a position, even though it was clearly a minor one, on Europe's foreign policy agenda. This might be a little surprising considering the other priorities of the Union. On the other hand, it is obvious that Africa's security problems were taken more and more seriously by the Europeans. Here, Alvaro Vasconcelos argued that:

> although no vital security interests of the European Union or of individual member states are apparently at stake in sub-Saharan Africa, there are a number of reasons, quite apart from any sense of responsibility . . . why the Union and WEU should adopt a common policy on conflict prevention and resolution in Africa. These reasons are . . . values, security concerns and a mixture of national and EU interests linked to Europe's search for a role as a world power. (Vasconcelos, in Khüne et al., 1995: 4)

During the 1990s, there were two processes going on within the European institutions which might very well have an impact on Europe's Africa policy in the current decade. First, there was the drive towards establishing a viable and strong CFSP, which placed the Council of Ministers in a crucial position within the Union. It seems as if the Council thinks in very operational terms about preventing conflicts by military means, which is perceived as having positive consequences for the foreign policy profile of Europe. This means that one of the reasons for Africa to have a position on the list of European foreign policy priorities is tied to the ambitions to establish a CFSP and thus to give the European Union a role in world politics. Interpreted in this way, Africa can to a large extent play a symbolic role for Europe. This statement can be backed by the attempts of the Council, with Javier Solana as the main actor, to establish a coherent European strategy for Africa which to a large extent focuses on conflict management and conflict prevention, and much less on development policy instruments such as aid (*Berlingske Tidende*, 20 March 2000).

The second trend was related to the development prospects of the region and especially to the concerns that conflicts and crises could hamper the development efforts of the continent (Cardoso et al., 2000: 2ff). This trend was carried by the Commission and especially by DG VIII. The core of the thinking of the Commission was probably expressed by the former Development Commissioner, Joao de Deus Pinheiro, who wrote that: 'development cooperation is indisputably the single most important instrument for an effective policy of peace-building in developing countries' (Pinheiro, 1999: 5–6).

In summary, Africa is of very limited national interest to Europe, apart from, perhaps, France and to some extent the UK. This may explain why the two old colonial powers apparently joined forces towards the end of the 1990s. If Africa is going to have another, more important position within Europe's overall foreign policy priorities, it has to be explained by the possible symbolic value of the ambitions of making Europe an important and significant player on the world scene. It is possible to argue that this great power ambition is within the realms of the 'national interest' of the European Union as a separate entity. Africa's place in this context is to play the symbolic role of a continent with enormous human suffering where the EU tries to prevent and manage conflicts. If this is correct, the development of the CFSP directed to Africa will depend on a bargaining process between actors, mainly within the Council of Ministers, favouring a prominent international role of the EU, and other actors, both in Brussels and in the member states, that do not share this ambition of using Africa as a symbol of the EU's international role.

Conclusions

A basic theoretical assumption of this chapter was that decision making within the European Union is highly fragmented. Furthermore, it was assumed that it is possible to distinguish between the individual national interests in Africa on the one hand and the European Union's interests in Africa on the other. Apart from the section on development aid, the analyses of the chapter concentrated on decisions related to the Common European Position on humanitarian assistance and on the CFSP. The dual analysis of development aid indicated that the national interests in giving development aid to sub-Saharan Africa diminished during the 1990s. This led to dramatic cuts in most bilateral aid budgets, and also in successive cuts in the common aid budget under the Lomé Conventions. The decreasing European interests in giving development aid to Africa did not repeat themselves in the humanitarian aid policy. There it was concluded that this special form of aid should remain a considerable size, among other factors because of the combination of a positive popular opinion and strong media focus on crises and emergencies.

The strong media focus and the strong emotions involved in emergency situations more or less forced politicians, both at the national and at the EU level, to react. Because of the immense symbolic value attached to acting in complex political emergencies, the political benefits from giving humanitarian aid to Africa were much greater than the benefits from giving development aid.

Thus the growing European foreign policy attention to Africa during the 1990s is explained by the real concerns in Europe for the security situation in Africa, combined with need and interest to develop the European Union into a strong international actor among certain groups in Europe and also certain member states, such as France. So, if there a European prioritisation of Africa in the future, this will be because the continent can play a role for European ambitions to become a significant player on the international scene. Based on the analysis in this chapter, this symbolic role of Africa can most adequately be fulfilled by the European initiatives on conflict prevention and crisis management. That is in line with the efforts of the Council and the High Representative Javier Solana to establish a coherent Africa policy of the European Union, as was argued before the first EU–Africa Summit in Cairo in the spring of 2000.

Even though military intervention under some kind of humanitarian heading will be the most spectacular instrument to be used, its effectiveness is highly questionable, as was underlined by the situation in Kosovo in the spring of 2000. This recognition of course opens space for the massive use of emergency aid as a supportive means for European efforts to manage and prevent crises in Africa. Also, and most significantly, it opens the door for a new role for development aid, in line with the proposals of the Commission. The latter point does not imply that there will be growth in European development aid to Africa. Rather, it means that development aid as we know it today will change quite considerably in order to buttress the endeavours of the Council to manage future conflicts in Africa. Such a conclusion seems to be in agreement with the arguments in the Reflection Paper presented by the Portuguese Presidency at the informal summit of the Development Ministers in Lisbon in January 2000. This says, among other things, that 'the creation of the CFSP brings to the debate the need to consider the European–African policies in a context that is broader than the traditional development aid framework' (Cardoso et al., 2000: 1). That things have moved in that direction within a few months was partly confirmed by the debate in the Council of Foreign Ministers on 22 May 2000, where the situation in Sierra Leone was on the agenda. The Ministers agreed that it was urgent 'to consider what practical support the Union can give for helping the UN to fulfil its mandate. Also, there was considerable agreement that political solutions in Africa can only be found if the EU is ready to use the big pools of aid money to motivate the countries to find peaceful solutions' (*Politiken*, 23 May 2000).

Note

1 Some of the information presented in this chapter was obtained via personal interviews carried out in Brussels in November and December 1999. Because of requests for anonymity, these are only indicated by the date of the interview involved.

Bibliography

Brüne, S. (1995), *Die Französische Afrikapolitik. Hegemonialinteressen und Entwicklungsanspruch*, Baden-Baden: Nomos-Verlangsgesellschaft.
Cafruny, A. and P. Peters (eds) (1998), *The Union and the World: Economy of a Common European Foreign Policy*, The Hague: Kluwer Law International.
Cardoso, F. J., W. Khüne and J. B. Honwana (2000), *Reflection Paper. Priorities in EU Development Cooperation in Africa: Beyond 2000*, Brussels: Council of Ministers.
CEC (1996), 'Green Paper on Relations between the European Union and the ACP Countries on the Eve of the 21st Century. Challenges and Options for a New Partnership', Brussels: CEC 14 November.
Conclusions, 1995, 'The conclusions of the Presidency. The European Summit', Madrid, 15–16 December.
Crawford, G. (1996), 'Whither Lomé? The mid-term review and the decline of partnership', *Journal of Modern African Studies*, 34:3, pp. 503–18.
DAC (Development Assistance Committee of the OECD) (1999), 'Financial flows to developing countries in 1998', PAC/COM/NEWS (99) 60, Paris, 10 June.
ECHO (1994), *L'Année de la Tragédie Rwandaise*, Rapport Annuel, Bruxelles: ECHO.
ECHO (1995), *The Year They Gave Peace a Chance in ex-Yugoslavia*, ECHO annual review, Brussels: ECHO.
ECHO (1996), *Return to Rwanda*, ECHO annual review, Brussels: ECHO.
ECHO (1998), *Caught in the Eye of the Storm*, ECHO annual review, Brussels: ECHO.
Eliassen, K. (ed.) (1998), *Foreign and Security Policy in the European Union*, London: Sage Publications.
Ginsberg, R. (1989), *Foreign Policy Actions of the EC*, Boulder: Lynne Rienner.
Ginsberg, R. (1999), 'Conceptualizing the European Union as an international actor: narrowing the theoretical capability–expectations gap', *Journal of Common Market Studies*, 37:3, pp. 429–54.
Gowing, N. (1994), 'Real-time television coverage of armed conflicts and diplomatic crises: does it pressure or distort foreign policy decisions?', Cambridge, MA: The Joan Shorestein Barone Center on the Press, Politics and Public Policy, John F. Kennedy School of Government, Harvard University, Working Paper 94–1, June.
Grilli, E. R. (1993), *The European Community and the Developing Countries*, Cambridge: Cambridge University Press.
Hill, C. (1993), 'The capability–expectations gap, or conceptualizing Europe's international role', *Journal of Common Market Studies*, 31:3, pp. 305–28.
Hill, C. and W. Wallace (1996), 'Introduction: actors and actions', in C. Hill (ed.), *The Actors in Europe's Foreign Policy*, London and New York: Routledge.
Holland, M. (1997), 'The Joint Action on South Africa: a successful experiment?', in M. Holland (ed.), *Common Foreign and Security Policy. Record and Reforms*, London: Pinter.
Khüne, W., G. Lenzi and A. Vasconcelos (1995), *WEU's Role in Crisis Management and Conflict Resolution in Sub-Saharan Africa*, Paris: Institute for Security Studies of WEU.
Landgraf, M. (1998), 'Peace-building and conflict prevention in Africa: a view from the European Commission', in U. Engel and A. Mehler (eds.), *Gewaltsame Konflikte und ihre Prävention in Afrika*, Hamburg: Institut für Afrika-Kunde.
Lister, M. (1997), *The European Union and the South. Relations with Developing Countries*, London: Routledge.

Lund, M. and A. Mehler (1999), *Peace-Building and Conflict Prevention in Developing Countries: A Practical Guide*, Brussels and Ebenhausen: SWP-CPN.

Marchal, R. (1998), 'France and Africa: the emergence of essential reforms?', *International Affairs*, 74:2, pp. 355–72.

Martin, G. (1995), 'Continuity and change in Franco-African relations'. *Journal of Modern African Studies*, 33:1, pp. 1–20.

Moravcsik, G. (1993), 'Preference and power in the European Community: a liberal intergovernmentalist approach', *Journal of Common Market Studies*, 31:4, pp. 473–524.

OECD (1996), *Efforts and Policies of the Members of the Development Assistance Committee*, Development Cooperation, 1995 Report, Paris: OECD.

OECD (1997), *Efforts and Policies of the Members of the Development Assistance Committee*, Development Cooperation, 1996 Report, Paris: OECD.

OECD (1998), *Efforts and Policies of the Members of the Development Assistance Committee*, Development Cooperation, 1997 Report, Paris: OECD.

Peters, B. G. (1992), 'Bureaucratic politics and institutions of the European Community', in A. M. Sbragia (ed.), *Euro-Politics. Institutions and Policymaking in the 'New' European Community*, Washington, DC: The Brookings Institute.

Peters, B. G. (1997), 'Escaping the joint-decision trap: repetition and sectoral politics in the European Union', *West European Politics*, 20:2, pp. 22–36.

Piening, C. (1997), *Global Europe. The European Union in World Affairs*, Boulder: Lynne Rienner.

Pinheiro, J. de D. (1999), *Peace-Building and Conflict Prevention in Africa*, Brussels: European Commission, Directorate General for Development.

Rhodes, C. (ed.) (1998), *The European Union in the World Community*, Boulder: Lynne Rienner.

Riddell, R. (1999), 'The end of foreign aid to Africa? Concerns about donor policies', *African Affairs*, 98:392, pp. 309–35.

Riesse-Kappen, T. (1996), 'Exploring the nature of the beast: international relations theory and comparative policy analysis meet the European Union', *Journal of Common Market Studies*, 34:1, pp. 53–80.

Robinson, P. (1999), 'The CNN effect: can the news media drive foreign policy?', *Review of International Studies*, 25:2, pp. 301–9.

Rosati, J. A. (1981), 'Developing a systematic decision-making framework: bureaucratic politics in perspective', *World Politics*, 33:2, pp. 234–52.

Rothberg, R. I. and T. G. Weiss (eds) (1996), *From Massacres to Genocide. The Media, Public Policy, and Humanitarian Crises*, Washington, DC: The Brookings Institution.

Shaw, M. (1996), *Civil Society and Media in Global Crises. Representing Distant Violence*, London and New York: Pinter.

Smilie, I. (1996), 'Mixed messages: public opinion and development assistance in the 1990s', in C. Foy and H. Helmich (eds), *Public Support for International Development*, Paris: OECD.

Smith, M. (1996), 'The EU as an international actor', in J. Richardson (ed.), *European Union Power and Policy-Making*, London and New York: Routledge.

Solana, J. (2000a), 'More punch to the Union' (in Danish), *Berlingske Tidende*, 10 February.

Solana, J. (2000b), 'A stronger and more responsible Europe' (in Danish), *Berlingske Tidende*, 25 January.

Thérien, J.-P. and C. Lloyd (2000), 'Development assistance on the brink', *Third World Quarterly*, 21:1, pp. 21–38.
Walle, N. van de (1999), 'Aid's crisis of legitimacy: current proposals and future prospects', *African Affairs*, 98:392, pp. 337–52.
World Bank (1989), *Sub-Saharan Africa. From Crisis to Sustainable Growth. A Lone-Term Perspective Study*, Washington: World Bank.

6

Changing interests in EU development cooperation: the impact of EU membership and advancing integration

Karin Arts

This chapter examines two main lines of developments *within* the European Union that have affected the geographical scope of, political priority for, and substantive orientation of, its development cooperation policy. They are, respectively, the changes in EU membership over time and the ever advancing European integration process. These two processes functioned both as incentives and as restraining factors for the elaboration of EU development cooperation policy and programmes. This chapter shows that their overall impact on development policy has been significant, especially since the 1990s. In particular, (prospects of) expanding EU membership, Constituent Treaty changes, the Common Foreign and Security Policy, and the pressure to increase accountability, transparency and efficiency, have diluted the Union's interest in development cooperation with the South.

The implications of changing EU membership for development cooperation

Between 1957 and 1995, the original six-member European Economic Community grew to the current fifteen-member European Union. The changes in EU membership that occurred over time have clearly influenced the geographical scope of, and political climate for, EU development cooperation policy. Further such changes can be expected in the first decades of the twenty-first century, as the Union's membership is likely to grow significantly in the near feature by enlargement with perhaps another thirteen countries in central, (south-) eastern and southern Europe. For Cyprus, Estonia, Hungary, Latvia, Lithuania, Malta, Poland, Slovakia, Slovenia and the Czech Republic are likely to accede to the European Union in 2004. In early 2000, preparations began for the accession of Bulgaria and Romania (Werts, 2002a, b). The accession of Turkey might be anticipated as well, but perhaps at a different pace.

Influencing the geographical scope of EC development policy and programmes
It is well known that since the early days of the European integration process some individual member states directed the external relations agenda towards the interests of particular (groups of) developing countries with which they had close (colonial and post-colonial) relations. France did so most openly and forcefully by making its accession to the to-be-established European Economic Community dependent on a preferential regime for its 'overseas countries and territories' (see also chapter 7). This resulted in the start of Community development cooperation policy in the form of the 'association paragraph' of the Rome Treaty, which applied to a specified list of developing countries, mainly African and Francophone.

When the United Kingdom first negotiated accession to the European Community in 1961–62, it also made a strong point of accommodating the interests of its own former colonies. This would be repeated during the second round of its accession negotiations in the early 1970s (Tulloch, 1975: 37, 101–3; Grilli, 1993: 16; Todd, 1999: 62–3). As a result, when the UK finally joined the European Community in 1973, the group of recipients of EC development assistance was drastically expanded to include a large number of the UK's Commonwealth cooperation partners in Anglophone Africa, the Caribbean and the Pacific (Glaser, 1990: 27). Thereafter, the UK tabled proposals effectively to expand further the range of aid beneficiaries in Asia (Tulloch, 1975: 108; McMahon, 1998: 171; Bonet, 1999: 255).

After the accession of Greece in 1981, and especially that of Spain and Portugal in 1986, a process of increasing attention to the development needs of countries in Latin America and the Mediterranean took off. Spain also played a leading role, in the 1980s and early 1990s, in forging closer cooperation between the EU and Cuba (Byron, 2000: 28–9).

The reasons for the changes in the relations with Latin America, which consisted of increasing aid allocations and intensifying trade relations, were at least three-fold. Firstly, there was optimism about the continent's development prospects, especially its trade potential. Secondly, the traditional historical and linguistic ties between countries in Latin America, Spain and Portugal played a part. Thirdly, the Spanish Development Commissioner Manuel Marin made important personal efforts (see also Barbé, 1998 and McMahon, 1998: 137–70).

In relation to the Mediterranean, the accession to the European Community of the three northern Mediterranean countries, Spain, Portugal and Greece, created a number of problems for agricultural products such as wine, olive oil, citrus fruits and tomatoes, produced both by member and non-member Mediterranean countries (Tsoukalis, 1981: 222–32, 252). Recognition of these problems, in combination with protectionism in favour of agricultural products produced within the European Community, could well explain the pattern of change that has occurred in the sectoral allocation of EC assistance to the Mediterranean (and the Middle East) since. Overall, the assistance programme for the Mediterranean has grown significantly. However, between 1986 and 1998 allocable aid for the sensitive agricultural sector dropped from a major share of 23 per cent to 5 per cent. Instead, non-controversial aid for water supply projects, education and health rose steeply (Cox and Chapman, 1999: 76). Through the years, existing Mediterranean member states have stimulated EU attention for the Mediterranean. Spain in particular, playing the card of geographical proximity, promoted increased concern within Europe about (real or perceived) security issues, including the areas of migration, drug trafficking and the environment. This led to an intensification of contacts between the EU and the Mediterranean (Lister, 1997: 30–4, 83–90, 106; Barbé, 1998: 119, 125–6; van Reisen, 1999: 46–52).

Accordingly, there has been a historical pattern of new European Community member states influencing the geographical scope of EC development policy and programmes. Can such effects already be traced as a consequence of the joining of the newest member states, Austria, Finland and Sweden, that obtained European Union membership in 1995? While it is hard to substantiate such an influence firmly, it seems obvious that, by their geographical location and history, these countries are likely to be among the Union members most interested in the political, economic and social development of Central and Eastern Europe. This could well turn out to be a source of additional support for the already clearly established trend to step up assistance efforts for countries in that region. The latter trend will be dealt with further in the next section of this chapter. Also, the accession of Austria, Finland and Sweden has increased the number of EU member states that are not tied to a (significant) colonial past and do not necessarily share the automatic attention and preference for Europe's traditional developing country partners. This came, for example, to the fore in the post-Lomé discussions on the possible extension of the ACP group to non-ACP LDCs (e.g. Bhutan and Nepal), which the Nordic countries were in favour of (van Reisen, 1997: 164; see also Grilli, 1993: 65–71). Accordingly, the accession of Austria, Finland and Sweden is likely to give additional clout to the long-time position of those member states that since the 1960s have argued in favour of a globalisation of Community development policy. The balance between EU member states which are in favour of a development policy that primarily targets a limited number of traditional developing country cooperation partners (e.g. Belgium and France), and those which, equally principled, are in favour of extending the same treatment to a broader group of developing countries in need of support (e.g. Germany, the Netherlands, Finland and Sweden) has definitely changed. This might lead to small further changes in the geographical scope of EC development policy and programmes in the future.

Substantive changes

Hand in hand with the changes that took place in the regional and country orientation of EC development cooperation, through the years its substantive direction and the overall policy climate also changed as a result of the expanding Community membership. An example of the latter was presented above, concerning the shift away from support for the agricultural sector of the southern Mediterranean. More broadly, a growing group of so-called 'like-minded countries' emerged that distinguish themselves from other member states by a relatively large priority and budget for development cooperation and/or by pronounced ideas about the policy area. In this context, the like-minded countries are Germany, Denmark, Finland, the Netherlands, Sweden and the United Kingdom. When deemed necessary, these countries consult each other intensively before important meetings of the Development Council of Ministers, the EDF Committee and other important bodies, to maximise the chances of their voices being heard and proposals being adopted. Within this group, the Nordic EU member states' Development Ministers meet regularly to coordinate their policies (Arnórsson, 1999: 91–2). More recently, the (all female) Development Ministers of Germany, the Netherlands, Norway and the UK came to meet for similar purposes in the so-called 'Utstein Group'. Under the influence of the like-minded countries, a number of new issues and foci entered the European Community development cooperation agenda. Among such new issues are, for example, gender, debt relief, and the quality and efficiency of aid. The clearest example of a new focus is poverty alleviation (see, for example, Cox et al., 1997: 139; Arnórsson, 1999: 102–3; Todd, 1999: 66–7; Turner, 1999).

So far, the accession of new member states has increased economic and political divergence within the Union (see, for example, Tsoukalis, 1981: 252–4, Barbé, 1998: 126), resulting both in geographic and substantive policy changes. The implications of the current European Union enlargement process and the further changes in EU membership that are likely to occur in that context are difficult to forecast at this stage. In any case, there will be an increase in the number of member states that are facing serious development challenges and problems themselves. One would expect this circumstance to be likely to reduce general support, and perhaps available resources, for EC development cooperation.

Advancing European integration

The European integration process was for quite some time primarily internally directed. Efforts to establish the single European market and European Monetary Union, and all the complicated details that arose in these domains, enjoyed clear priority. As an economic actor, the European Community gained importance and strength. However, apart from the traditional and/or unavoidable external activities of the European Community and its member states in the spheres of development cooperation and trade respectively, the Union at large lacked both the mandate and the means to build a coherent and comprehensive external relations face. For example, until 1992 hardly any common objectives had been formulated for Community development cooperation or European Political Cooperation. This contradiction between an internally ever more integrated Europe and an externally under-developed entity, or between an economic giant and political dwarf (after Lister, 1997: 18; see also van Reisen, 1999), gradually came to be seen as undesirable, both within the Union/Community and their institutions themselves and by other relevant actors such as non-governmental organisations and academics.

Constituent Treaty changes

The 1992 Maastricht Treaty on European Union heralded the beginning of serious change in the internal–external dichotomy described above. Its Title V formally established the Common Foreign and Security Policy, set the CFSP objectives and provided some instruments through which they might be realised. These provisions were slightly elaborated and streamlined in the 1997 Treaty of Amsterdam. According to the latter's Article 11, the CFSP shall pursue to safeguard the common values, fundamental interests, independence and integrity of the Union; strengthen the security of the Union in all ways; preserve peace and strengthen international security; promote international cooperation and develop and consolidate democracy and the rule of law, and respect for human rights and fundamental freedoms. According to Article 12, the CFSP instruments are: the definition of CFSP principles and general guidelines, common strategies, joint actions, Common Positions and the strengthening of systematic cooperation between the member states. Similarly, the Maastricht Treaty extended a formal Constituent Treaty-based mandate for development cooperation policy to the European Community and listed the direct objectives to be 'fostered' by it. They are: 'the sustainable economic and social development of the developing countries, and more particularly the most disadvantaged among them'; 'the smooth and gradual integration of the developing countries into the world economy'; and 'the campaign against poverty in the developing countries'. In addition, EC development policy is supposed to contribute to a goal that was also set for the CFSP. This is 'the general objective of developing and consolidating democracy and the rule of law, and to that of respecting human rights and fundamental freedoms' (Articles 3q and 130u of the 1992 Maastricht version of the EC Treaty). The Treaty of Amsterdam, in slightly more elaborate wording, reiterated the (especially in the context of overlapping mandates) crucially important consistency principle that had already been introduced in Maastricht: 'The Union shall in particular ensure the consistency of its external activities as a whole in the context of its external relations, security, economic and development policies.' Such consistency is to be safeguarded by the Council and the Commission, which shall cooperate to this end (Article 3 of the 1997 Amsterdam version of the EU Treaty).

The sum total of these Constituent Treaty changes firmly established the Community/Union mandates and procedures in the spheres of development cooperation and foreign policy. That achievement by itself is likely to trigger an increase in Community/Union activities in these fields. In his general analysis of the impact of the EU's institutional framework or evolving 'acquis communautaire' on member states' choices concerning cooperation, for example in European foreign economic policy, Young (2000: 93–116) argued that 'the EU's evolving institutional framework structures the member governments' choices about cooperation in new policy areas'. Oberthür dealt with similar aspects in the environmental sphere (1999: 641–59). He concluded that the EU 'has had difficulties in leading on issues not firmly established on its policy agenda. On subjects for which European legislation existed, coherent EU leadership at the international level has been more frequent.' Accordingly, the Treaty changes in the sphere of development referred to above should be seen as important potential incentives for stepping up both the making and implementation of development cooperation policy. However, the newly established mandates are all shared with the member states. In other words, next to the European Community/Union's competence in development cooperation and foreign policy, the member states maintain their own individual competence as well. Experience has shown that such a sharing of mandates opens up a whole range of uncertainty and possibilities for individual member states to fall back on their national competence and interests if the Community/Union's line does not please them. Such patterns have been described by Meunier and Nicolaïdis (1999: 477–501, esp. 497–8) for the area of trade, and by this author for the area of human rights and development cooperation (Arts, 2000: 165, 254–5; 371). They are a serious potential obstacle to further stepping up development policy efforts, especially as regards implementation.

Consistency in EU external relations
Another interesting possible effect of the Constituent Treaty changes which were set out above lies in the aspect of consistency. Much more explicitly than before, the Treaties now formally link together the political, security, economic and development aspects of EU external relations at large. This is done, as mentioned already, through codification of the general principle of consistency for EU external relations and through more detailed Articles on coherence in the development cooperation Title of the EC Treaty. The creation of the office of the 'High Representative for the Common Foreign and Security Policy', currently taken up by Javier Solana, could perhaps also be seen as a means to increase consistency in external relations, although his summary mandate does not refer to this at all (Article 26 of the 1997 Amsterdam version of the Treaty on European Union). The implications of this are uncertain and not necessarily positive for development cooperation policy and especially not for its implementation.

However, if the consistency assignment is interpreted as requiring coordination of all policy measures and instruments, so as to ensure that they mutually reinforce each other rather than contradict, this element of change might work out positively for development cooperation. For example, development is an essential (though not the only) condition for security, respect for human rights, democracy, and so on. In that light, the linking of all external policy aspects could well point to the need to increase development assistance to a particular country or region. On the other hand, the newly prescribed consistency element could also work out negatively for development cooperation. In particular, this would be the case when some aspects of external relations, such as overall political relations, would be regarded as of primary importance and others, such as development cooperation, as in the service thereof. This would lead to an undesirable further politicisation of European Community development cooperation. Unfortunately, this is not an unlikely option, as illustrated by the following remarks by Development Commissioner Poul Nielson, made in April 2000: 'Being more active collectively could strengthen our hand in foreign policy. And as foreign policy is increasingly becoming a joint European effort, development cooperation should logically follow and support' (Nielson, 2000: 5).

The intensification of efforts to elaborate the Constituent Treaty provisions concerning foreign policy and development cooperation reflects the existence of at least some political will to strengthen the European Union's external face to make it match its – by now pretty strong – internal face. More broadly, at the beginning of the twenty-first century, the search for a stronger external identity and greater visibility and public appreciation of the European Union's international political and developmental efforts has become a fairly important push factor for the EU's agenda and its level and means of action. For example, at least partly as a consequence of these considerations, the Union has thrown itself into a mass programme for supporting reconstruction and humanitarian relief for Kosovo, assigning itself a leadership role but also stretching its implementation capacity to the very limit (see, for example, Haglund, 2001). And, according to Commissioner Nielson, one of the major reasons for reformulating the European Community's development policy, as announced in an April 2000 Commission Communication, was that 'an explanation is overdue of why European Community development cooperation matters and what place it should have in the world of international donors' (Nielson, 2000: 1). More specifically, this apparently has inspired a new determination on the side of the Commission to create a stronger profile for the European Union in relevant multilateral fora, as announced in its April 2000 'Communication on the European Community's Development Policy'. According to the Commission, 'it has to be recognised that the EU's large-scale disbursement does not entail proportional influence' (CEC, 2000a: 14). For example, the EU 'as a whole, financed . . . 64 per cent of the cost of structural adjustment programmes in Africa, while the cumulated voting right of the Member States in the IMF is only 27 per cent' (CEC, 2000a: 15). The Commission now explicitly seeks to reinforce the Union's position in 'the discussions on economic reform policies or other major topics which constitute key issues for developing economies' (CEC, 2000a: 15). In May 2000, External Relations

Commissioner Chris Patten justified yet another Commission reform in the sphere of the management of external assistance programmes with the argument that it 'will restore its credibility as a foreign policy actor in one of the major fields of external EU action' (CEC, 2000b; see also CEC, 2000c).

Increasing accountability, transparency and efficiency
Another major cluster of, again, both potential incentives for and obstacles to elaborating European Community development cooperation policy is found in the overall pressure on the EC/EU to increase accountability, transparency and efficiency. During the 1990s, persistent reports about such things as inefficient spending of resources in various policy areas, corruption within the Commission, fraud by members of the European Parliament and other negative features, seriously affected the public image of the Community/Union. This trend, together with the strengthening powers of the European Parliament and rising interest in 'Europe' in national politics in the member states, has created a climate in which justifying the EC/EU's involvement in a particular issue and accounting for the ensuing results has rapidly gained importance. Specifically for development cooperation, this trend has, among others, directly resulted in greater attention to evaluation exercises within the Commission. Roughly since 1995, ever more frequently and systematically, evaluations of Community development cooperation activities have been undertaken. While there is still a lot of scope for improvement in this field, the increase in number and depth of evaluations has been facilitated by supportive policy-making efforts in the various relevant Evaluation Units of the Commission (e.g. in former DG VIII and the Joint Service for External Relations). The main results of a number of major evaluations of Community development assistance (1986–95) and humanitarian aid (1991–96) exposed some common problems which, if addressed, will bring about an intensification of policy making and implementation in the field of development cooperation (ICEA/DPPC, 1999).

In the opinion of the Commission, essentially these problems are growing pains 'where policies and structures have not been adapted sufficiently fast to meet the growing responsibilities of the Community in the more-and-more complex area of development cooperation' (CEC, 2000a: 14). In line with many of its critics, the Commission, for example, has found the EC aid system to be 'too complex and fragmented' and that '[p]olicies are guided by the instruments rather than by policy objectives and clearly defined priorities' (CEC, 2000a: 14). It also signalled staffing problems. For managing 10 million US dollars of aid, the Commission has 2.9 staff members. Compared with 4.3 at the World Bank and between 4 and 9 in the major member states, this is indeed not generous. On the other hand, according to some (including the Dutch Minister for Development Cooperation Eveline Herfkens), with a better monitoring of the quality of Commission staff in combination with better use of multilateral development cooperation channels, expansion of Commission development staff would not be justified.

Among the signs of concrete changes being made to remedy some of the evaluation results are the May 2000 'Commission Communication on the reform of the management of external assistance' and the post-Lomé changes in ACP–EC relations. The Cotonou Agreement, for example, abandons Stabex and Sysmin. For all except the least developed countries among the ACP, Cotonou replaces the general preferential trade regime by still to be negotiated regional free trade arrangements. Thus long-standing Lomé instruments, which already for quite some time have been criticised for being outdated and ineffective, finally are being replaced. Unfortunately, it is not so clear that the newly proposed instruments, including the post-Lomé regional free trade arrangements, will indeed bring positive change. The 'integrated framework for Community activities' in development cooperation that the Commission proposed as another element of a possible solution (CEC, 2000a: 23) is rather disappointing. It is very general and hardly adds anything to what was already derived from the Constituent Treaty texts. If the relevant actors do not succeed in identifying and providing remedies to the established shortcomings of Community development cooperation, in the long run this may lead to a decrease of activity in this area and perhaps a retreat to the bilateral policies of the member states. At this stage, it is impossible to forecast which of the two possible scenarios – that is, an increase or a decrease of priority for Community development cooperation – ultimately will materialise as a result of the greater scrutiny of the effectiveness of relevant Community activities.

Another line that the European Community institutions have taken, at least partly in response to the increasing criticism of the quality and effectiveness of European development cooperation, lies in the involvement of civil society. For a long time the role of non-governmental actors in the making and implementation of European development policy was fairly limited. Since the late 1990s, however, the Commission and Council of Ministers have made more serious attempts to open up to civil society. Accordingly, on several occasions since the mid-1990s, relatively broad processes of consultation took place before major policy changes were finally decided upon. Examples include the consultations on the November 1996 Green Paper (CEC, 1996) the civil society input into the subsequent broader debate on the future of the Lomé Convention, and the preparatory process of the April 2000 Commission 'Communication on the European Community's Development Policy'. In the latter, the Commission stated that it now 'considers civil society one of the key pillars of its development policy' (CEC, 2000a: 28). In order to involve civil society actors in Community development policy, the Commission now aims to define 'methodologies and framework' for the:

- Information, consultation and dialogue with civil society actors on the establishment of development policies and strategies.
- Reinforcement of the capacities of civil society actors.

- The involvement of civil society actors in the design and implementation of cooperation programmes.
- Decentralised cooperation whereby actors at the local level take direct responsibility for the drawing up and implementation of cooperation programmes.' (CEC 2000a: 28–9)

Whether the new space for civil society will bring about an increase or a decrease in the Community development programme again is not so clear. The greater emphases on the value of consulting civil society actors and on the need to strengthen civil society's capacity to take part in the designing and planning of development cooperation programmes or projects may well lead to an increase initially. However, particularly for the implementation of such programmes and projects, if the new policy line is pursued seriously, and if successful, in the long run this may well result in a shift away from the Community to civil society itself as the main implementing actor. In any case it is clear that the days of strictly intergovernmental Community development cooperation are over.

Conclusion

In broad terms, this chapter has explored some of the current general determinants of the geographical and substantive scope of European Community development cooperation. In particular over the last decade, these have changed rather drastically. The accession of new members to the European Community/Union during the 1970s and 1980s brought clear changes to both elements of scope. However, perhaps the most bold of such changes are still to come as a result of the expected enlargement of the Union with Central and (south-) Eastern European countries. Through the years, the group of recipients of Community development aid and preferential trade arrangements has grown significantly. The traditionally preferred partners in development cooperation of the European Union, largely its former colonies, have definitely lost this position and are unlikely to recapture it.

The advancing process of European integration has resulted in a dynamic complex of new determinants. These include new Constituent Treaty mandates, the drive for consistency and overall strengthening of the European Union's external dimension, and the related current trend to push for greater accountability, transparency and efficiency of Community/Union actions, among other factors through greater civil society involvement. For most of these determinants it is hard to foresee at this stage whether ultimately they will result in a stepping up or a scaling down of the European Union's development activities.

Overall, however, at the beginning of the twenty-first century the general scene for EU development cooperation looks drastically different from what it was in the almost four decades of experience in the previous century. A very wide spectrum of considerations and interests, much beyond those relating to the needs of developing countries in the South, now directs the European Union's agenda and policy-making efforts. In other words, interest in development cooperation with the South clearly has diluted. The exact implications of this evolution, however, will only become visible in the course of the next decade.

Bibliography

ACP Secretariat (2000), 'Press release on the conclusion of the successor agreement to the Lomé Convention', www.acpsec.org/gb/press/037900_e.htm, as on 23 May 2000, p. 2.

Arnórsson, A. (1999), 'The Nordic contribution to the development cooperation of the European Union', in C. Cosgrove-Sacks and G. Scappucci (eds), *The European Union and Developing Countries*, Houndmills: Macmillan.

Arts, K. (2000), *Integrating Human Rights into Development Cooperation: The Case of the Lomé Convention*, The Hague/London/Boston: Kluwer Law International.

Barbé, E. (1996), 'Spain: the uses of foreign policy cooperation', in C. Hill (ed.), *The Actors in Europe's Foreign Policy*, London and New York: Routledge.

Barbé, E. (1998), 'Balancing Europe's Eastern and Southern dimensions', in J. Zielonka (ed.), *Paradoxes of European Foreign Policy*, The Hague/London/Boston: Kluwer Law International.

Bonet, M. (1999), 'EU–ASEAN relations', in C. Cosgrove-Sacks and G. Scappucci (eds), *The European Union and Developing Countries*, Houndmills: Macmillan.

Byron, J. (2000), 'Square dance diplomacy: Cuba and CARIFORUM, the European Union and the United States', *European Review of Latin American and Caribbean Studies*, no. 68, pp. 23–45.

CEC (1996), 'Green Paper on Relations between the European Union and the ACP Countries on the Eve of the 21st Century: Challenges and Options for a New Partnership', COM(96) 570 final, Brussels, 20 November.

CEC (2000a), 'Communication on the European Community's Development Policy', COM(2000) 212 final, 26 April, Brussels.

CEC (2000b), 'Commission shakes up management of external assistance', press release IP/00/480, Brussels, 16 May.

CEC (2000c), 'Communication on the reform of the management of external assistance', Brussels, 16 May.

CEC (2000d), 'The new ACP–EU Agreement', http://europa.eu.int/comm/development/document/acp_eu_agreement_en.htm, as on 20 April, pp. 3–4.

Council of Ministers of the European Communities (1991), 'Resolution on human rights, democracy and development', *Bulletin of the European Communities*, 24:11, pp. 122–23.

Cox, A. and J. Chapman (1999), *The European Community External Cooperation Programmes. Policies, Management and Distribution*, Brussels: European Commission.

Cox, A., J. Healey and A. Koning (1997), *How European Aid Works: A Comparison of Management Systems and Effectiveness*, London: Overseas Development Institute.

Glaser, T. (1990), 'EEC–ACP cooperation: the historical perspective', *The Courier*, no. 120, pp. 24–8.

Grilli, E. R. (1993), *The European Community and the Developing Countries*, Cambridge: Cambridge University Press.

Haglund, A. (2001), 'The European Union and humanitarian assistance: definition, international context and developments', in C. Cosgrove-Sacks (ed.), *Europe, Diplomacy and Development: New Issues in EU Relations with Developing Countries*, Houndmills and New York: Palgrave.

ICEA/DPPC (1999), *Synthesis Report of EC (ACP, MED, ALA, Humanitarian) Aid Evaluation*, Brussels, May.

Lister, M. (1997), *The European Union and the South*, London and New York: Routledge.

McMahon, J. A. (1998), *the Development Cooperation Policy of the EC*, The Hague/London/Boston: Kluwer Law International.

Meunier, S. and K. Nicolaïdis (1999), 'Who speaks for Europe? The delegation of trade authority in the EU', *Journal of Common Market Studies*, 37:3, September, pp. 477–501.

Nielson, P. (2000), 'A new focus and a better organisation for the European Communities' development cooperation', speech at a Conference on European development policy in Berlin on 12 April, SPEECH/00/135.

Oberthür, S. (1999), 'The EU as an international actor: the protection of the ozone layer', *Journal of Common Market Studies*, 37:4, pp. 641–59.

Reisen, M. van (1997), 'European Union', in J. Randal and T. German (eds), *The Reality of Aid. An Independent Review of Development Cooperation 1997–1998*, London: Earthscan.

Reisen, M. van (1999), *EU 'Global Player'. The North–South Policy of the European Union*, Utrecht: International Books.

Todd, P. (1999), 'Britain and the Lomé Convention', in C. Cosgrove-Sacks and G. Scappucci (eds), *The European Union and Developing Countries*, Houndmills: Macmillan.

Tsoukalis, L. (1981), *The European Community and its Mediterranean Enlargement*, London: George Allen & Unwin.

Tulloch, P. (1975), *The Politics of Preferences*, London: Croom Helm/Overseas Development Institute.

Turner, E. (1999), 'The EU's development policy and gender', in M. Lister (ed.), *New Perspectives on European Union Development Cooperation*, Boulder/Oxford: Westview Press.

Werts, J. (2002a), 'Commission shepherds ten countries into the EU for the price of six' (in Dutch), *Europa van Morgen*, 32:2, 13 February, pp. 24–5.

Werts, J. (2002b), 'Candidate EU member states are delighted after 'historical compromise' (in Dutch), *Europa van Morgen*, 32:16, 6 November, p. 1.

Young, A. R. (2000), 'The adaptation of European foreign economic policy: from Rome to Seattle', *Journal of Common Market Studies*, 38:1, pp. 93–116.

7

'Sense and sensibility': the role of France and French interests in European development policy since 1957

Anne-Sophie Claeys

Since 1957, France has been heavily involved in the definition and implementation of a European development policy. It has considered this to be a way to maintain French interests and influence over Africa, while sharing the costs of such a policy with the other EU member states. More recently, the French approach towards European development policy has been challenged by the enlargement of the European Union, reforms in the Commission and international factors such as the growing role of the international financial institutions and the end of the Cold War. These changes simultaneously contribute to a process of reshaping French bilateral and multilateral development policies. At a time when France and Europe are in the process of reforming their approach, a case study of France is relevant for several reasons. It allows for observation of cross-cutting influences, for analysis of both national and European interests in development policy, and an assessment of the levels of coordination, coherence and complementarity between the Commission and member states and within member states.

The use of the expression 'sense and sensibility' (after Jane Austen's novel) in this chapter can be understood as a reference to the construction of the European Union as well as to French behaviour towards, and its attachment to, Africa. 'Sense' relates to France's choice for Europe. 'Sensibility' refers to the highly politicised relations between France and its former colonies, which explain the difficulties or impossibility to reform the 'familial' relations with French-speaking Black Africa. Economic reasons pushed France towards Europe, while political and symbolic motivations prevented it from leaving Africa. From the initial decision not to sacrifice its African vocation for the construction of the EEC, France has been hesitating between Europe and Africa, unable to choose which link should be privileged. France tried to win on both counts. Europe contributed much to the rebuilding of France's economy and to shaping it as a modern country, while Africa was still considered a major instrument in maintaining the rank of France on the international scene. This non-choice generated inefficiency, incoherence and competition between bilateral and multilateral policies, and disillusion among public opinion. Gradually, European concerns moved to the top of the agenda, while Africa became of minor interest. However, there are obvious and positive signs of change in French African policy. From the 1990s onwards, things have been evolving more quickly and a lot of factors have had an influence in France, in Europe and in Africa, contributing to the reshaping of this three-pole relationship.

This chapter focuses on the French impact on EC development policy and explains how its influence evolved over time.[1] The first part shows the different channels used by France to contribute to the elaboration of the European development policy. The second part explains the reasons for its influence. The third part presents recent changes and the decrease in France's presence and impact.

In order to define 'how' and 'why' France had a major impact on the conception and the making of the European development policy, some theoretical tools are necessary. Both Europe and France have to be comprehended as complex subjects. Europe is not only a group of states and states are not monolithic actors. Plurality of national actors, non-state mechanisms and actors, diversity of administrative cultures (even within one country), and the capacity of European institutions to acquire some autonomy, all have to be taken into account in order to understand the making of European public policies and to measure the role played by member states, administrations, parliaments, pressure groups and others. Neo-institutionalism, federalism, neo-functionalism and theories about a European model of governance enable one to go beyond intergovernmental approaches, mainly represented by the neo-realist theories (Hoffmann, 1993; Moravcsik, 1999 and 2000), which are still useful for analysing French positions on the international scene and comparing them with those of other state actors (Lequesne, 1998).

Different channels to shape EC development policy

France has contributed largely to the formulation and implementation of European development cooperation policy. It did so through offering institutional models, people, funding, ideas and policies.

Organisational models and human resources

French influence over the initial structure of the Commission was large. Originally, the Commission was built according to French administrative specifications, implemented by its long-term secretary Emile Noel. The impact of this structure was aptly illustrated by a highly placed European civil servant from the Netherlands: 'we live under a 19th century French administrative system. A reporter reports to a deputy head of department, who reports to the head of department, who reports to the director, who reports to an assistant of the

Director General, who reports to the DG, who talks to the Commission Cabinet which finally talks to the Commissioner himself' (quoted by Page, 1997: 8). It is difficult to refer to a European model of administration seen as a particular system, for 'Directorates-General themselves have developed very distinct traditions' (Rouban, 1998: 92). Nevertheless, over the years harmonisation increased, through the progressive sharing of common knowledge, common interests and common know-how. In early times, French civil servants were interested in a European career, as the national political situation was uncertain (France changed regime in 1958). The room of manoeuvre of the first civil servants was large because they lacked guidelines from their ministries. They had to work on an institutional model for the Commission with their colleagues of the other member states. The model of the French ministerial cabinets was adopted by European Commissioners.

On the administrative level, France has always been heavily involved in the making and implementation of European development policy. At the beginning, many French civil servants worked within the Directorate-General of the Commission in charge of development issues and many of them remained within that DG for their whole career. For long, as a kind of implicit rule, the Development Commissioner was French. From 1958 to 1985, all Development Commissioners were French (Lemaignen, Rochereau, Deniau, Cheysson, Pisani). The choice of a French Commissioner was perceived as logical because the African Associates expressed their preference for an already known interlocutor, and because France had greater experience and presence in Africa (Lemaignen, 1964: 57). Moreover, some former *'administrateurs coloniaux'* (high civil servants in the colonies) were re-oriented within the DG Development after decolonisation occurred in the early 1960s. For instance, Jacques Ferrandi entered the Commission in 1958 and left his mark on the shaping of DG VIII and the creation of the EDF. At that time, France was very much interested in the work of two Directorates-General: Development and, above all, Agriculture. It would be erroneous to think that French civil servants recruited by the Commission follow instructions given by the French Permanent Representation (PR) in Brussels. Nevertheless, they still have privileged relationships with their colleagues from the PR. According to Lequesne (1993: 202): 'French civil servants within the Commission do not seem to be confronted by a conflict of loyalty between France and the Community but feel entrusted with a double loyalty to both of them.' A French administrator at the Commission quoted by Lequesne stated: 'I particularly inform the French Representation because, as a European civil servant and as a Frenchman, I do consider as a priority that the community dimension be well understood and perceived in my own country.' It cannot be denied that Commissioners in general are not subordinated but linked to their governments (personal communication, 2000a).

The choice of language is another sensitive point for people at the Commission. At the beginning there was no rule on this matter. Until the first enlargement, the French language was the only medium of reflection and decision within the European Community. It was even suggested that the French President Pompidou conditioned the EC membership of the United Kingdom to the arrival at the Commission of bilingual English civil servants (Guérivière, 1992: 54)! Progressively, the use of the English language has taken over that of French, which was still prevailing in DG VIII/DG DEV until the nomination of Danish Commissioner Nielson in 1999.

The financial channel

The financial influence of France on European development policy has mainly been exerted within the framework of the specific policy towards Africa and later the ACP. The main instrument for the programming and implementation of Lomé/Cotonou aid is the EDF. The structure and functioning of this fund were inspired by French methods. As early as 1946 the FIDES (Investment Fund for Economic and Social Development) was created in France in order to re-launch agricultural activities in the colonies by public funds. In the same year, Jean Monnet himself initiated a four-year project for the modernisation and economic equipment of the *métropole* and the overseas territories. The FIDES inspired the first FEDOM (Overseas European Development Fund), which became the EDF. The EDF is programmed for five years and does not belong to the Community budget. Its resources come from national contributions on a more or less voluntary basis and are controlled by the member states, without the involvement of the European Parliament. These features clearly distinguish the EDF and EC development cooperation from other relevant actors. As phrased by Delphin (1992: 44): 'the multilateral institutions like the World Bank and the International Monetary Fund have a sound economic approach, while the EDF philosophy of action allows to accept projects that can produce political or symbolic benefits even if their economic profitability is low'.

The EDF Committee can be a theatre for negotiations and bargaining between the member states, and between the Commission and some member states, above all when projects imply political interests. The EDF Committee is led by the Commission and composed of representatives of the member states. A funding proposal has to be accepted by qualified majority. This is a fundamental step within the project cycle. ACP countries usually tend to privilege their 'boss' for market attribution (Ravenhill, 1995). This kind of re-bilateralisation of ACP–EU relations can be explained through clientelism (Ravenhill, 1995) or paternalism (Delphin, 1992). Power does not lie in the ACP–EU joint institutions but in Community bodies such as the Commission, the Council of Ministers and the EDF Committee, and also in the EC member states themselves.

Thus the permanency of bilateral relationship between some ACP countries and some powerful member states within the European scheme is understandable. This situation is strengthened by the lack of coherence and cooperation between the ACP states as a whole. They do not defend common interests and do not gather their forces to negotiate. Former French colonies spontaneously kept on dealing with France first, even for European matters. As a former colonial power, France lobbies for projects presented by its privileged African partners. One should also bear in mind that, before 1995, France was among the greatest contributors to the EDF. Now it is the biggest contributor. According to Delphin (1992: 74): 'The political aspect is *de facto* strengthened by the voting mechanism and the largest contributors have the heaviest weight in the decision process.' During Lomé I, II and III, France imposed to allocate aid towards best performing or promising countries and to countries which had a longer association with the EC. This inheritance of a trend in French colonial aid has now moved towards aid for the poorest under the pressure and the preferences of most of the other member states, and along with the enlargement of the EU (Anyadike-Danes and Anyadike-Danes, 1992).

A philosophy of action

The 'philosophy of action' conveyed by France has long relied on its will and capacity to transpose its bilateral positions within the Community approach. The Lomé model, inherited from the Treaty of Rome and the Yaoundé Convention, was progressively adapted according to the positions of some other member states and changes on the world scene. Nevertheless, the maintenance of a specific link with Africa, especially initially, can be understood as an expression of France's will.

The Lomé Convention was long considered to be an embodiment of the New International Economic Order: political neutrality of the EC, equality of the partners, interdependence and mutual interests, non-reciprocal trade preferences, additional aid, joint management of aid and new cooperation instruments (Stabex) were the innovative and promising principles that structured that model of North–South relationship. However, this supposedly new relationship still relied on a colonial basis although some countries, such as Nigeria, Kenya and Uganda, started to negotiate an association with Europe as early as the end of the 1960s (Lister, 1988: 60). In 1973, new negotiations between the EC and its African Associates were to lead to a successor agreement to the second Yaoundé Convention, which would come to an end in 1975. During those negotiations, France and Great Britain did not have the same interests nor the same weight. France accepted that some British colonies should join the Association, as long as its own relations with the AAMS (Associated African and Malagasy States) and the franc zone African countries would not be affected. Then, France maintained that only African and Caribbean British colonies should become signatories of the new agreement. The African states of the Commonwealth were considered 'associable' while the Asian states of the Commonwealth were not (Grilli, 1993: 26). France believed that the entry of Asian states would unbalance the privileged relation that Europe set up with Africa. The arrival of new African countries in the agreement was accepted precisely because it strengthened the coherence of a regional approach. The shift from Yaoundé to Lomé shows the permanency of a regional approach defended by the French, against a more global framework for European policy as advocated by Britain, the Netherlands and Germany. In 1957, France had strong arguments to impose its own conception of a European development policy. 'By contrast, when Britain sought admission, the EEC was already established. The Community could exist perfectly well without the UK; thus Britain had less bargaining power than France had possessed' (Lister, 1988: 62).

Another element of France's philosophy of action is the way in which it has transposed its will of being 'the champion of the Third World' and 'an advocate for the poor among the rich' to Europe (Naudet, 1997: 166). Lomé as *the* model for cooperation with the South expresses this idea. Nevertheless, despite interesting and innovative principles about development cooperation, Europe and France did not have sufficient financial means and lacked the political will to achieve that goal. The Lomé model has not been applied to the other developing continents and has not become *the* European development cooperation model. Lomé was, and will remain, an ad hoc response to a given situation.

To summarise briefly, one can say that, through different channels, France has durably influenced European development policy. It did so via the administrative and institutional level, with French civil servants, and thanks to development cooperation instruments such as the EDF. In addition, its philosophy of action played a part, in which Lomé has been perceived as the preservation of a specific relationship with Africa and as part of the European foreign policy on the world scene.

The reasons for France's influence

In 1957 and the following years, France was the main actor within the construction of an institutional link between Europe and Africa. The reasons for the French involvement in European development policies arose from the strong economic, historical, political and strategic links between France and Africa. Although the neo-realistic approach as such is insufficient to explain all that is at stake here, it is useful to understand French imperatives as regards the European construction in the late 1950s. Firstly, France had to maintain independence in French diplomacy. Secondly, the construction of a Western European entity should give France the means to reach some of the national goals that it could not achieve on its own any longer. Thirdly, France had to preserve a sphere of influence abroad, mainly in Africa and in the Middle East (Hoffmann, 1993: 128–9). Moravcsik, who also considers the state as the main actor on the international scene, refutes the idea that the prime interests that underlie French politics rely on political and strategic considerations such as the *grandeur* of France or military security. According to him, French involvement in the European construction was motivated by the preferential trade advantages that could be obtained for industry and agriculture in order to modernise the French economy (Moravcsik, 1999 and 2000). One can also consider both arguments – the political one and the economic one – as complementary. The French will to achieve a European 'African policy' was definitely linked to these economic and political considerations.

The French need for a European development policy: the idea of EurAfrica
According to Ravenhill (1995: 105): 'France's determination not only to maintain but also to expand its sphere of influence on Africa has set it apart from the other European former colonial powers.' The relation between France and Africa was more than an economic arrangement and relied on more complex determinants. This can be explained thanks to concepts such as history, duty, civilising mission and familial relationship. Many francophone African political leaders were involved in French political life, as Members of Parliament or even as ministers. As François Mitterrand stated in 1957: 'Without Africa, there will be no History of France in the 21st century' (Mitterrand, 1957: 237). Just after the signing of the Rome Treaty, France entered a process of institutional change: de Gaulle was called back to power, a new constitutional regime was set up and the African colonies were offered independence within a new organisation called 'the French Community', designed to be a transitional body. All colonies approved this new framework by referendum except Guinea-Conakry.

The newly established European Community became a kind of obligatory associate for Africa. In 1957, four of the six signatories of the Rome Treaty had overseas territories, mostly in Africa. At that time, French territories were the recipients of reciprocal preferences within a privileged market, protected by a common monetary zone guaranteed by the French franc. Progressively, French aid to the colonies placed a huge burden on the French Treasury. The necessary but costly modernisation of the colonies and the *métropole* can explain why France instigated the so-called 'particular relationship' between Europe and Africa. In fact, France simply laid down the association regime as a *conditio sine qua non* for the ratification of the Rome Treaty. According to Gaston Defferre – the French Minister for overseas territories – the costs of the French colonies were so great that 'a symbiosis between the two processes of integration' became necessary and led to 'the idea of a Eurafrican market' (quoted in Schreurs, 1994: 83). Even if the association regime did not make sense for each of the EC member states (such as Germany and the Netherlands), the concept of Eurafrica started to develop from that moment and was seen as an equitable partnership which was going to promote African economic and social development. According to Senghor it was 'an idealised vision of Eurafrican cooperation, yet underlying it was essentially the same rationale that appealed to the Europeans: it was a way of creating a third force on world politics capable of resisting the hegemony of the superpowers' (Chazan *et al.*, 1992: 387). Then, in the 1950s, Africa was seen as the necessary opening of Europe towards the world. From the very beginning of the negotiation process, France refused to choose between 'divorce and bigamy' (Delorme, 1972). Using that metaphor, one could say that France wanted to conclude a marriage contract with Europe, as long as this contract took into account its existing spouse. 'France has multilateralised its aid and preferential trade relations through the treaty of Rome' (Zartman, 1993: 4). That is true to the extent that only a part of the relations was multilateralised: France shared economic costs but not political influence over Africa.

French interests and arguments

In the late 1950s, France no longer had sufficient means for its external ambitions. The strong economic links that existed between the European colonial powers and their territories could not be denied at the very moment when European countries were negotiating the sharing of their resources and harmonisation of economic policies, which also affected overseas territories' markets and products. Although political and symbolic arguments already existed when the association regime was negotiated, one has to bear in mind that in 1957 African countries were still colonies and the question of France's influence over them was not at stake. This issue rose in priority as soon as the colonies got independence. The return of de Gaulle and the development of a policy of independence for France on the international scene contributed to a refocusing of interests from economic to political matters. So when the EEC Treaty was under negotiation, French interests were mainly economic. Stating that France was a net recipient of its involvement in the African colonies would be simplistic. Trade relations between the territories and France were organised along with the capacities of the former to satisfy the needs of the latter. The colonial pact was constituted by trade and financial links which guaranteed the economic balance of the empire.

In 1957, the debate between profits and losses generated by the colonies was not solved. French politicians were aware that the colonies brought about heavy costs. Nevertheless, they were not convinced that leaving them was a good choice, strategically speaking. Archives of the French Ministry of Foreign Affairs reflect the preoccupations of the EEC Treaty negotiators: France would enter the common market only if its colonies were included. One of the main ideas was that the European project looked very much like the French association model: 'The links between France and the overseas territories are constituted by the two fundamental aspects which are under consideration in the European project: a free trade area which implements free circulation of goods, services, capital and people, and duty free imports within the Community which triggers a system of reciprocal preferences' (French Ministry of Foreign Affairs, Archives, 1956). The same document even stated that the *Union Française* was a more achieved model than the European one because members of the Franco-African community shared a common currency. There were three major French objectives. Firstly, achieving a non-discriminatory economic relationship between Europe and associated territories. Secondly, strengthening the institutional and economic cohesion of the *Union Française* through the spillover effect generated by the creation of the common market. And thirdly, compatibility with the GATT rules (Schreurs, 1994). The bargaining base was a European financial involvement against access to the African market for the EC member states, under certain conditions.

To summarise briefly the relationship between France and Africa is no easy task. The links between the two are not only economic but can also be qualified as historical, privileged and political. They have even been labelled as blood ties but are also considered neo-colonial, personalised, clientelist, constraining and costly. One could specifically mention the 'diplomacy of affection' and the 'imaginary family links' here (Constantin, 1993). The search for independence and the preservation of France's status as a great power is a *leitmotiv* in French foreign policy. The African *pré carré*, a military presence on the continent and the CFA (Communauté Financière Africaine) franc zone serve its ambitions. A strong position in the UN, the defence of *la Francophonie* and the claim to be the advocate of the Third World contribute to the appearance of France in the world. Moreover, 'French policy towards Africa is best understood as one of the most important components of France's claim to middle power or mini-superpower status (together with its independent nuclear arsenal and its efforts to play a leading role in promoting European integration) and of its determination to pursue an independent and active foreign policy' (Ravenhill, 1995: 106).

It has often been said that the French organisation of cooperation with Africa settled by de Gaulle's administration at the time of decolonisation was a means to leave in order better to stay. France did whatever was possible to preserve economic and political links such as military positions with its former colonies, most of which were demanding this type of assistance. It seems legitimate to ask whether links with newly independent African countries were preserved as a means to help that continent, as an element of foreign policy or to serve French interests. One could say that all factors apply and this can explain why France was the main defender of the renewal of the association.

From a granted association to a negotiated association

Decolonisation implied a change in the association regime for the newly independent African countries. To convince the reluctant member states to maintain the substance of the association regime after 1960, France argued that the association was primarily a solution for OCTs exports and development problems, and was not serving a political purpose. The EEC Council decided to perpetuate the agreement until 1962. The French idea of a Euro-African group which could serve both European and developing countries' interests survived after the independence of the associates. As the Netherlands and Germany considered the first association to be a transitional period, they were opposed to a renewal of the partnership. France, Belgium and the Commission were in favour. African countries insisted on their homogeneity as a group, their economic weakness and the responsibility of colonial powers. They expressed their will to maintain the association. Then, 'Yaoundé I de facto multilateralised the existing regime between the EEC and former colonies while maintaining intact the aid system that had been set up by the Treaty of Rome' (Grilli, 1993: 20). This Convention indeed embodied the institutionalisation of the association regime.

In 1963, France was the only member state that opposed the accession of Great Britain to the EEC, at least until the UK reorganised its economy. The disappointment of Germany and the Netherlands was strengthened by the failure to enlarge the association to Nigeria and the East African Community. Negotiations occurred but some member states did not ratify the agreements. Moreover, despite the non-discrimination principle, the first Yaoundé Convention did not succeed in setting up real equality between member states in the repartition of financial and technical cooperation markets. French industries and companies kept on obtaining the majority of EDF-related work in the associate states (Delorme, 1972: 209). During the whole Yaoundé period, member states confronted the diverging opinions about the future of the association. The Netherlands wanted to suppress both the trade and aid parts and to establish a world-wide system of development assistance. On the other hand, France fought to preserve the privileged relation with African associates. France was not opposed to the coexistence of two systems of preferences, as long as the AAMS remained privileged as compared with other developing countries (Delorme, 1972: 207). The second Yaoundé Convention resulted from a compromise between globalists and regionalists. Reciprocal concessions were made between the two European camps, to the detriment of the associates.

As seen in the first part of this chapter, France has heavily contributed to maintaining geographical coherence among the recipients of Lomé/Cotonou aid and the specific relationship with Africa. The argument that the Lomé Convention perpetuated the colonial relationship – generally justified – has always been used by opponents of the French model of European development policy. During the first fifteen years of Lomé, no adaptation of the Lomé model was proposed. ACP countries as much as European countries continued to benefit from the system without trying to improve it, despite identified limits and problems. All participants found the game profitable but instead of sharing common interests, Europe at one side and the ACP at the other progressively started to perpetuate the Convention for their own interests. The spirit of Lomé moved slightly and European development cooperation entered a ten-year period of deep mutation.

Changing context, changing interests

The 1990s were characterised by dramatic changes in the world. With the end of the Cold War and the acceleration of globalisation, North–South relationships were reshaped on several levels. Multilateral institutions played a greater role, the ACP was economically marginalised. Europe and France had to reset their priorities and to reform their cooperation system. Many factors can explain the rising disinterest of France towards Africa, both bilaterally and through the European channel.

Upheavals on the world scene

Many changes have taken place since 1975, economically as well as politically. The New International Economic Order did not become the way to rule the world economy. As for interdependence between developed and developing countries, what is left is a one-way dependence of the Third World countries on the industrialised ones. One of the core concepts of the Lomé Convention has thus disappeared. The limits of the Lomé trade model have been heavily analysed. Non-reciprocal trade preferences did not really benefit the ACP countries, except for a very small number of countries such as Mauritius. The ACP's share of international trade declined from 3 per cent in the middle of the 1970s to 1.5 per cent in the 1990s, despite an increase in the number of ACP countries. In other words, the EU's privileged partners suffer from the 'unimportance of being preferred' (Davenport, 1992: 233). Non-ACP developing countries that only benefit from the Generalised System of Preferences, less advantageous than the Lomé regime, managed to maintain or even to increase their share of European trade. The economic situation of the ACP could even have been worse without trade preferences. Whether true or not, that marginal result cannot be satisfactory.

Along with bad trade performances, the debt problem has been on the rise for many ACP countries. African states increasingly had to conclude agreements with the international financial institutions (IFIs) in order to get loans. These loans have been more and more subjected to strong economic conditionalities, including reform of their economies, control of expenses and implementation of sound macroeconomic policies. Instead of trying to formulate an alternative model to the 'Washington consensus', the European Union and the member states have progressively aligned their policies according to the approach of the IFIs (see chapter 2). If the effects of structural adjustment were criticised, the rationale of the programme itself has not been contested. As for France, in 1993 then French Prime Minister Edouard Balladur announced the so-called 'Abdijan doctrine'. This entailed that, from that moment onwards, any new French loan was conditioned to a prior agreement with the IMF or the World Bank. French-speaking African countries were among the last to sign Structural Adjustment Programmes with the IFIs because previously they were protected within the frame of the Franc zone.

The Abdijan doctrine necessarily implied the devaluation of the CFA franc, which occurred in 1994 (Lelart, 1998: 203).

The fall of the Berlin Wall also had a fundamental impact on development issues. Consequences are manifold, both for Europe and Africa. The situation described earlier (about the French imperatives) had one fundamental precondition: Germany could not reunify and become more powerful than France within the EU (Hoffmann, 1993). As for the ACP countries, especially the African ones, they suddenly lost the bargaining power they could use when two opposite blocs were leading the world. African countries were no longer the object of international attention, they ceased being a field for peripheral East–West conflicts and they lost a geo-strategic rent. As for Europe, it is commonly believed that the EU was unable to fill the vacuum when Soviet ideology disappeared. The European Union showed its limits as an achieved political body and could not offer a distinct position from the dominant American model. As long as the bipolar world existed, Europe was seen as (and tried to be) the champion of the Third World, a politically neutral partner which could offer an alternative to communism and liberalism. As soon as the Wall fell, the EU did nothing more than align itself with the dominant thought. The same thing happened with France, which considered itself as the advocate of developing countries and as an alternative model. For France 'being anti-Americanist or anti-communist appear less as *a priori* ideological positions than as a rational attitude chosen in order to let France best maintain its international role' (Touraine, 1993: 808). This French position was only defendable until one of the two adversaries disappeared.

The shift to the Euro in 1999 generated a debate about the status of the CFA franc. This currency had been pegged to the French franc since 1948. France had to convince its European partners of the Euro zone that the link between French and CFA francs is a budgetary arrangement and not a monetary agreement. On 23 November 1998, the Council of the EU gave a positive opinion (through decision 98/683/CE) stipulating that France could maintain these agreements. Technically speaking, the French Treasury is still guaranteeing free convertibility, fixed parity and centralised management. It was important for France that the launching of the Euro would not modify the bilateral dimension of the relationship between Franc zone countries and France. However, the monetary cooperation is extended to the European Union, which replaces France as an 'agency of restraint' (Collier *et al.*, 1997: 301). Franc zone countries were more interested than Europe in the future of their monetary link with France. For Europe, 'this question was a very small issue within the whole debate about the Euro' (personal communication, 2000b).

New European concerns for Central and Eastern European countries (CEEC) contributed to a reorientation of aid. European priorities are not strategically defined but reflect answers to ad hoc situations. Along with a massive amount of aid for the CEEC, the EU re-launched a big development and cooperation programme with the Mediterranean countries in an attempt to strengthen their security and to stabilise the area. Two kinds of reaction can be distinguished about the French attitude towards the relative withdrawal of Europe from Africa. Firstly, France agreed with Europe. It became conscious that, rather than in Africa, new political and economic opportunities are elsewhere. At the Community level, France is more interested in issues such as enlargement, structural funds, Common Foreign and Security Policy, Common Agricultural Policy, reform of the European institutions, the Euro, and so on. Priorities are more in economy and internal issues than in development policy. Secondly, France considers its involvement in Africa still to be useful for its political image, as well as for the economic interests of French private companies, and because of a solidarity based on history. It therefore tries to limit the total disinterest in, and disillusion of, some EU member states about the Lomé Conventions, mainly through keeping up its contribution to the EDF and defending the renewal of the Lomé Convention, despite the critics and the unwillingness of other member states to remain in a regional framework.

The place of France within the post-Lomé negotiations

During the post-Lomé negotiations, France no longer played the role of *the* guarantor of the Convention. It remained one of its defenders because 'the Lomé Convention conveys a European model of development cooperation, largely inspired by France' (Khoury, 2000: 2). The position of France evolved around the preservation of a specific global agreement and a different trade regime with the ACP countries. France defended the regional-based approach designed by the Commission in order to create Regional Economic Partnership Agreements. France wanted to avoid the standardisation of the EU–ACP relationship. 'For the French, the most important issue of the negotiations was trade. We were tempted to be more flexible on political issues as long as we could get more about this specific trade regime' (personal communication, 2000c). According to the Commission proposals, France also defended the creation of an environment that favours investment and economic growth (Secrétariat Général de l'Union Européenne, 1997; Posthumus, 1998) and the idea of creating an inter-African peace-keeping corps. Recognising the progressive alignment of the EU to the model shaped by the IFIs, France has been attempting to formulate different ideas. It advocated a 'fight against inequalities' rather than a struggle against poverty. It brought out questions on structural adjustment and it considered the concept of good governance as too vague a notion. However, this criticism or distance exists in words rather than in deeds.

The EU's negotiation mandate mentioned the non-renewal of Stabex. Along with a few ACP countries benefiting from these instruments, France was the only country that really defended the mechanism. The Cotonou Agreement admits that instability in export earnings jeopardises development policies and economic reforms in ACP countries but it only gives additional support included within the financial envelope for long-term development support.

France considers that this is not adapted to one-off external shocks. The question of instability of markets is not solved in the new Agreement. France is right in arguing that this point is fundamental, but it has to be mentioned that France had a distinct interest in preserving this instrument. After all, the main recipients of the Stabex were two faithful friends of France, that is Côte d'Ivoire and Cameroon.

The debate about including the EDF in the Community budget is relevant to understand France's change of attitude towards the importance of the EU–ACP relationship. The French, the Danes and the Luxemburgers contribute proportionally more to the EDF than to the Community budget. France provides 24.3 per cent of the EDF while it funds 'only' 17 per cent of the Community budget. This position as first EDF contributor gives France a certain legitimacy among both donors and recipients of aid, as well as symbolic and political power. However, France has now been converted to the idea of including the EDF in the Community budget and tries to convince its reluctant partners. One can ask if France now thinks that, compared to its high financial involvement in the EU–ACP partnership, political feedback is insufficient. It appears that the economic rationale defended by the Ministry of Economy and Finances carries off the philosophy of the Ministry of Foreign Affairs. This example shows that French internal divergences have an impact on the definition of France's official position towards European policy. In the Cotonou Agreement, the EDF is still based on state contributions but France has officially asked DG DEV to study inclusion of the fund in the Community budget.

Reform of the European and French development policies
The point here is not to describe the reform processes of development policy in France and in Europe, but to explain how these changes will modify the role of France within EU development policy. The making of French African policy is a multi-polar and multilevel exercise. There are roles for the Ministry of Foreign Affairs, the Ministry of Economy and Finances, the Treasury, some technical ministries, the AFD (French Development Agency), the SGCI (General Secretariat for Inter-ministerial Coordination), the African cell of the Presidency, some French private companies, civil society at large, public opinion, NGOs, and others. French cooperation is a galaxy, an institutional nebula. As far as development policy is concerned, France consists of 'a multiplicity of decision centres which do not work in cooperation with each other, in harmony' (Bayart, 1983: 13). This complexity favoured personal links between African and French actors and one of the main characteristics of French cooperation has long been lack of transparency. The necessary reform process has been going on since 1998. The reform pursues more coherence, transparency in policies and better coordination with other bilateral and multilateral donors. It also aims at restoring the credibility of France in Africa, democratising the African policy, reforming aid and associating civil society actors.

The French Ministry of Development Cooperation has been amalgamated within the Ministry of Foreign Affairs. Many observers and actors (both from France and the Commission) state that the already decreasing presence of France in the international and European debate on cooperation is even more pronounced since the Ministry of Development Cooperation disappeared. The dilution of responsibility in Paris does not favour influence on the elaboration of European strategies. Until recently, every great European development policy was inspired by France. Today, the thought about development is Anglo-Saxon. According to a former Director-General at the Commission, 'every French civil servant in Brussels can confirm the decrease in the French presence' (HCCI, 2000). The bi-polarisation between the Ministry of Economy (which manages more than half of the cooperation budget) and the Ministry of Foreign Affairs could jeopardise the future of development policy. How could international cooperation maintain a degree of autonomy if it is torn between budgetary constraints and diplomatic considerations? The recent heavy cut in French bilateral ODA contributes to the trend of normalising France among the other donors and can de-legitimate the leading role of France. Moreover, French MEPs no longer contribute to conveying French ideas. For example, the Development and Cooperation Committee is no longer chaired by well-known French politicians such as Bernard Kouchner and Michel Rocard.

The new-born Haut Conseil de la Coopération Internationale is expected to fill the gap between the authorities and civil society, as 'French policymakers have long tended to forget that this second world exists' (Brüne, 1994: 56). This institution includes representatives from NGOs, MPs, trade unions, researchers and actors of decentralised cooperation and contributes to the making of development cooperation policy. To enlarge the traditional privileged *champ*, a 'zone of prior solidarity' has been created. It mainly covers the ACP group as a whole, which reflects the search for more coordination and coherence between the Commission and France. They are both trying to lose the image of post-colonial paternalism which has characterised Franco-African relations and influenced the European development policy.

The geographical division of aid zones in the Community organisation of development cooperation is a fundamental element in the relation between France, Europe and Africa. Until recently, the European administrative hard core of this work was DG VIII. This structure began with managing the Community's aid and trade relations with member states' former colonies. This field of action was under negotiation every time that enlargement of the EU introduced the problem of the candidate's former colonies, which were supposed to join the other recipients of European aid. The geographical organisation of the Commission's external relations has now gradually shifted towards a thematic framework: DG External Relations, DG Trade, DG Enlargement, DG Development, ECHO and EuropeAid compose 'the RELEX group'. As for the reform of development policy within the European Commission, a recent assessment document concluded that (1) the reform of the RELEX group was seen as an 'urgent and vital priority'; (2) 'the overall policy direction seems quite logical and coherent'; (3) 'implementation will be the real test', and (4) 'some critical dimensions merit greater attention'. The document recommends to Europe to develop 'its own specificity as a global player and donor' (Bossuyt et al., 2000: 28–30). When one uses the words 'Europe' and 'Commission', the same kind of analysis as for France can be made about where and by whom European development policy is elaborated. There are a lot of diverging positions within the member states, and there is some incoherence between certain Community sector-related policies. The Commission has to organise a minimum consensus. Some actors say that the Commission only results from the will of the fifteen EU member states (personal communication, 2000d). Others state that it cannot be denied that the Commission produces thoughts on its own.

The current reforms in France and Europe show some parallels in major themes as well as in cooperation mechanisms. This common vision is perceptible through new matters and objectives such as the integration of developing countries in the world economy, regional integration and the fight against poverty. These principles constitute the European development policy aims as included in the Maastricht Treaty. French and European development cooperation have to face decreasing aid budgets and new priorities in development matters. Africa's position as Europe's and France's privileged partner is challenged by new concerns for the near-abroad. French and European official positions about development use the same wording and concepts: rationalisation of technical and financial cooperation instruments, governance, ownership, efficiency, profitability, private sector, competitiveness, regionalism, trade *and* aid approach. This convergence should be interpreted as a standardisation more than a revival of the EU–ACP relationship.

The French position on European development policy is both supportive and critical at the same time. France strongly supports the principle of European development cooperation but criticises methods and results. France calls for more coordination and complementarity with member states, asks for better aid efficiency and serious evaluation. It proposes to strengthen sector-related coherence and to improve Community procedures (CICID, 2000). Many French official reports advocate strict application of the principle of subsidiarity: the EC should limit its action to fields where it can offer value added. In other sectors, implementation of Community aid should be delegated to a member state when it is a leader in the sector involved (Tavernier, 1999; CICID, 2000). This idea of *chefs de file* already exists within the framework of operational coordination between the EU delegations and member states' agencies in the field (personal communication, 2000e). The Commission has recently accepted the principle of a division of labour between itself and the member states (CEC, 2000; Nielson, 2000). This example shows that France has not lost all the influence on policy making that it used to have. Nevertheless, the whole statement shows that the French position within Europe is now more or less standardised compared with the other European Union member states and compared with what it used to be.

Conclusion

It cannot be denied that France played a great role in shaping a development policy model for the European Community, and that it lost a large part of its influence along with successive enlargements of the Community and the choice of other national and European priorities. French disengagement from Africa is firstly occurring at a bilateral level: by military withdrawal, decrease in ODA and normalisation of the political relationship. One could have expected this disengagement to be compensated by a stronger involvement in Community development policy. But the combination of two types of factor limits the role of France in European development policy towards Africa. There are 'objective factors' (such as enlargement of the EU to member states which do not agree with the French geographical approach to development, new priorities and partners, the dominant role of the IFIs) and 'French factors' (such as the will to budgetise the EDF and reduce its own contribution, weak presence in the European and international debate on development, decreasing human investment in and impact on the Commission).

It seems that France, at the end of the twentieth century, has chosen sense rather than sensibility. A study of the main themes within Mitterrand's public addresses showed that 'Europe' progressively gained importance. Constructing Europe was Mitterrand's main preoccupation, above all during his second mandate as President. Comparatively, 'Africa' was not a fundamental item in his speeches on French foreign policy (Labbé, 1990). Two quotes can further illustrate the feeling of sense overriding sensibility. At the end of his second mandate, President Mitterrand stated: 'Never separate French greatness from the construction of Europe. This is our new dimension and our ambition for the next century.' Secondly: 'In the past, France was an imperial nation, exercising influence over the Mediterranean and Africa, and having world-wide dreams. Nowadays, and above all thanks to its economy (trade, investments, industrial and scientific cooperation), France is essentially European' (Moreau-Desfarges, 1994: 70). It seems difficult to imagine that France could or would wish to make Africa a priority for Europe as long as it is not one of its own priorities.

Note

1   This research builds on participant observation, carried out through: a five-month internship at the Post-Lomé Negotiation Task Force of the Commission's DG VIII (October 1998–February 1999); participation in the work of the French High Council for International Cooperation on coherence between bilateral and

multilateral development policies (1999–2002); and interviews with French and European Commission civil servants.

Bibliography

Anyadike-Danes, M. K. and M. N. Anyadike-Danes (1992), 'The geographic allocation of the European Development Fund under the Lomé Conventions', *World Development*, 20:11, pp. 1647–61.

Archives MAE (Ministère Français des Affaires Etrangères) (1956), DE–CE Marché Commun 719. Territoires d'Outre-Mer (PTOM). Mai 1956–Décembre 1956. Letter by Gaston Defferre to the President of the Council, 17 May 1956.

Bayart, J. F. (1983), *La Politique Africaine de Mitterrand*, Paris: Karthala.

Bossuyt, J., T. Lehtinen, A. Simon, G. Laporte and G. Corre (2000), 'Assessing trends in EC development policy. An independent review of the European Commission's external aid reform process', *ECDPM Discussion Paper*, no. 16, May.

Brüne, S. (1994), 'Under pressure for reform: French policies towards South of the Sahara', in S. Brüne, J. Betz and W. Kühne (eds), *Africa and Europe: Relations of Two Continents in Transition*, Hamburg: Lit Verlag.

CEC (2000), 'Communication de la Commission au Conseil sur la politique de développement de la Communauté Européenne', COM (2000) 212 final, Brussels.

Chazan, N., R. Mortimer, J. Ravenhill and D. Rothschild (1992), *Politics and Society in Contemporary Africa*, Boulder: Lynne Rienner.

CICID (Comité Interministériel de la Coopération Internationale) (2000), *La Coopération Française au Développement: une Refondation*, Paris: La documentation française.

Collier, P., P. Guillaumont, S. Guillaumont and J.W. Gunning (1997), 'The future of Lomé: Europe's role in African growth', *World Economy*, 20:3, pp. 285–305.

Constantin, F. (1993), 'Patronage et cardinalité', in D. C. Bach and A. Kirk-Greene (eds), *Etats et Sociétés en Afrique Francophone*, Paris: Economica.

Davenport, M. (1992), 'Africa: the unimportance of being preferred', *Journal of Common Market Studies*, 30:2, pp. 233–48.

Delorme, N. (1972), *L'association des Etats Africains et Malgache à la Communauté Economique Européenne*, Paris: LGDJ.

Delphin, H. (1992), *Partenariat ou Paternalisme? Les Relations CE–ACP dans le Cadre de la Mise en Œuvre de la Convention de Lomé*, Thèse en vue de l'obtention du diplôme d'Etudes Administratives Européennes Approfondies, Bruges: Collège d'Europe.

Grilli, E. (1993), *The European Community and the Developing Countries*, Cambridge: Cambridge University Press.

Guérivière de la, J. (1992), *Voyage à l'Intérieur de l'Eurocratie*, Paris: Le Monde Editions.

HCCI (Haut Conseil de la Coopération Internationale) (2000), Communication by Philippe Soubestre, Former Director-General of the European Commission, HCCI audience, 15 June.

Hoffmann, S. (1993), 'French dilemmas and strategies in the new Europe', in R. O. Keohane, J. S. Nye and S. Hoffmann, *After the Cold War. International Institutions and State Strategies in Europe, 1989–1991*, Cambridge: Harvard University Press.

Khoury el, Z. (2000), 'La nouvelle politique européenne de coopération', *Les Notes Bleues de Bercy*, no. 187, pp. 1–12.

Labbé, D. (1990), *Le Vocabulaire de François Mitterrand*, Paris: Presses de la Fondation Nationale de Sciences Politiques.

Lelart, M. (1998), 'La zone franc et l'intégration monétaire européenne', in D. Bach (ed.), *Regionalisation, Mondialisation et Fragmentation en Afrique Subsaharienne*, Paris: Karthala.
Lemaignen, R. (1964), *L'Europe au Berceau. Souvenirs d'un Technocrate*, Paris: Plon.
Lequesne, C. (1993), *Paris–Bruxelles. Comment se Fait la Politique Européenne de la France*, Paris: Presses de la Fondation Nationale des Sciences Politiques.
Lequesne, C. (1998), 'Comment penser l'union européenne?', in M.-C. Smouts (ed.), *Les Nouvelles Relations Internationales. Pratiques et Théories*, Paris: Presses de la Fondation Nationale de Science Politique.
Lister, M. R. (1988), *The European Community and the Developing World*, Aldershot: Avebury.
Mitterrand, F. (1957), *Présence Française et Abandon*, Paris: Plon.
Moravcsik, A. (1999 and 2000), 'Le grain et la grandeur: les origines économiques de la politique européenne du Général de Gaulle', *Revue Française de Science Politique* 49: 4–5, pp. 507–43 (première partie); 50: 1, pp. 73–122 (deuxième partie).
Moreau-Desfarges, Ph. (1994), *La France dans le Monde au XXème Siècle*, Paris: Hachette.
Naudet, D. (1997), 'French development aid', in A. Cox, J. Healy and A. Koning (eds), *How European Aid Works. A Comparison of Management Systems and Effectiveness*, London: Overseas Development Institute.
Nielson, P. (2000), 'A new focus and a better organisation for the European Communities' development cooperation', speech given at a Conference on European development policy in Berlin on 12 April, SPEECH/00/135.
Page, E. (1997), *People Who Run Europe*, Oxford: Clarendon Press.
Personal communication (2000a), from a member of Edgar Pisani's cabinet, June.
Personal communication (2000b), from Y. T. de Silguy, European Commissioner for Financial and Monetary Affairs, April.
Personal communication (2000c), from Z. el Khoury, SGCI, July.
Personal communication (2000d), from a member of the French Permanent Representation, January.
Personal communication (2000e), from a member of the EU delegation in Cameroon, Yaoundé, February.
Posthumus, B. (1998), 'Au delà de Lomé IV: points de vues préliminaires des gouvernements européens sur les relations futures ACP–UE', *ECDPM Working Paper*, no. 53.
Ravenhill, J. (1985), *Collective Clientelism. The Lomé Convention and North–South Relations*, New York: Columbia University Press.
Ravenhill, J. (1995), 'Dependent by default: Africa's relations with the European Union', in W. Harbeson and D. Rothschild (eds), *Africa in World Politics. Post War Challenges*, Boulder: Westview Press.
Rouban, L. (1998), *La Fin des Technocrates*, Paris: Presses de Sciences Po.
Schreurs, R. (1994), 'L'Eurafrique dans les négociations du Traité de Rome', *Politique Africaine*, no. 49, pp. 82–92.
Secrétariat Général de l'Union Européenne (1997), 'Note à l'attention des membres des groupes ACP et Coopération au développement. Seconde contribution française sur l'avenir des relations UE/ACP', doc no. 250/97 (ACP/CODEV), Bruxelles.
Tavernier, Y. (1999), '*La Coopération Française au Développement*', rapport au Premier Ministre, Paris: La documentation française.

Touraine, M. (1993), 'La représentation de l'adversaire dans la politique extérieure de la France depuis 1981', *Revue Française de Science Politique*, 43:5, pp. 807–22.

Zartman, W. (1993), *Europe and Africa: The New Phase*, Boulder and London: Lynne Rienner.

8

The Commission and development policy: bureaucratic politics in EU aid – from the Lomé leap forward to the difficulties of adapting to the twenty-first century

Adrian Hewitt and Kaye Whiteman

To integrate or to surpass the French neo-colonial system: the Commission's choice

From the time that a united Europe was a gleam in the eye of Jean Monnet to the signing of the Treaty of Rome in 1957, the institution of the Commission was central to the European idea. Rather than just a European civil service or a think-tank, it was also intended to be the motor of European unity. Much of the subsequent debate on how to take Europe forward has been around the role the Commission might or might not play. And, when it has seemed to be stagnating, there has been a wringing of hands by Europeanists over the waning of the power of the Commission in relation to the Council of Ministers, much more seriously under the control of the member states, and, more recently, in relation to the Parliament. Every time the European project has been taken forward there has been an initiative from the Commission, usually impelled by a creative President such as Roy Jenkins (Economic and Monetary Union) and, most spectacularly, Jacques Delors (the setting up of the single European market in 1993, the European Union and the Maastricht Treaty). Under weaker Presidents, however, the Commission was revealed to be perhaps the least accountable European institution of all, and this caused periodic crises of legitimacy as well as policy, most strikingly in 1999 under Jacques Santer.

In the Treaty of Rome, the presence of the kernel of what was later to become a development policy was found in Part IV. It had been included in the manner that has come to be the trademark of European policy making: as a result of last minute horse trading by member states. In 1957 France, Belgium, the Netherlands and even Italy all still had some colonial ties, described euphemistically in the Treaty as 'special relationships'. Algeria at that time was even politically part of France, though it would not remain so for many more years. It had not been envisaged, however, that the new democratic Europe should have colonial entanglements associated with the past era of aggressive nationalism, least of all by the Dutch (who had already lost Indonesia) and by the newly democratic Germans who saw empire as one more trapping of the Wilhelmine and Prussian past. Thus a relationship with a few parts of what was to be described as the developing world was wished on the Community almost as an afterthought, but a very French afterthought, deftly anticipating burden sharing with Bonn. Still it was important enough for the French government of Guy Mollet to make it, in February 1957, a condition of signing up to the Rome Treaty. The key elements were trade access to the EEC with reciprocity – for these were still colonies and protectorates – and a European Development Fund to which Germany and France were to contribute one-third each, even though the principal beneficiaries were French territories.

The association provisions of the Rome Treaty were all the more significant as at that time France's African territories were not yet independent, and it was not even envisaged that independence would automatically come. The late Algerian war meant that France's empire was in a crisis of decline. It took the arrival of de Gaulle on the ruins of the Fourth Republic in 1958, and the foundering of his French Community project in the wake of Guinea's rejection of de Gaulle's plans in the referendum of that year, to force the issue. The unexpected arrival of nearly all of France's African territories at independence in 1960, with those of Belgium rapidly in their wake, as well as the former Italian possession of Somalia, meant that a reformulation was necessary. The rest of the six original EEC member states had no desire to take on excess post-colonial baggage and resolved to treat France's (and Belgium's) ex-colonies as, at best, Europe's 'near-abroad'. They insisted that development policy remain subservient to the guiding EEC policies and doctrines, not least Europe's own economic integration and the protection of its agriculture. After some serious intra-European negotiation, and a certain amount of arm twisting on the part of the African associates over the amount of money offered in the second European Development Fund, there emerged the treaty which became the Yaoundé Convention of 1963. The tough part of the negotiation was between France, supported by Belgium and Italy, and the Dutch and Germans, who were unhappy at the strong French bias of Yaoundé. Fourteen of the eighteen countries were former French territories with continuing monetary ties to the former mother country and seventeen of the eighteen were broadly considered 'francophone'.

The Commission at that time largely favoured the French position, as the structures established in 1958 were heavily weighted in its direction, and managed to carry along the other nationalities in support of the association experiment. From 1958 until 1984 the Commissioner responsible for the association (as from 1975 succeeded by a partnership of equals) was French, most notably Jean-Francois Deniau, there at the time of British accession; Claude Cheysson, the first Commissioner to be designated 'Development Commissioner'; and Edgar Pisani, who very much picked up where Cheysson left off. In 1984 the development portfolio was split to accommodate Cheysson's return after his spell as Mitterand's External Affairs Minister. The split initiated more than a decade of uncertainty in the Commission's development policy. This was a reflection of the extent to which France attached importance to the relationship and made it a political priority through its critical early years, as well as the years of adaptation to British entry and the emergence of a global approach to the subject, during which France felt that its interests needed to be protected.

French hegemony was counter-balanced by a remarkable continuity of German officials who held the post of Director-General of DG VIII, the Directorate-General responsible for the association, which evolved into the Development DG. These Directors-General in the early years were loyal executors of policy, by and large reflecting the official German view that this was a policy included to keep the French happy. It used to be said that the Commission was a heavy French administration implemented by Germans – that is, they took it too seriously. There certainly grew up a generation of francophile Germans in DG VIII, who embraced the association policy with almost missionary zeal and were puzzled when it became subjected to serious criticisms, especially in Africa itself.

There was some variation of personalities. If Hans-Broder Krohn, a career Commission official, implemented the evolving policy of the early 1970s correctly (as befitted a former officer in the German army) but without imagination, his successor Klaus Meyer was simply a transplant from the Foreign Ministry in Bonn. The most influential of German Directors-General was certainly Dieter Frisch, who came in after Meyer in 1984. He was a DG VIII career official. He had started in the Commission as an interpreter, and had been very involved in Cheysson's grand designs of the 1970s. Frisch managed to impose his personality on both the Directorate and policy, paving the way for a Commission initiative to include development policy in the Maastricht Treaty of 1992, for the first time as an element in its own right. He believed that once a 'critical mass' of harmonised policy was achieved, a real European development policy would evolve. In this he was perhaps being ambitious, in view of the turmoil which later beset the different development instruments in the Commission. The larger member states with distinctive bilateral policies (notably the British and the French) still felt that theirs was superior to that which was dispensed from Brussels, but they were compelled by treaty arrangement to put an important share of their development cooperation budgets into the European pot. They retaliated to Commission aggrandisement by maintaining the separate off-budget status of the European Development Fund (essentially for the African ex-colonies), which they continued to control while the European Parliament and other parts of the Commission expanded tariff policy and budget spending to other parts of the developing (and later transitional) world. Of course, in the end the tail wagged the dog.

As important as the retention of the Commissioner post in this early period was the nomination, right from the beginning, of a French Director of the European Development Fund, in the shape of a highly autocratic former colonial official, the Corsican Jacques Ferrandi. He held the post from the beginning of 1958 through to 1976, when he resigned after a conflict with Cheysson (a French socialist with greater powers of forward thinking) that was almost predestined – a clash of rival development philosophies. Ferrandi's universe was entirely confined to French-speaking Africa, and he adjusted badly to the world of Lomé and more so to that of development policy. In contrast, the Lomé Convention was the Commission's high water mark in development policy. It was admired for the achievement, not only within Europe and among the developing countries, but by a much broader international audience, especially during the first five years (1975–79) of Lomé I.

Ferrandi established a network of EDF delegates in each of the eighteen countries of Yaoundé, even the smaller mini-states, accountable to him personally. Essentially he created an empire within the empire of DG VIII, subjected to specific codified regulations, 'instructions aux délégués', down to the regulation black Mercedes for each delegate, as part of the maintenance of the prestige of the EDF. Predictably, Frenchmen who often were in position for long periods held the key delegations in Dakar and Abidjan (nodal points of the French sphere of influence in Africa). The EDF was run through an agency outside the Commission (the 'Agence Européenne de Coopération' – technically, in fact, a Belgian company), which gave greater flexibility and independence, out of the control of the Community's own budget. The EDF was also endowed for a period of five years, which gave greater stability than were it to be dependent annually on the caprices of the Community budget. This also made it a potentially more reliable source of aid than member states' own bilateral programmes. The existence and power of Ferrandi underlined the figurehead nature of the Directors-General of DG VIII, up to the point of Ferrandi's resignation. Even then, despite several restructurings, the resilience of the Ferrandist system initially proved hard to eliminate. An equivalent structure limped on under the Frenchman Philippe Soubestre until February 2000, when even that empire was broken up and operations (AIDCO) were entirely separated from what passed as policy (DG DEV).

France's concern to keep a strong handle on European policy brought its own dividends. Under Yaoundé, although the French put in one-third of the total funds, because of the preponderance of former French territories among the associated states, the contracts awarded to French firms still showed a surplus. This situation continued under the Lomé Convention up to the mid-1980s, in part because it took the new entrants time to adapt to the EDF's systems. Every technically exciting innovation, such as Stabex (from 1975), initially put the lion's share of resources the way of francophone West Africa, and particularly Senegal and Côte d'Ivoire, ostensibly as a counterweight to the non-EDF-funded Sugar Protocol inherited when Britain joined. By the later years of Stabex the pie was being shared more equally. However, it was only at the end of the 1980s that a more equitable overall balance was achieved.

Cooperation or development

The period of 'the association', essentially from the Rome Treaty up to the opening of the Lomé negotiations in 1973, was one in which the Europe of the six discovered through the French as intermediary the modalities of a 'cooperation policy'. Even the use of the word 'cooperation' is an illustration of the way in which the French introduced into the European context their own nomenclature, which they had developed to describe their own development policy in 1961. The same applied to the emotive and subsequently discredited word 'association', which had strong Gaullist overtones dating from the abortive Franco-African Community of 1958 which was also an 'association'. And of course the EU itself was a Community, or a series of Communities, after the French model, until very recently.

At the same time the other members of the EEC discovered the limitations and distortions of the French perspective. For various reasons, the Commission was not in the forefront of those who pushed for change. It lacked a strong internal policy unit, although there were those who were aware of the inadequacies of what was happening. For the countries of 'the association' (officially the AAMS) were very much perceived as being 'Europe's chosen few'. (This term was coined by Morton and Tulloch (1977). Tulloch also published *The Seven Outside* (1973), referring to Asian countries which later became high achievers despite being excluded from the EEC's charmed circle.) Not surprisingly, the relationship was much criticised in the new nationalist Africa, by leaders such as Kwame Nkrumah of Ghana and Sekou Touré of Guinea. There was much suspicion of the idea of 'Eurafrica' which some of the more enthusiastic proponents of the association tended to promote. It appeared not just paternalistic, but had unfortunate historical associations with both Hitler and Vichy, and tended to conflate the charge of neo-colonialism laid against the whole Yaoundé relationship. Later, the narrower concept of 'Françafrique' became a cynical jibe of French youth (not just of the French left) as France found itself faced with taking tough decisions on the reform of economic and foreign policy in an era of globalisation.

One of the main conditions that the Germans and the Dutch imposed for agreeing to Yaoundé was nonetheless a commitment on the part of the European Community to negotiate association agreements with other countries at similar stages of development elsewhere in Africa. This was taken up by Nigeria, which in spite of reservations about Yaoundé negotiated a trade accord. Typically this was never implemented because of the significantly pro-Biafra posture adopted by France and many of the other original EEC member states during the Nigerian civil war (1967–70). In 1967 the German/Dutch pressure bore more positive, if still modest, fruit in the association agreement with the East African Community. This was still limited in scope and concessions compared with the sweeping nature of the Yaoundé Convention. The East African Community itself split up shortly afterwards. In 1972 an association agreement was reached with Mauritius, whose deal with the EEC included an aid component. This privilege was accorded in part because it did not cost very much, but also because, as a country with a minority francophone population, a formal link to the EC was a consolidation of French efforts to lure the country into its own sphere of influence. The Mauritians were smartly using this to get in ahead of the field at the moment of British entry. Surprisingly, in the 1950s and 1960s (and by some even as late as 1972) Mauritius was seen as a hopeless case of a labour-surplus economy with a declining core commodity. In fact it used its European links more extensively than any other and Mauritius is currently referred to not only as a Lomé role-model but also as one of the few ACP countries (perhaps the only) really to have developed from the relationship.

It is hard now to recall the curious political climate in Europe. De Gaulle's celebrated '*non*' to British entry of February 1963 (greatly to the disappointment of the Dutch and Germans) was one of the factors that led to the almost fatalistic acceptance of the loaded Yaoundé deal a few months later. Without the British and their colonial baggage the other countries of the Community were left with little choice but to go ahead with 'the association' on French terms, recognising that it at least offered them wider market access and connections in Africa. But it was still France's affair.

The President of Gabon, Omar Bongo, for long led one of France's most conspicuous client states. This went up to the extent that via the aid relationship he became the paymaster of several French parties. In the 1990s Omar Bongo wrote that in the 1960s he had asked General de Gaulle why he was so reticent about British entry ('*mais pourquoi, mon Général?*'). The General replied 'It is because of you others, the francophone Africans. For you in this affair of the European Community, everything happens pro rata because of demography, so when you see the giants, Nigeria, Tanzania, Kenya beside Gabon, one must be vigilant' (Bongo 90, 1994). India, Pakistan, Malaysia, and even the later poverty-stricken Bangladesh, were commensurately beyond the pale, outclassed by size and size of economic threat. This concern to maximise the influence and advantage for the francophones found further expression once British entry returned to the agenda, in the pursuit of the 'acquis' – that the Lomé Convention had to provide an expansion of aid and should not lead to loss of advantage for the once-favoured ones. This became one of the sub-texts of the eighteen-month negotiations for Lomé in 1973–75.

One has to observe that in the first fifteen years of the EEC, up to the early 1970s, faced with French domination of the association debate, the Commission, far from playing the dynamic role which is its prescribed vocation in the Community, appeared frequently to be passively supporting the interests of a member state in a partial way. That presented a distorted picture of the Community internationally, at a time when the Commission under President Hallstein was in many directions carving out its innovative role in relation to the Council of Ministers, and also taking on the ardent nationalist ulterior motives ('*arrières-pensees*') of de Gaulle. Obviously there were those in the Commission, including in DG VIII, who felt that the policy as it stood was inadequate, but it took time for their views to be heard because of the overall context. The resignation of de Gaulle in 1969 led to a considerable easing of the pressures on the Commission in many directions, notably with regard to the British. This had important implications for the whole association policy: eventually it enabled the creation of a development policy.

Thus in 1972 British entry brought a remarkable sea-of-change, as the blockages imposed by de Gaulle seemed to melt away because of the various understandings reached between President Pompidou and Prime Minister Edward Heath. The very fact of accession opened up perspectives – initially simply because of necessity, as existing Commonwealth accords had to be squared or buried. But the fact was, as we have already shown, that other Community members, notably the Germans and the Dutch, wanted to give the Community a more serious approach to developing countries. They felt the need to open up the association in Africa because they saw the need for relations where they had better markets, especially since the Association Agreements, notably that with the East African Community, had come to seem very small beer. Even the French had a school of thought, to which Pompidou subscribed, that felt that the '*pré carré*' or backyard (as it was known) did not bring French business enough rewards, and that not just the rest of Africa but other parts of the world, including Asia, the Middle East and Latin America, offered more opportunities. President Giscard d'Estaing became a relatively youthful exponent of this idea, though held back in his time by the powerful French Africa business and security lobby as well as the realities of party funding. It is marginally reassuring to find the same Giscard presiding over some EU forward thinking in his old age.

The whole process of putting together the new relationship that eventually was to become the Lomé Convention involved setting up a deal that best responded to the needs of what were now the nine member states. This was the time for the Commission to play a constructive role in pursuing that objective. The crucial Commission memorandum of April 1973, prepared while Jean-Francois Deniau was still Commissioner, contained many of the seeds for the future. It held a number of pioneering ideas but at the same time came on the cusp between two very different policies. It hauled in a lot of old colonial baggage and burdened Europe's development policy with it for decades to come. Some parts of the memorandum still seemed astonishingly to talk in terms of the out-dated and much criticised language of 'Eurafrica' and the association, for example:

> The policy of association with the AAMS goes far beyond the mere application of preferential trade measures and of technical and financial aid. Most authoritative voices in the AAMS stress, unceasingly and emphatically, the fact that association is, in the first place, a political option which aims at the maintenance and development of privileged relations of every kind between Europe and Africa. (CEC 1973)

An alternative Commission 'Fresco of Community Action Tomorrow', dating from 1974, in contrast received short shrift. It was seen as impossibly global for the time. Yet it still comes across as fresh today (CEC, 1974).

The Deniau report came at a time soon after British entry when there was still an apparent impasse between the 'associates' and those who, for a brief period, inelegantly came to be called 'the associables'. Deniau was, after all, a conventional Gaullist and a classic operator of the French system. He thought the process could be controlled. During this period some seemed to contemplate Yaoundé remaining as a fast-track closed accord, while the associables could remain part of an outer circle. Such ideas were largely marginalised with the appointment of Claude Cheysson, who may legitimately be described as Pompidou's gift to the British, which helped break through the resistance to non-reciprocity. The linguistic change was significant here; that is, the elimination of the hated expression 'association', so redolent of neo-colonialism. It was not simply a cosmetic change, but the style mattered. Many of the anglophone African leaders would not have signed up to anything less. That was Cheysson's particular contribution. He was credible with the reformers, grasping change with both hands, but was still able to preserve enough of what mattered to the French.

The Commission was in charge of the Lomé negotiations, as it had been in charge of the Yaoundé negotiations, but this was the biggest venture in the field of relations with developing countries that the Commission had ever handled. Both Commissioner and Director-General were supposed to be chief negotiators, with the Council of Ministers providing the secretariat, jointly with first the Associated African and Malagasy States and then the ACP. A special place was accorded to Maurice Foley, who had been brought in early in 1973 by the Commission, obviously with the support of the British, to be one of three Deputy Directors-General of DG VIII. A former Foreign Office minister and a convinced European, his particular role was to bring at least Africa, the Caribbean and the Pacific into a wide-ranging negotiation, and to ensure that the idea of keeping the Yaoundé countries as a privileged inner circle would be totally squashed.

Foley and other newcomers in DG VIII brought an important injection of new blood and progressive thinking. This occurred especially through selling the idea of a Pan-African dimension and by bringing in the Organisation of African Unity (even if north Africa was excluded since it was embarking on separate accords with the Community). A particular task allotted to Foley was selling the idea to the Nigerians, who had been suspicious, and the Pan-African ticket was one of his means. It was no longer simply something for former colonies, even if that still formed the core. The crucial success was to raise the possibility of accepting non-reciprocity, which made its way somewhat enigmatically into the text of the Deniau report. The infusion of Caribbean negotiating skills, not least in the person of Shridath Ramphal, complemented the African heavyweights and crucially helped to create and sustain solidarity among the new ACP group.

With the arrival of the more imaginative and unconventional Cheysson, who had had a sometimes brilliant but very chequered diplomatic career, non-reciprocity and its successor – 'partnership' – became an article of faith. The progressive elements of DG VIII came to the fore after the 1974 oil crisis. Lomé did represent a compromise with the acquis so beloved of the francophones, which was guaranteed by the Community. The aspiration for a 'global development policy' espoused by the like-minded Judith Hart of Britain and Jan Pronk of the Netherlands, both development ministers at the time who formed a working alliance (the 'Hart–Pronk axis'), was only half materialised, but Lomé still represented a giant step forward. Even in British circles it was accepted that in practice a treaty that encompassed the Indian sub-continent and south-east Asia might be over-ambitious, and need a different approach from Lomé. Nevertheless there was still pressure for opening up elsewhere, which over the years came to pass, even if the growth was, in true Community fashion, ad hoc and piecemeal.

There was at the time much talk of the changed philosophy embodied in Lomé that took account of the New International Economic Order. This was a new deal between supposedly or declaredly equal partners, a reflection of 'genuine' interdependence, thereby going a long way to answering the heavy criticisms that had been made of Europe's attitudes. The presence of all Africa was psychologically very important, as was that of the Caribbean and the Pacific, at least as a concession to globalism and a step away from the dubious idea of 'Eurafrica'. The use of an all-embracing and innovative accord to bring African countries together, especially in a way that bridged the anglophone/francophone divide, was also a plus point for the European Community as it helped to heal the old colonial wounds created at the time of the partition of Africa in the nineteenth century.

Other Community institutions – notably the European Parliament, the Court of Auditors and the Economic and Social Committee – were relatively powerless then (and on into the 1980s). The Commission was at the height of its powers and delivered the goods, the first Lomé Convention. To cap it all, the Commission mastered the spin that was needed to sell the Convention, not just to developing country governments but to ordinary Europeans.

The Commission, and especially the duo Cheysson and Foley, moved to the forefront of this change of attitude and concept. One has to recall that in 1974, right in the middle of the negotiations, Cheysson launched a document called

'The Fresco' on the basis of a blueprint furnished by DG VIII intellectuals (CEC, 1974). The artistic imagery was vivid, as it conveyed for the first time a vast panoramic picture of a global development policy that was only in the course of being painted, with a number of different elements, both geographical and thematic. Humanitarian issues were raised for the first time. The Fresco was doubtless ahead of its time. It paved the way for many things that came to pass later, again in an overly piecemeal and ultimately incoherent fashion. It was a project that only the Commission could have done and represented the sort of leap of imagination that is expected of the Commission at its best.

On another level, the same can be said of the serious attempts to radicalise Europe's policy towards southern Africa. This was a result of a conscious Commission bid to play the Pan-African card. Southern African issues came in as well, notably the running sore of the Rhodesian war (which was a problem that the British brought with them to Brussels), the wider issue of apartheid in South Africa, and the related matters of the destabilisation by the Pretoria regime of the newly decolonised Portuguese territories of Angola and Mozambique as part of its attempt to seek support from those in the west who simply saw the world in Cold War terms. The Commission had begun to find allies in the reinforced EEC–ACP parliamentary association (which came to be called the Joint Assembly) of the Lomé Convention. Like the joint parliamentary association, this had initially very much been a compliant 'Eurafrica' support body. However, the arrival of the British and the Danes reinforced those with a broader political agenda, and the Commission found useful allies in its efforts.

This was very much adopted by Cheysson, especially as he declared his hand as an ally of the French Socialist Party (which caused him to secure the post of External Affairs Minister when Mitterrand won the election in 1981). But the policy was that of Foley, with particular support from an influential but low profile British DG VIII official, John Scott. Like Scott, Foley had excellent contacts in southern Africa, including in the liberation movements. These were able to help shift Commission positions in the sub-region, enabling advantage to be taken when, for example, the breakthrough finally came in Rhodesia with Lancaster House, and Zimbabwe became independent in 1980, immediately applying to join the Lomé Convention. The role of Foley and Scott with the delegate in Botswana, David Anderson, in encouraging the establishment of the Southern African Development Coordination Conference which (now as the South African Development Community) is still perceived to be one of Africa's more successful regional groupings, is not to be underestimated. Foley's creative role is worth signalling for the history books, but it should also be recorded that he received little back-up from his home government, even though his old party (Labour) was in power from 1974 to 1979. He never became Development Commissioner or even Director-General in the 1978 rotation of the Commission, even though at that stage development was the second largest budget in Brussels after agriculture. It was not among Foreign Office priorities in Europe, and this sadly appears to have been accepted in Downing Street. British diplomats dealing with Brussels have always considered DG VIII as something that was both a low priority and that had escaped from their grasp. Only from 1997 under the more aggressive Clare Short did they have to change, but by then she had a lot to criticise the Commission for too and the entire Commission had to resign in 1999.

In the 1980s the tradition of a pioneering role for the EC/EU in the international campaign against apartheid in South Africa, though this became less in the late 1980s after the departure of Cheysson and Pisani. The latter had very much maintained Cheysson's line in many respects. But by then the precedents had been established and the ball had started rolling. The key conflicts had been with British and German officials in DG I, who were more susceptible to pressure from the South Africans. There were also western pressures articulated through the Council at the time of the Shaba crisis in May–June 1978, after President Giscard d'Estaing's supposedly humanitarian intervention to save the Mobutu regime (and Africa from communism). But scepticism and divisions within the ranks of NATO itself meant that any European initiative could be firmly discounted. On the whole, it proved possible for the Commission, and hence Europe, to play a political role even without the institutional framework to carry it out, apart from the tenuous European Political Cooperation. There may now be more institutional back-up after Maastricht and Amsterdam. There are now three, arguably four, Commissioners working on policies relevant to developing countries. The Council even has a single External Affairs voice, Javier Solana (the 'Monsieur PESC' so wanted before), but does one dare to suggest that the European dimension to policy formation has borne fewer results?

The commitment to southern Africa, especially democracy in South Africa, was not followed up in the four and a half years of negotiations for the South Africa agreement, in which the EU has been shown at its worst and most selfish. One feels that Philip Lowe as Director-General did try to do his best. However, with a weaker Commissioner (Pinheiro) and the general decline of Commission prestige and influence, as well as the still apparent lack of influence of the Parliament, which with its left majority might have made a difference, the story has been a sorry one. At all costs a repetition must be avoided when the former Lomé countries have to accept reciprocity, that is extend reverse preferences to the EU, and negotiate to form REPAs under the 2000–20 Cotonou Agreement. But the ACP is weaker and less organised to negotiate now than it has ever been.

The turning point

The 1978–79 negotiations to renew Lomé marked the first nail in the coffin of the Lomé idea – equality and interdependence. The spirit went after that, along with producer power, and the NIEO, and the North–South dialogue. Never again did the Commission really appear to be on the side of international radical thinking on development. The running was later taken up by the Parliament, and then by leading NGOs. Lomé itself became an increasing embarrassment and slowly slid down the scale of Commission priorities. The bolting on to development 'policy' of other continents, and the separate existence of a badly run Humanitarian Office (ECHO), brought the lie to the Maastricht Treaty telling us that the EU really had a coherent development policy. Much has been devoted to burying Lomé without appearing to do so. By Lomé IV in 1990 it was arguably brain-dead, if a Convention can so be. Yet it was renewed for a further ambitious ten years, and not five as before. Cotonou capped that in the EU fantasy world of 2000 by being signed for *twenty* years.

The 1980s and 1990s saw a huge African crisis – more than the 'lost decade' of Adedeji (Executive Secretary of the UN Economic Commission for Africa from 1975 to 1991). This meant that equality (always a fiction anyway) went out of the window. The ACP, faced with decline, felt increasingly that Lomé was less of a negotiating battleground, except perhaps when it came to the size of the EDF, where, after the play-acting, the ACP had to accept what it was given. In fact, the conflicts were as much among member states as with the ACP. At the same time, other disadvantages of Lomé became more apparent. Also, the spirit shown by the Commission became submerged in pressures from the Bretton Woods institutions in the era of Reagan/Thatcher, after the Berg report from the World Bank in 1981 which stridently articulated structural reform and free market liberalisation. This translated into the acceptance by the Commission of 'policy dialogues' (conditionalities which failed) and led the policies to be increasingly prescriptive of the form of governance which would be acceptable to Europe in return for trade concessions and aid. Without a Commission machinery to apply the results, however, even the new policies became discredited in the eyes of the member states.

Fragmentation: Cotonou, MEDA, PHARE–TACIS and the near-abroad

The fragmentation of development within the Commission in the 1990s called for radical solutions – or an exit strategy from development cooperation in favour of the member states' own programmes. Since development was always more than just aid, the latter option was hardly real.

Yet the decade of the 1990s had started well. With the Maastricht Treaty came the first mention of development as a core European policy (rather than a Part Four add-on, hitherto very partial and Africa focused). In the late 1990s there was even a formal Statement of Development Policy which claimed to put poverty-focus at the core (despite the realities of bestowing EU aid and trade privileges). As the Lomé relationship with the ACP was clearly foundering and a multiplicity of other new Community relations and EU development policies were blooming, though also adding further to the Commission's confusion, especially when it barely mastered them. As early as 1976 the European

Parliament had insisted on at least token programmes of support for Asia and Latin America (ALA). When Spain and Portugal became members, the Latin American links were reinforced. Spain also insisted on a Mediterranean programme (MEDA), including most of the developing countries of North Africa, which the Commission was largely unable to control. No more than its member states, the EC could not be insensitive to Live Aid and the entreaties of the relief charities. Earlier the Commission had a strong controlling influence over the NGOs. Then ECHO was allowed almost complete autonomy to spend wildly. Only the Court of Auditors seemed able to keep some elements in check. The biggest change of all ought to have been the most obvious to Europe, for the end of the Cold War started in the European Community's direct neighbour, Hungary, when it allowed GDR refugees to escape through its territory into the EC, and in Berlin itself when the Wall dividing West and East came down in 1989. Programmes of assistance and to underpin reform for transition states (for Poland and Hungary initially, hence PHARE: Polan–Hungady Assistance for the Reconstruction of the Economy) and technical cooperation with Russia and the states of the former Soviet Union (TACIS) were quickly succeeded by programmes of support and adjustment which regarded the former as potential accession states to the EU itself – though not before a lot of criticism over the quality of funding and targeting under PHARE and TACIS.

This meant that the ACP, the original core of poor, weak, deserving but non-threatening countries in the long-lived Lomé arrangement had been comprehensively overtaken by 'other interests' – by all the other interests, really. Eastern Europe, the direct neighbour of the member states, and Russia itself had become the EU's near-abroad on which the best accession or cooperation policies would be lavished – just as the African colonies had been, politically, the EEC's near-abroad when the relationship started forty years earlier. From the ACP point of view, the Commission had failed to defend it (though it was hardly astute in safeguarding its own interests). From the viewpoint of Brussels, however, the Commission had simply moved on.

Some would argue that the Commission made one last attempt to retrieve the situation with a consultative document, the 1996 'Green Paper on Relations between the European Union and the ACP Countries on the Eve of the 21st Century' (CEC, 1996). The consultation was however peremptory, and the Commission was itself in deep difficulty by 1998 to 1999. ACP interests were so little defended that the Green Paper foreshadowed what followed in the Cotonou Agreement: the return of reverse preferences (and reciprocity in other domains); the disbandment of the commodity protocols and the Stabex mechanism; sub-regional arrangements further undermining ACP solidarity and partnership; enforceable political conditionality with the active use of Article 96 sanctions; and not just a standstill on the overall aid envelope, but the replacement of fixed five-year allocations with ceilings which are now fiendishly difficult to draw down. In a charitable move, EU ministers even consigned the enormous pipeline of unspent EDF balances into debt relief, including for the undeserving, so proving that moral hazard still applies. There is no ACP state which sees Cotonou as an improvement on what went before. Many see so little of interest in the new agreement, especially in its REPA elements for WTO-compatible trade (though the Commission never tested the alternative), that they are unwilling to sign up for a regional partnership when the time comes, unless they suffer a withdrawal of aid as a sanction. If they are classified as least developed (in UN and now WTO terminology) they need not bother to sign. For, only months after the June 2000 Cotonou Agreement was signed, another part of the Commission, Pascal Lamy's Trade Directorate-General, launched 'Everything But Arms', a facility under which all non-lethal exports from precisely half the ACP countries (plus other least developed, notably in Asia) enter the European Union market duty free and quota unrestricted. These are the new Lomé beneficiaries but unfortunately the old Lomé states were neither considered nor consulted, such is the fragmentation of policy now within the Commission.

After these disruptions, however, and after the reformation of the Commission subsequent to the resignation of the Santer Commission in 1999, the development section of the Commission became its own worst enemy. Already heavily outpaced by other Commissioners successfully fighting their own turf wars, notably Pascal Lamy on Trade and Christopher Pattern on External Relations, the Development Commissioner Poul Nielson divided his Directorate into two. He separated the operational side (effectively aid programming and the delegations) from policy (of which there had been little constructive development in recent years). This damaged internal morale and further eroded Development's position in the EC hierarchy. The process also dismayed its clients – especially those of longest standing, the ACP. There could even be worse to come for the latter. For the 'near abroad' states of Central and Eastern Europe, having recently received the benefits of aid diversion, now form the core of the ten accession states which swell the EU to twenty-five in 2004. Not having any strong tradition of development cooperation policy in the communist era, being in the main of an income level closer to developing countries than that of previous applicant states, and being keen to compete, they are unlikely to be supportive of generous development cooperation policies for Africa, the ACP or the ALA – at least not beyond that required by conformity to the European 'acquis'.

If the first Lomé Convention of 1975–79 was the peak of the Commission's development influence, the current period of enlargement and post-Lomé consolidation for the ACP during 2002 to 2007 is likely to prove the most challenging ever for the Commission. The Development Commissioner must start by reintegrating policy with operations. He (or when succeeded perhaps she) then needs to earn the respect of the governments of the critical member states (which no longer resist saying that they can do better under bilateral operations, and that the rules of subsidiarity shall apply), not least through a more transparent working pattern. And third, it is essential that the Commissioner for Development tackles the EU's own internal incoherence and contradictions, particularly in respect of agricultural protectionism. In that context, perhaps the Lamy 'Everything But Arms' initiative is less a poisoned chalice (for poor non least-developed countries such as Kenya, Jamaica, Guyana and India which cannot benefit) than a litmus test of the EU's own generosity. When least developed countries from Bangladesh down to Lesotho are really allowed to export into the EU any agricultural product they can produce domestically, without unreasonable labelling or phytosanitary impediments or surge factors, and when conversely their own markets for sugar or grains or beef are not distorted by the EU's own subsidy policies, then that test will be passed. European Community development policy will then get its second wind, and the Commission will again be a major player with the USA, Japan and its own member states.

Bibliography

Bongo, O. (1994), *Confidences d'un Africain: Entretiens avec Christian Casteran*, Paris: Albin Michel.

CEC (1973), 'Deniau Commission Memorandum', Brussels.

CEC (1974), 'Communication on development aid: fresco of Community action tomorrow', *Bulletin of the European Communities*, 7: supplement 8.

CEC (1996), 'Green Paper on Relations between the European Union and the ACP Countries on the Eve of the 21st Century. Challenges and Options for a New Partnership', Brussels, 14 November.

Cox, A. and A. Koning with A. Hewitt, J. Howell and A. Marr (1997), *Understanding European Community Aid*, London/Brussels: Overseas Development Institute/European Commission.

Davenport, M., A. Hewitt and A. Koning (1995), *Europe's Preferred Partners? The Lomé Countries in World Trade*, London: Overseas Development Institute.

GEMDEV (1998), *La Convention de Lomé en Questions*, Paris: Karthala.

Grilli, E. (1993), *The European Community and the Developing Countries*, Cambridge: Cambridge University Press.

Hewitt, A. (1983), 'Stabex: an evaluation of the economic impact over the first five years', *World Development*, 11:12, pp. 1005–27.

Hewitt, A. (1994), *Crisis or Transition in Foreign Aid*, London: Overseas Development Institute.

Hewitt, A. (2001), 'Beyond poverty? The new UK policy on international development and globalisation', *Third World Quarterly*, 22:2, pp. 291–6.

Lister, M. (1998), *European Union Development Policy*, Basingstoke: Macmillan.

Mortimer, E. (1969), *France and the Africans*, London: Faber and Faber.

Morton, K. and P. Tulloch (1977), *Trade and Developing Countries*, London: Overseas Development Institute.

Page, S. and A. Hewitt (2002), 'The new European trade preferences: does "Everything But Arms" help the poor?', *Development Policy Review*, 20:1, pp. 91–102.

Raffer, K. (2001), *Cotonou: Slowly Undoing Lomé's Concept of Partnership*, Development Studies Association Paper, Mimeo.

Ravenhill, J. (1985), *Collective Clientelism: The Lomé Conventions and North South Relations*, New York: Columbia University Press.

Tulloch, P. (1973), *The Seven Outside: Commonwealth Asia's Trade with the Enlarged EEC*, London: Overseas Development Institute.

Whiteman, K. (1998), 'Africa, the ACP and Europe: the lessons of 25 years', *Development Policy Review*, 16:1, pp. 29–37.

9

Conclusions: the potential and limits of EU development cooperation policy

Karin Arts and Anna K. Dickson

On 23 June 2000 the Cotonou Agreement was signed, replacing the twenty-five-year-old Lomé Convention. There was a distinct feeling of change in Cotonou and the new Agreement is seen as radically overhauling its predecessors and setting a new basis for partnership between the ACP and EU states. It is too early to provide in-depth analysis of the Cotonou Agreement, not least because in many ways Cotonou provides a kind of interregnum between the existing Lomé Conventions and future, as yet to be determined, Regional Economic Partnership Agreements. This is most obvious in the case of the trade-related aspects of the Agreement. Negotiations started in September 2002 for progressive implementation from 2008 onwards, creating, in effect, a ten-year transition period.

It has been argued in various corners that Lomé was in need of overhaul. Not only were the instruments less than effective, but the international context had changed so drastically over the period involved that the articles of agreement appeared anachronistic. It is hard to disagree with this analysis, although many of Lomé's failings lay not so much in the actual policies (some of which, as we have pointed out, were highly commendable) but in their management and implementation. The Cotonou Agreement places key emphasis on political dialogue (Article 8). It makes good governance a fundamental and positive element, while respect for human rights, democratic values and the rule of law become essential elements (Article 9). Peace-building policies and conflict prevention and resolution feature more prominently than before (Article 11). The inclusion of migration extends the agreement and accommodates growing European concerns explicitly (Article 13). The Cotonou Agreement also proposes finally to end the preferential trade margins accorded to non-least developed ACP states in favour of more liberal free trade agreements strongly shaped by the WTO agenda (Article 36).

These changes need to be seen in the context of the April 2000 elaboration of new Commission guidelines for development policy. These include the desire to maximise the impact of development policy by identifying priorities for action and concentrating Community action in a limited number of spheres in which the Community provides value added. The principal aim of development policy is now to reduce, and eventually to eliminate, poverty and to this end there will be new emphasis on pro-poor policies. The Council, Parliament and Commission have agreed to focus on six main areas: trade, regional cooperation, macroeconomic support, transport, food security and capacity building, especially for good governance and the rule of law (CEC, 2001).

Cotonou's new emphasis on poverty reduction and eradication (Article 1) is to be welcomed. It is difficult to believe that this has not been the goal of EU development policy thus far. Development assistance in all its forms should surely be directed at the poor wherever they might be located. The conception of poverty used by the Commission is also to be commended as it moves away from a *lack of resources* approach towards a more multifaceted conception that includes issues of vulnerability that might not be reflected in income-based statistics alone (CEC, 2001). We have two main reservations. Firstly, it remains unclear how this primary focus on poverty reduction as an end can be squared with the increased emphasis on political conditionalities evident in the Cotonou Agreement. Secondly, it is also uncertain how a pro-poor focus can be compatible with the desire to facilitate global economic competitiveness in less poor economies for which preferential trade margins will no longer exist. These are matters for further research.

Our aim throughout has been to assess the record of development cooperation from the Treaty of Rome to Lomé, and beyond to Cotonou, and to offer an informed analysis of the significant trends over the period. We have also sought to assess the implications of the trends identified for future development policy and so to conceptualise the role of EU external action in the realm of development. It is in the realm of external action that the EU increasingly displays its foreign policy goals (Smith, 1998). Development policy thus constitutes a key aspect of EU foreign policy.

Most authors identify the gap between the promise and the performance of development policy as a key determinant of development policy outcomes. Performance in development policy has been hindered by three fundamental defects which intensified after 1989. Firstly a lack of value added; that is, the absence of novel or unique policies and of the political will to create them. There is instead a tendency to follow global trends rather than to set them. To this end we have seen the dissolution of that which was novel, including Stabex and Sysmin, the commodity protocols and, most significantly, non-reciprocity and political neutrality. Although a third position would be a desirable counterweight to the prevailing neo-liberal consensus, the absence of it is not costly to the EU. This fact leads to a degree of inertia in this regard.

Secondly, Community development policy has become less focused on a single group of beneficiaries. Since 1989 in particular we have seen the widening of the geographical focus based on geopolitical interests rather than need. This widening leads to dilution and overstretch, and increases the capability–expectations gap. The recently launched Everything but Arms initiative allows duty free entry for all goods and services (except arms) from the least developed countries. While this does focus on the poorest, it is not at present economically costly to the EU and does not refute the above criticism.

Thirdly, we identify a Community overly concerned with creating the image of a significant world actor. Development policies have thus become more concerned with form than substance. This is evident in the declaring essential of certain political conditionalities such as democracy and good governance but having difficulty in applying criteria consistently. It is also evident in the new focus on conflict resolution which can be dealt with more easily than poverty and/or for which the EU will at least gain public credibility for trying.

These defects are exacerbated by those factors which the Council and Commission have identified as being problematic in the policy-making process, namely the lack of coherence between different sectors of Community policy and inconsistencies between Community policy and member states' national policies. This is evident in French inability, for so long, to decide whether it wished to put Europe or Africa at the centre of its external policy. It is also evident in the bureaucratic nightmare of multiple Directorates and agencies dealing separately with issues concerning and impinging upon development, and creating, in effect, incoherence between policies.

The negotiations for future ACP–EU trade relations began in September 2002. These negotiations aim to create free trade areas between the EC and sub-regions of the ACP group. The implications of this are significant for all ACP states, as well as the ACP group as a whole. The new Economic Partnership Agreements will be shaped by the emerging WTO agenda in which the European Union is inescapably a major player. The failure of the WTO in Seattle has set hopes for the Doha Development Round; however, there are no guarantees. Moreover, the Development Round will not alter the fact of European domination in ACP–EU relations. The ACP for its part will need a common negotiating platform and a list of minimum objectives if it is not to be marginalised in this process.

In line with evolving European Union policy in recent years, and especially after the events of 11 September 2001 in the USA, the political dimension of the relationship is likely to increase. Even the economic dimensions will have political implications. Thus the Lomé era has certainly ended, the neo-colonial past has been put to rest and a new era of development cooperation is in the process of being created. However, the EU is also deeply involved in its own processes of further integration and enlargement, and the dilemmas of widening or deepening will temper the colour of future development cooperation.

References

CEC (2001), 'Speech by Commissioner Nielson to the German Parliament 12 December 2001', Europa/comm/commissioners/neilson/speech/20011212_en.htm.

Smith, M. (1998), 'Does the flag follow trade? Politicisation and the emergence of a European foreign policy', in J. Peterson and H. Sjursen (eds), *A Common Foreign Policy for Europe?*, London: Routledge.

Index

ACP states *see* Cotonou Agreement; Lomé Conventions
ACP market share 46, 123
aid
 allocation patterns of 8–9, 62, 71, 86, 103
 effectiveness of 14, 108
 geographical scope of 5, 60–1, 62, 71, 103, 137, 139
Africa
 EU–Africa Summit (Cairo, 2000) 69, 81, 97
 see also Cotonou Agreement; Lomé Conventions
agriculture *see* Common Agricultural Policy
Algeria 65, 133
Angola 90, 142
ASEAN 7, 72
Asia 66, 72–3, 117, 137, 139, 145
Asia–Europe Meeting (ASEM) 63, 73
Associated African and Malagasy States (AASM) 117, 122, 137, 140

bananas 50, 53–6
beef 50, 147
bilateralism *see* development cooperation policy
Botswana 47, 142
Burkina Faso 37

CAP *see* Common Agricultural Policy
Caribbean 53, 55, 74, 117, 141

see also Cotonou Agreement; Lomé Conventions
Central America 63, 66, 73
Central and Eastern Europe 62, 75–6, 124
see also enlargement
Cheysson, C. 115, 134, 136, 140, 141, 142, 143
civil society 28, 31, 37, 109–10, 126, 127
coherence 83, 106, 113, 114, 126, 127, 144, 147, 151
Cold War (end of) 2, 4, 8, 25, 43, 60–3, 80, 91, 123
Commission
 communication on development policy in the run-up to 2000 (1992) 6, 34
 communication on EC development policy (2000) 8
 Green Paper on relations between the EU and ACP (1997) 4, 48–9, 109, 145
 role and mandate of 7, 48, 127
Common Agricultural Policy 48, 51–2, 125, 147
Common Foreign and Security Policy (CFSP) 7, 62, 66, 69, 70, 80, 82, 91–6, 105
Commonwealth 44, 102, 117, 139
complementarity 6, 83, 113, 128
conflict prevention 66, 69, 92–3, 149

153

Index

consistency 7, 105, 106, 110
corruption 10, 26, 35, 85, 108
Côte d'Ivoire 47, 94, 126, 136
Cotonou Agreement 2, 34–7, 68–9, 81, 145, 149
  corruption 10, 35
  good governance 10, 35
  terms of aid 36–7
  terms of trade 109
Council of Ministers (EU)
  resolution on human rights, democracy and development (1991) 9, 27, 61
Court of Auditors 141, 145
Cuba 7, 14, 74, 102

debt issues 31–3, 36, 37, 104, 123, 145
democracy (promotion of) 24, 26, 27–8, 65, 66
Deniau, J.-F. 115, 134, 139, 140
development cooperation policy
  bilateral vs. common 5–6, 7, 83, 86, 94, 106, 117, 118, 122
  objectives of 7, 35, 45, 66, 128
  see also coherence; complementarity; consistency

East African Community 122, 138, 139
Eastern Europe see enlargement, with Central and Eastern European states
ECHO see humanitarian aid
Economic and Monetary Union 2, 124
Economic Partnership Agreements see Regional Economic Partnership Agreements
Ecuador 55, 56
enlargement of EU
  with Central and Eastern European states 75, 101
  with Greece 102
  with Spain and Portugal 70, 73, 102, 145
  with Sweden, Austria and Finland 85, 103
  with UK 60, 102, 118, 139
European Development Fund (EDF) 62, 68, 116, 118, 126, 134, 135

European Parliament 28, 68, 83, 135, 141
European Political Cooperation (EPC) 61, 70, 105, 141
Everything but Arms initiative 49–50, 56, 146, 147, 151

Ferrandi, J. 136
Fiji 47
France 5, 14, 24, 44, 51, 52, 85, 86, 96, 102, 113–32

Gaulle, C. de 119, 120, 121, 134, 138
GATT 44, 54
  see also trade preferences
gender 30, 104
Generalised System of Preferences (GSP) 9, 42, 47, 69, 123
Germany 5, 8, 24, 52, 60, 86, 95, 119, 124
Ghana 94, 137
globalisation 4, 46, 50, 123, 137
good governance 10, 25, 35, 69, 85, 149
Greece 5, 70
Green Paper on relations between the EU and ACP (Commission, 1997) 4, 48–9, 109, 145

highly indebted poor countries initiative (HIPC) 31–3, 36, 37
humanitarian aid 83, 87–91, 144
human rights 9, 24, 27, 65, 66, 149

International Financial Institutions see International Monetary Fund; World Bank
International Monetary Fund 4, 6, 19–24, 45, 116
  (enhanced) structural adjustment facility 19, 30

Jamaica 47, 147
Japan 24, 72, 147
Joint Assembly (ACP-EU) 28, 68, 142

Kenya 117, 138, 147
Kosovo 76, 81, 89, 90, 97, 107
Kurdistan 89, 90

Index

Latin America 63, 66, 73–4, 102, 139, 145
least developed countries 5, 49, 69, 103, 109, 146
Liberia 89, 90
Lomé Conventions 1–2, 14, 68–9, 81, 117–18, 136, 144, 149
   political conditionality of 9, 27–9, 68, 85
   and structural adjustment 20–34, 45
   terms of aid 17–34
   terms of trade 43–4
Lomé I 18, 44, 136, 140–1
Lomé IV 27
   mid-term review 28, 46, 85
   structural adjustment 22–4, 48

Maastricht Treaty (1992) *see* development cooperation policy, objectives of
Marin, M. 28, 70, 102
mass media 88–91
Matutes, A. 70
Mauritius 46, 123, 137
Mediterranean 51, 62, 65, 70–2, 102–3, 124, 145
Mercosur 7, 74
Middle East 67, 70, 71, 139
Mozambique 33, 90, 142

National Indicative Programme 22–3, 36
neo-liberalism 44–5
Netherlands 5, 60, 86, 119
New International Economic Order (NIEO) 2, 44, 117, 123, 143
Nielson, P. 36, 50, 106, 116, 146
Nigeria 117, 122, 137, 138

Organisation for Economic Cooperation and Development (OECD) 30, 33, 36
Organisation of African Unity (OAU) 93, 140

Pacific 141
   see also Cotonou Agreement; Lomé Conventions

peace building 93, 149
Pinheiro, J. de Deus 91, 96, 143
Pisani, E. 115, 135, 143
political conditionality 9, 24–9, 34–5, 45, 48, 75, 85, 144, 145, 150–1
poverty reduction/alleviation 29–30, 32, 35, 37, 46, 50, 104, 144, 150

Regional Economic Partnership Agreements (REPAs) 49, 50, 125, 143, 146, 149, 151
rum 50
Russia 62, 65, 76

security issues 64, 65–6, 95
Sierra Leone 89, 90, 97
Solana, J. 80, 95, 97, 106, 143
Somalia 89, 90, 134
South Africa 92, 142
Stabex 2, 23, 44, 50, 109, 117, 125, 136–7, 145, 150
structural adjustment programmes 19, 21, 25, 123
Sudan 89, 90
sugar 44, 50, 136, 147
Sysmin 2, 44, 50, 109, 150

trade liberalisation 4, 53
trade preferences 123
   WTO compatibility of 47, 49, 50, 56, 69, 121, 146, 149
Turkey 70, 71, 101

Uganda 33, 117
Ukraine 62, 65, 76
United Kingdom 5, 14, 24, 44, 51, 86, 96
United States of America 2, 6, 24, 52, 55, 64, 66, 73, 147, 151
Uruguay Round 47, 52
Utstein Group 104

Washington consensus 20, 33, 36, 123
Western European Union 93–4, 95
Windward Islands 53–6

World Bank 4, 6, 19–26, 31, 45, 50, 54, 116
World Trade Organisation 4, 47, 49, 52, 54–6, 69, 151
  see also trade preferences, WTO compatibility of

Yaoundé Conventions 44, 117, 122, 134, 138

Zimbabwe 24, 47, 142

Lightning Source UK Ltd.
Milton Keynes UK
22 October 2010

161719UK00003B/27/P